S0-CAZ-113

THE GLOBAL COMMON GOOD TOWARDS A MORE INCLUSIVE ECONOMY

Casina Pio IV, Vatican City
11-12 July, 2014

LIBRERIA EDITRICE VATICANA

© Copyright 2016 - Libreria Editrice Vaticana
00120 Vatican City
Tel. 06.698.81032 - Fax 06.698.84716

ISBN 978-88-209-9906-3

www.libreriaeditricevaticana.va
www.iustitiaetpax.va

TABLE OF CONTENTS

APPENDIX

FOREWORD

The Pontifical Council for Justice and Peace is happy to publish the *Proceedings* of a two-day Seminar on the theme *The Global Common Good: towards a more Inclusive Economy*, held on July 11th and 12th, 2014, at the Pontifical Academy of Sciences, Casina Pio IV, in Vatican City.

This invitational Seminar brought together leaders and experts from a number of areas. Economists, bankers, and heads of international and intergovernmental organizations joined representatives of the Church and non-governmental organizations. Names and qualifications can be found in the *List of participants* at the end of this volume.

The Holy Father is responsible for both the idea for the Seminar and the impulse to have it take place. Indeed, I believe all participants would agree that the Holy Father's welcome, the luncheon spent in his company, the words he addressed to us, were high water marks of the Seminar.

In his Apostolic Exhortation *Evangelii Gaudium* (EG), Pope Francis calls us to share the joy of the Gospel with everybody and in all places. The Gospel provides grounds for hope in a world that so seriously lacks it: "No one is excluded from the joy brought by the Lord" (EG 3), because He is in our midst in order to help us live our lives to the fullest, regardless of the many difficulties we daily face. Yet the prevailing economy presents serious barriers to a full and joyful life. For example, extreme poverty, pervasive inequality and the exclusion of millions from the processes of development generate a world where many people live with "precious little dignity" (EG, 52) and where only a minority today enjoy prosperity (EG, 56). There is a need to create new economic models and tools to respond to the spreading "globalisation of indifference" (EG, 54).

The Pope recognizes the great contributions made by business and finance to human development over the centuries. The world's economic leaders "have demonstrated their aptitude for being innovative and for improving the lives of many people by their ingenuity and professional expertise"(*Message of Pope Francis to the Executive Chairman of the World Economic Forum of Davos*, 2014). Global business and financial communities "can further contribute by putting their skills at the service of those who are still living in dire poverty" *(ibid.)*.

This Seminar helped the Pontifical Council for Justice and Peace to reflect on how the economy might extend the benefits and reverse the gaping inequalities and worsening exclusions. We continue to seek additional insights and help in better understanding how to improve the shared lot of humankind within a globalised economy, and enable an estimated two billion people to escape from dire poverty. The seminar materials confirm that Catholic Social Teaching does not oppose a market-based economy, so long as it is not an oligarchy. That is, an acceptable market-based economy operates in a coordinated fashion, is oriented toward the common good and is marked by inclusivity, stability, transparency and democracy. Such an economy considers its political and philosophical base as well as its financial impact.

I would like to emphasize our gratitude to our guests, who generously suspended their professional and academic engagements for some days to join us in Rome. Moreover, they kindly agreed to send in their Reflections as a follow-up to the meeting. It is this collection of various essays of different size and structure that we are now publishing, together with the *Questionnaire* sent to all guests before the Seminar, and all the speeches during the meeting. The

Discussion Paper and the *Research Working Paper* – written to facilitate both the reflections and reactions of the participants – can be found in the *Appendix* of this book.

Finally, my gratitude goes to all contributors and especially to our Scientific Committee for their untiring collaboration in the preparation of the meeting and of this volume of essays.

Cardinal Peter K. A. Turkson

President of the Pontifical Council for Justice and Peace

ADDRESS OF POPE FRANCIS AT THE CONCLUSION OF LUNCHEON WITH THE PARTICIPANTS IN THE INTERNATIONAL SEMINAR ON THE POPE'S PROPOSAL "TOWARDS A MORE INCLUSIVE ECONOMY" MADE IN THE APOSTOLIC EXHORTATION *EVANGELII GAUDIUM*

Casina Pio IV in the Vatican
Saturday, 12 July 2014

I thank the Cardinal President for his words, I thank you for your fellowship, for the invitation, and for your work. What you are doing is so important: to reflect on reality, but to reflect without fear, to reflect with intelligence. Without fear and with intelligence. And this is a service.

One of you spoke to me about the three reductionisms, but I will speak only of the first: anthropological reductionism. I think that this moment is the most pronounced time of anthropological reductionism. The same thing happens to man as happens when wine becomes grappa: it passes through an organizational still. It is no longer wine, it is something else: perhaps more useful, more specialized, but it's not wine! It is the same for man: man passes through this still and ends up — and I say this seriously — losing humanity and becoming an instrument of the system, the social system, economic system, a system where imbalance reigns. When man loses his humanity, what can we expect? What happens is what I would call in common parlance: a policy, a sociology, a "throwaway" attitude. One discards what is not needed, because man is not at the centre. And when man is not at the centre, another thing is at the centre and man is at the service of this other thing. The aim therefore is to save man, in the sense that he may return to the centre: to the centre of society, to the centre of thought, the centre of reflection. To bring man once again to the centre. And this is laudable work, and you are doing it. I thank you for this work. You study, reflect, hold these conferences for this, so that man is not thrown away. Children are thrown away, because the birth rate — at least here in Europe — everyone knows it; the elderly are thrown away, because they are of no use. And now? A generation of young people is being thrown away, and this is most serious! I saw a figure: 75 million young people, under 25 years of age, without work. The young "neither-nors" neither studying nor working. They don't study because they don't have the means, they don't work because there are no jobs. More waste. What will be the next thing thrown away? We must stop before it's too late, please!

I thank you. I thank you for the help that you give with your work, with your reflection, to restore this unbalanced situation and to recover man and bring him back to the centre of reflection and the centre of life. He is the king of the universe! And this is not theology, it is not philosophy — it is human reality. With this we will go forward. Thank you, thank you truly. Thank you!

WELCOME AND INTRODUCTORY REMARKS

Cardinal Peter K.A. Turkson
President of the Pontifical Council for Justice and Peace

It is my pleasure to welcome you to Rome on this beautiful sunny July afternoon. We are very pleased to have you join us at in this historic Pontifical Academy of Sciences within the Vatican Gardens. I thank God for your safe arrival here. You represent many different components and sectors of the economy and society. In advance I appreciate the effort each one will make to add your complementary perspectives to the upcoming discussions. May God guide us towards solid understanding and promising proposals in view of a more inclusive economy and the global common good.

Critique of current shortcomings

In November 2013, Pope Francis issued his Apostolic Exhortation *Evangelii Gaudium,* in which he calls us to share the joy of the Gospel with everybody and everywhere. The Gospel, he asserts, provides grounds for hope in a world that so seriously lacks it: "No one is excluded from the joy that comes out from God, because He is in our midst in order to help us live a life to the full, regardless of the many difficulties we daily face" (4-5).[1]

Yet the prevailing economy presents serious barriers to a full and joyful life. For example, extreme poverty, pervasive inequality and the marginalization of millions from the processes of development, generate a world where many people live with "precious little dignity" (52) and where only a minority today enjoy prosperity (56). The world's financial system seems to function well for

---

[1] The citations in this form are to sections of *Evangelii Gaudium.*

relatively few, rather than serving the entirety of mankind and the common good (57). But rather than present a diagnosis of the current economic malaise, I want to stress the need to create new economic models and tools to respond to the spreading "globalisation of indifference" (54).

How to deal with these shortcomings and improve present economics is the main reason we are here today. This is not an easy task. The challenges are enormous, particularly because "certain present realities, unless effectively dealt with, are capable of setting off processes of dehumanization which would then be hard to reverse" (51). In addition, there is no consensus on the best ways to respond to the economic challenges.

Still, as Pope Francis pointed out at the 2014 World Economic Forum in Davos, business and economic vocations, as well as political vocations, are indeed noble. Economic decisions in a globalised world can bring about a great deal of good.

In this spirit, our ambitious goal for this seminar is to inspire everyone to discover and deploy our creative capacities to develop an "economy of inclusion".

The Meaning of "Economy"

I would like to share a personal story with you. It may help to explain our topic.

My father was a carpenter at a mine in Ghana, my mother sold vegetables, and they were in charge of a household with ten children. As parents imbued with Christian values, neither of them would ever consider the possibility of having a joyful life if some of their children were unable to live well, much less well than the others.

In like manner, the management of our planet, our common home, should not be considered a success while more than half our brothers and sisters subsist in miserable conditions, living incomparably less well than the rest of us. Such conditions do not promote hope, joy and peace.

To me, this is what economics is all about. As you know, the original meaning of the word comes from ancient Greek. It combines *oikos* (which means house or home) and *nomos* (which refers to law, rule, or management), giving us *oikonomia* or economics.

For the Greeks, this meant there had to be a practical wisdom of household management. And according to *Evangelii Gaudium*, economy should be "the art of achieving a fitting management of our common home, which is the world as a whole" (206).

So what does this mean for us?

A home is a busy place. Many different things occur in a household and sustain it. Yet it is one home. It is not a haphazard collection of disparate pieces, much less fragments in conflict.

If we take this to the level of society, we should not ignore the whole in favour of the parts; nor lose sight of the parts by concentrating exclusively on the whole. We recognize broad social movements or activities. We should see society functioning as an integrated whole. At the same time we readily perceive various aspects or dimensions: economic, juridical, moral, aesthetic, religious, mythological, social and cultural among others. Societies are not divided up into unrelated spheres of activity and responsibility.

To sum up: our common home is both many parts and a whole. If we ignore the whole, we cannot interpret any part correctly. If we neglect, misrepresent or exaggerate any part, we misunderstand the whole.

Exchange provides a useful tool for understanding societal action at both the broadest and the most granular levels. Many social phenomena can be incorporated under the general rubric of exchange. No one should be excluded from the "great exchange" we call society.

To return to my family example, if several of my brothers and sisters had been excluded from the various forms of exchange – if several or even the majority were to suffer, while the parents and a few of the children did well – then the Turkson household would not at all have been in order. The *oikonomia* would not have been functioning justly or harmoniously.

Certainly it was not easy for my parents to be creative and energetic in generating wellbeing for all of us, taking into account our modest rest resources and each one's needs. Similarly, to conceive of a more inclusive and just economy, a better-managed system with human dignity at its heart, where nobody is left on the peripheries, may not be easy – but it seems like an eminently worthwhile and timely challenge.

Prospects for an economics of common good and human dignity

With these ideals in mind, I believe that the Holy Father has laid out the task before us. Pope Francis encourages us to use "tools of creativity in the hope that they might enrich the discussions" and "recognize the fundamental role that modern business activity has in bringing about changes, by stimulating and developing the immense resources of human intelligence," as he said at Davos earlier this year.

Let us turn our attention to two aspects of today's economy: how the different participants in the economy relate to each other; and how resources (labour, capital, raw materials, technology, know-how) are used within it.

Everyone has something to contribute. At Davos, Pope Francis emphasised that the various economic and political sectors are charged with "promoting an inclusive approach which takes into consideration the dignity of every human person and the common good."

I ask myself, and invite each of you to ask: can the system make room for what Pope Francis seeks? Can the world be brought out of the most devastating forms of poverty that particularly harm the excluded and the poor?

Our Church has asked such basic questions for many years – systematically, since Pope Leo XIII's *Rerum Novarum* of 1891. More recently, in 2009, President Barack Obama knew what challenges his newly formed government would face following the 2008 financial crisis. Broader accountability would need to come to bear at a global level. In his inaugural address, President Obama spoke of how the United States economy was badly weakened as a consequence of greed and irresponsibility. "To those nations like ours that enjoy relative plenty, we say we can no longer afford indifference to suffering outside our borders; nor can we consume the world's resources without regard to effect." Yet now, five years later, consuming "the world's resources without regard to effect" continues to prevail.

Many of you have spoken about this as well. From among your many important publications, I select a few remarks especially pertinent to our topic of promoting a more inclusive economy that is better oriented towards the truly common good:

- Earlier this month in Paris, José Ángel Gurría, Secretary-General of the OECD, said that "Understanding what drives economic and social progress is crucial to understanding how to improve wellbeing" and that "Addressing the multidimensional nature of progress lies at the heart of this endeavour."

- In June of 2011, Pascal Lamy, Director-General of the WTO, identified the essential problem today as "too little governance of globalisation. Our institutions, policies, and mindsets have not caught up with the integrated and interconnected world that we have created. The first age of globalisation fell apart because there was no effective political and policy response to profoundly changing economic and social conditions. Stating the problem is the easy part. Providing answers is more difficult, and implementing them is more difficult still." I must think that this is true for us here today.

- Jeffrey Sachs from Columbia University said that "We need to defend the interests of those whom we've never met and never will." Moreover, the current situation reminded him "too much of the fable of the farmer whose chickens are dying. The local priest gives one remedy after another – prayers, potions, oaths – until all of the chickens are dead. 'Too bad,' says the priest, 'I had so many other good ideas.'" I trust the parable applies not only to priests and farmers, but more generally to the economy's practitioners and custodians!

- In May 2014, Mark Carney, Governor of the Bank of England, said that "We simply cannot take the capitalist system, which produces such plenty and so many solutions, for granted. Prosperity requires not just investment in economic capital, but investment in social capital." He also said that "Unchecked market fundamentalism can devour the social capital essential for the long-term dynamism of capitalism itself. To counteract this tendency, individuals and their firms must have a sense of their responsibilities for the broader system."

- Kofi Annan, former Secretary-General of the United Nations and now Chairman of the Africa Progress Panel, declared that "Poverty is not a mono-dimensional problem involving just a lack of income. Extreme poverty represents a complex multifaceted set of phenomena involving the denial of opportunities across many areas of life, causing and reinforcing each other. Part of poverty is a lack of income, yes, but so too is a lack of education, health-care, nutrition, access to safe drinking water, the subjugation of women and environmental degradation."

- Finally, Muhammed Yunus, winner of the 2006 Nobel Peace Prize, called poverty "the absence of all human rights. The frustrations, hostility and anger generated by abject poverty cannot sustain peace in any society. To overcome poverty and the flaws of the economic crisis in our society, we need to envision our social life. We have to free our mind, imagine what has never happened before and write social fiction. We need to imagine things to make them happen. If you don't imagine, it will never happen."

To me, all these pertinent remarks point in one converging direction. As a fundamental matter of the rights of the poor and of our solidarity with them, it is imperative that the poor participate effectively in the development and implementation of solutions to their own problems and to society's problems as well.

Welcome to our Seminar

We all come with many questions and much to seek out and learn. With the help of our Research Working Paper, of your expert inputs, and in dialogue with each other, we have an opportunity to propose a better direction. It is important to discuss the concepts and theories and debate the ideas. At the same time, let us bravely consider what can concretely be put in place and as quickly as possible.

At Davos, the Holy Father noted the great achievements in the economic and technological realms. Then he quoted *Evangelii Gaudium:* "Business is – in fact – a vocation, and a noble vocation, provided that those engaged in it see themselves challenged by a greater meaning in life" (EG, 203) and then added that those in leadership "are able to serve more effectively the common good and to make the goods of this world more accessible to all." With admiration I recognize your track records as leaders solving many daunting problems and doing much to make the world a better place. So let us ask: can we not do this together now? Can we make the ideas and possibilities of more inclusive economy come to real life?

It is certainly my hope – a hope I trust you share – that we can make good progress towards this challenge over the next two days. Let us dare to rethink the economy and the administration or stewardship of our planet household for the benefit of all members of the human family.

Let us share the joy that comes from the Gospel, namely the Good News that all people have been rescued by Christ, which flows into rescuing creation from all manner of oppression, exploitation and despair (cf. EG, 215). This is to bring hope to the present world.

Let us aim, therefore, at establishing an economy in which the dignity of each person and the pursuit of the common good are neither overlooked nor sacrificed to lesser values. Let both local and global economy develop, which is to achieve progress, while respecting humanity – our brothers and sisters now, and future generations as well – and all creation that God gave us as our garden home (cf. EG, 220-221).

May the Lord bless this work and guide our efforts to make a genuine contribution for the sake of all. Let us be courageous in discussing the economy and brave in our search for how it can better benefit the truly common good.

QUESTIONNAIRE

This questionnaire was sent to the participants in preparation for the Seminar

Preamble

A wise American saying proclaims: never waste a crisis! This saying resonates with the famous expression used by St. Ambrose, bishop of Milan: "Happy the collapse [of the Roman empire] if the reconstruction will make the building more beautiful". The current financial and economic crisis affords us a rare opportunity to pause and reflect on where we have been going and where it leads. One of the most penetrating dangers of our epoch was stamped by the 20th Century writer C.S. Lewis as "chronological snobbery", that is, the uncritical acceptance of anything merely because it belongs to current intellectual trends. To repel such a danger, intelligent understanding of *res novae* and moral commitment are both required.

Some stylized facts

First, the political system has not been able, so far, to modify in a significant way the financial institutions responsible for the present crisis. Under these conditions, there is no guarantee that in the next 15-20 years another systemic bank and financial crisis can be avoided.

Second, the economic machinery continues to operate in a scandalously unfair way. Growing inequality jeopardizes both the efficiency and the stability of our societies. Inequality has become endogenous to the system and this generates not only economic costs (e.g. speculative bubbles; decreasing rate of investment; consumption distortions), but also social and human costs. It is a fact that an inequality rate exceeding a certain threshold reduces health and increases the mortality rate of people.

Third, the framework of the present market system tends to erode some of the values that sustain our civilization. Indeed, the process of creative destruction in Schumpeter's sense applies not only to firms and to inputs of production, but also to the very values that gave rise to market capitalism in the first place. In particular, the present market system tends to empower the strong over the weak.

Fourth, and as a consequence of the above, global capitalism as a model of social order has increasingly taken the characteristics of a religion, since it posits an overarching goal for human life and seeks to pursue it on the basis of a specific concept of human being. Today, the masking of the ideological nature of global capitalism takes place in two ways. On the one hand, decisions with moral content are presented in technological terms (e.g.: human rights have to be limited for the sake of labour flexibility). On the other hand, technical arguments are rendered as genuine moral alternatives (e.g.; the market versus State alternative is presented as if it were an ideological question). Isn't it urgent to try to de-mask the ideological nature of the global economic order?

Fifth, market capitalism is change incarnate. Yet, for all its fixation with change, the present system has lacked any theory to explain how a traditional society could become capitalist. This is the great paradox of capitalism's intellectual life. We know how change might take place within a market economy and the ensuing consequences. But economic science gives few accounts of how the economy might undergo non-linear changes.

What might be done

I. A global *government* seems to be at the same time desirable and necessary, in order to enforce strong redistributive policies, and undesirable and impossible, since it would reduce the space of legitimate freedom of both people and states. So, what should be done? Can the answer be found in global *governance*?

Rather than imagining a new world government, would it be advisable to focus attention on the existing global systems of governance – the UN with its network of international organizations; regional entities like the EU, Mercosur, Pacto Andino, G8, G20, etc. – in order to see what is working and what is not working and why.

II. While the protection of workers' rights remains mainly organized on a national basis, capital is fully globalized. It is this asymmetry that has guaranteed a new form of competition – the one between free labour and "slave" labour. Don't we need a world initiative similar to the GATT that has brought to the establishment of WTO? Can we conceive a General Agreement on Wages and Labour for the protection of workers' rights on a world scale?

It is known that the systematic violation of human rights (*iura hominum*) is associated with the action of about 70,000 multinational corporations operating at the world level. These have been able to create their own commercial code – a clear example of soft law. Can we be satisfied with the Guiding Principles prepared by the special "Ruggie Commission" on behalf of the UN – a commission instituted after the failure of the Mary Robinson Commission – and approved in the summer of 2011 by the UN (*Guiding Principles on Business and Human Rights. Implementing the United Nations 'Protect, Respect and Remedy' Framework*)? What should be done in order to implement effectively the project of social corporate responsibility if the aim is that of overcoming the present-day moral divide among countries?

III. An area where the lack of international governance is today particularly problematic is that of fiscal coordination among States. A reasonable level of tax competition is certainly positive in view of improving the allocation of resources. However, in the present conditions that level has been abundantly

23

overtaken: more than a few States have tax regulations especially suited to attract corporations unwilling to pay taxes in the countries where the resources have been created, to shelter purely speculative financial operations and to facilitate money laundering in the service of organized crime. What can be proposed to put an end or, at least, to curb such a trend?

IV. In May 2007, humanity witnessed a true turning point in world history. For the first time ever, just over half of the global population was confirmed as living in urban environments. No less than 95% of the current urban growth is accounted for in developing countries, all of which are absorbing five million people each and every month in cities, compared to a growth rate of half a million in developed countries.

Unlike the first wave of urbanization, today's process has been radically decoupled from industrialization, sometimes even from development *per se*. The present urbanization process is driven by nothing other than poverty. It is no longer true that "all roads lead to the towns" (F. Braudel); they lead to the slums. What form should new welfare policies take on in order to cope with this new phenomenon?

V. Recent empirical evidence shows that today market interactions causally affect the willingness to accept severe, negative consequences for a third party. This suggests that people do not care about the pecuniary externalities. It is well known that market price does not reflect the full social costs of the consequences of an economic choice; yet it is believed that the price system guarantees allocative efficiency.

However, there is a mirror image to the allocative function of market price: it also distributes incomes and wealth across the economy. Why does mainstream economics consider only technical externalities and give no attention to pecuniary externalities, those having to do with the distributive dimension of price changes? Is there a moral case for mitigating the most severe instances of pecuniary externalities? Is it acceptable that the pursuit of efficiency – a legitimate goal in itself – comes at the detriment of social justice? (From 2007 to 2012, the top 1% has increased incomes by 31% and the bottom 40% has decreased incomes by 6%).

VI. A pressing issue today concerns the way one should understand the construction of welfare programs. Granted that it is accepted that a welfare system should be based upon universalistic principles, how is it possible to design such a system without falling into the trap of "assistentialism"? Is it possible to combine solidarity (equity) and subsidiarity (reciprocity) in a credible and sustainable way?

It is known that there are a variety of modes of answering such questions. There is the way that can be called "laissez-faire" fundamentalism that advocates a plan for technological transformation driven by self-regulated systems, with the abdication of politics and the narrowing of scope for collective action. A second way is the neo-statist solution, which postulates a strong demand for public intervention in the social and economic spheres. Is a third way possible, where civil society organizations (NGOs, foundations, social enterprises, and voluntary associations) become active partners of public entities in the programming and managing of welfare services? As history confirms, these are true agents of radical change, via the accumulation of social capital and the provision of relational goods. Which conditions have to be met in order to allow these mission-driven organisations to perform more than a mere advocacy and denunciation function?

By way of conclusion

It is by now well-recognized that market systems are consistent with many cultures, conceived as organized systems of values. In turn, the type and degree of congruence of market systems with cultures is not without effects on the overall performance of the systems themselves: in general, the final outcome of market coordination will vary from culture to culture. Thus, one should expect that a culture of extreme individualism will produce different results from a culture of reciprocity where individuals, although motivated also by self-interest, entertain a sense of solidarity. In the same way, a culture of cooperation will certainly produce different results, on the economic front, than a culture of extreme positional competition.

But cultures are not to be taken for granted. Cultures respond to the investment of resources in cultural patterns. Indeed, how well an economic system performs depends also on whether certain conceptions and ways of life have achieved dominance. Contrary to what might be believed, economic phenomena have a primary interpersonal dimension. Individual behaviours are embedded in a pre-existing network of social relations which cannot be thought as a mere constraint; rather, they are one of the driving factors that prompt individual goals and motivations. People's aspirations are deeply conditioned by the conventional wisdom about what makes life worth living.

It is not wise to hide the difficulties lurking in the practical implementation of a cultural project targeted at nothing less than a "paradigm shift" in economic thinking. As in all human endeavours, it would be naïve to imagine that certain changes do not create conflict. The differences of vision and the interests at stake are enormous. It is no accident that a kind of widespread anguish about the future is running throughout society today. Some people and certain pressure groups are exploiting this anguish as a political tool, deriving from it, depending upon the circumstances, either a market-centered Machiavellianism or a state-centered Machiavellianism. Would it not be better for all and everyone to try to escape this dichotomous mode of thinking?

OVERVIEW OF THE RESPONSES TO THE PRE-CONFERENCE QUESTIONNAIRE

Rev. Prof. Helen Alford, op
Dean of the Faculty of Social Sciences
Pontifical University of St. Thomas Aquinas (the Angelicum)
Consultor of the Pontifical Council for Justice and Peace

Introduction

Thank you very much Cardinal Turkson and thank you also for being here. Without further ado, let's move on to try and synthesize the responses to the Questionnaire which you have received.

The first group of submissions were definitely organizational responses that often weren't signed by any one person but were presented as the response of a particular institution or organization. We also had some people who clearly represented organizations and a smaller number who responded in a rather personal way. However, I would say that they were presenting ideas that would be in line with the way the institutional staff is working, even though they were personally expressed. And then, we had individuals responding. I would just like to go over the questions that were posed in the questionnaire, then look at the responses with the idea of creating a sort of mosaic of the different elements and perhaps identifying the key elements that came out in the responses. This would be done with the view to helping the subsequent discussion. Perhaps, another image we could use would be that of creating small hooks to hold together our thinking and not to lose the richness that we had in this prior phase. That would then lead us on to open up the discussion, in the sense of looking at points of divergence and a point of convergence.

I find it beneficial for us to expand on convergence and divergence in light of a "pontifical" discussion. Here I thought it might be slightly funny, but also quite important, to say that this is a word which relates us to the fact that we're in a Pontifical Academy and this meeting is being jointly sponsored by the Pontifical Council for Justice and Peace. When, in English, we think of the word "pontificate," we think of somebody who is telling us what we are supposed to believe or not, whereas, as you probably know, the original meaning of the word is the pontifex, or a bridge builder. A bridge builder has to connect different positions. A bridge doesn't need to exist or has no purpose if we don't have differences. So it's very important that we have plurality and different ideas, this is very important for dealing with these complex problems that we face. So the pontifex needs to build the bridge between difference, and while differences are important, the bridge creates unity. So, we try to have diversity and plurality, but also some kind of deep unity, which is, of course, particularly important if we want to act. One of the things that so often blocks any way of responding to the problems we face – and everybody can see our problems – is that we don't have a sense of unity of what to do, and that, of course, stops everything from moving forward.

THE SIX QUESTIONS OF THE QUESTIONNAIRE

We had six main issues to look at.

1. The first one was: Is it sensible to think about the idea of global government. As the question said: On the one hand, it seems desirable and necessary, at the very same time it seems undesirable and impossible. So we are in this complex, various, almost contradictory situation. At the end, the question was saying "what is working and what is not working and why" in existing governance arrangements

2. The second question was looking at protecting workers' rights, and here we had, in a sense, a choice between a more

statutory type of protection, based on the treaties and mechanisms for enforcing treaties, and a more voluntary approach through CSR; even the UN *Guiding Principles on Human Rights* is a voluntary system at the moment.

3. Then, we moved to the third question on Fiscal Coordination among States.

4. The fourth one had quite a lot to do with organization but ended with a question about a type of welfare for the more urbanized societies we face today.

5. The fifth question looked at externalities and put its finger on pecuniary externalities. It is quite interesting that this question got the fewest responses out of all the questions, which might be interesting to reflect upon. So, we are looking at externalities that affect social justice and, in a way, if we have trade-offs between efficiency and inclusivity, how we should deal with this situation.

6. And then, the last one was looking at the role of civil society in welfare provision in particular.

I. GLOBAL GOVERNMENT

If we look at the first question – there were obviously very interesting and very wide and rich responses – let us try to draw out some key-points which could be useful for discussion. The first interesting point is that several people gave pointers dealing with the process itself. The OECD's response was especially interesting. Some people said the words are not so important. It isn't important whether we choose "government" or "governance": What is important is that we are trying to move towards a better situation than we are in now. The ICCR's response talked about an adaptive approach that is constantly shifting its focus and moving forward. So, the process is actually crucial. In regard to that, several of the responses talked about principles for global governance and global government, and we can briefly mention some underlying principles. The UNDP had pairs of ideas: efficiency and effectiveness, legitimacy and transparency, accountability and fairness. There was also an interesting point from *World Bank* about indicators: if we are going to govern well, we need to know how we measure how well we're doing. In particular, we may mention GDP which was referred to as "imperfect, but the best available measure of economic performance"; we might have some good discussion on that during the seminar. Then, some people made some more concrete proposals. In general, they refer to strengthening both global governance and multilateralism. People felt that these are two simultaneous tracks that have to go forward together. One respondent said that we should move some power from the *Security Council to the General Assembly* – a bit like what's been happening in Europe with the move from the European Council to the European Parliament, perhaps – and make more of regional organizations to increase inclusivity. Some people focused on words from the Catholic social tradition, including the idea of the "world political authority", initially launched by John XXIII and also mentioned by Benedict XVI in his recent Encyclical. Some people linked their comments to this idea. Michel Camdessus talked about a "supreme council" above the Bretton Woods organizations, a kind of transformation of the current G20. The CIDSE organization mentioned two reports from the 1990s, and their proposal to transform ECOSOC into an economic and social security council, so here again we have some more concrete proposals that are directly connected with ideas from Catholic Social Thought. The submission from the FAO also deals with governance in relation to food security, nutrition and the new developments that are occurring in these areas through the Committee on World Food Security.

II. PROTECTING WORKERS' RIGHTS

The second question looks at labour, and, in particular, at these two possible routes of dealing with labour protection, one more focused on statutory regulation such as the proposed *General Agre-*

ement on Wages and Labour, or something similar, and the other of a more voluntary type in which the term CSR, Corporate Social Responsibility, is a sort of central term, although the OECD also introduced the idea of *Responsible Business Conduct* (RBC) there. Several people said that if we are going to have CSR, if we are going to go along the voluntary route, it has to be taken up seriously; it cannot be a form of philanthropy or some kind of marketing; it has to be integrated into the way of running the business. Ferrero gave an example, and talked about a multi-stakeholder approach. The representative from the Cooperative Bank talked about how it is internalizing externalities. Some people raised the issue which is always raised, with regard to this approach, which is that especially when you are looking at human rights, a voluntary system will have drawbacks. CIDSE pointed out that only the good companies will do this voluntarily. There was also mention of minimum wages in general. As the ILO *World of Work* report showed very well last year, minimum wages don't tend to threaten the number of jobs and, furthermore, a well-applied system creates demand, to a much greater extent than allowing companies to keep more money and expecting them then to invest it. As we know, right now, there are huge cash mountains in the big multinational companies that are not being invested, and if some of that money had gone into wages we would have seen a quicker effect on demand and, of course, this would help inclusivity and growth as well. The *World Bank* talked about how they are now introducing a whole safeguards framework to do with the projects that they fund to ensure high standards of labour protection. They also emphasized that we need to think much more positively: they pushed against the idea of society mistrusting business; for them, we need to think about the possibility of private-sector-led development and that the private sector has a key role to play in dealing with exclusion and poverty. As a last point on voluntary mechanisms, the OECD reported that its *Guidelines on Multinational Enterprise* are beginning to move a bit closer to a statutory type of regulation. This is the only international instrument to which governments have committed themselves, and it includes a kind of grievance mechanism in it, so that we are beginning to see something approaching a legal mechanism within that system. If we now turn to look more at the statutory line of worker protection, a little bit less was said about this in response to this question. Several people mentioned the importance of the ILO and various points about that. The FAO emphasized that existing protections need to be extended to the rural and agricultural informal sectors before we even think about anything else. On the specific proposal about the idea of a *General Agreement on Wages and Labour*, some people were very much in favor – ICCR, for instance; others had some reservations and felt that it could be just a very long, drawn-out negotiation, which in the end would not necessarily achieve very much. Klaus Schwab from the *World Economic Forum* talked about technological change and how this could be a factor that is crucial in the way work develops in the future and the way labour can be protected.

III. FISCAL COORDINATION AMONG STATES

Our third question dealt with fiscal coordination among States. Here, the overwhelming impression you get from the replies is that this is a big problem and it is difficult to deal with it. All specific proposals should be read against that background and the difficulty of dealing with this issue as a whole. Several responses emphasized the importance of involving all countries, especially developing countries, which are losing a lot of income through tax havens or various kinds of mis-invoicing of trade, and the various initiatives to deal with that. The big issue, apart from transparency and cooperation, is actually confronting the offshore and tax haven problems. The three biggest offshore centres in the world are London, Tokyo and New York, so, of course we are not just talking about Bermuda and Niue and other small countries. So there is a very big problem here. Some respondents talked about a world tax authority, though not in much detail. *Oxfam* mentioned the importance of a tax for financing public services which we will come back to a little bit later when we look at welfare. Finally, a bit along the lines of Schwab's earlier point about technology, Michel Camdessus said: "just be careful, that we can't expect too much of a tax system, we can't expect a planetary redistribution of wealth, even though it can help to increase inclusion and lead to a better fiscal system".

IV. WELFARE FOR AN URBANIZING POPULATION

The fourth point regarded welfare policies for the new urbanization. We had a lot of responses here about the question of urbanization. What counts is urban poverty, its dimensions, the question of treating it or preventing it, relating also to the point made by CIDSE and FAO about supporting rural communities and stopping people from drifting, simply because of poverty, from the rural areas to urban areas, and only for that reason. The *World Bank* talked about how their research, or research they referred to, argues that we can deal with poverty, or at least, if we really want to confront poverty, we can deal with a significant part of it. They suggest that two thirds of the answer needs to come from growth, while one third is to do with redistribution. They support the idea that we cannot confront poverty just with policies to do with growth, and they very much support the idea of conditional cash transfers, a question which relates to some of the case studies below. The *Bolsa Familia* in Brazil, for instance, is one example where families are given support if they have their children vaccinated and send them to school; such a system very much increases positive outcomes for children. In all of their responses, *Transparency International* has talked about the importance of accountability; when we are talking about policies on urban development, accountability applies to city administrations, not just those at the national level. In response to this question, we had quite a lot of case studies that were interesting. The *Cooperative Sector* talked about how they are especially well placed to deal with questions of urban exclusion and poverty and urban welfare, because of the way cooperative businesses fund projects. Lastly, a lot of cities are crucial with regard to dealing with climate change, but many of them, especially in the South, are not really able, at the moment, to confront this problem. This makes the project called the *Low Carbon Livable Cities*, the initiative of the *World Bank,* especially important.

V. EXTERNALITIES, PECUNIARY, SOCIAL JUSTICE AND OTHERS

Our fifth question, on efficiency and pecuniary externalities, as we already said, had fewer responses than the others. The OECD in its response actually gave a reason why there would not be so many responses on this point, although some people contested the question, saying it is not true that the idea of pecuniary externalities is completely absent from economic theory or research. Anyway, the basic ideas behind mainstream economic thought tend to cover up this problem and tend to make it invisible. If you hold to the idea of *Pareto efficiency,* an assumption that people do not enter into transactions unless it increases their welfare, pecuniary externalities should not be a problem. But, of course, we know they are. As the OECD said, "there is a strong case for mitigating the most extreme examples of pecuniary externalities". In the agricultural system, we are very used to hearing about something which is not usually called a pecuniary externality, even if, in fact, it is such: the effects of international markets on the commodity prices of basic food products. The OECD has proposed compensatory measures, which are not just a sort of straight redistribution to people who are hit unfavorably by price changes, but what they call a "policy tool kit", especially with interventions at key moments in people's lives, early childhood, or, especially if we think of Europe now, young adulthood, that is, very targeted interventions that can help people at particularly vulnerable points in their lives. Cooperatives find it easier to combine efficiency and social justice; they don't have such a clear trade-off than perhaps, other economic actors have, especially because they can also take a longer term view. *Transparency International* talked about corruption as being one of the key factors which tends to increase exclusion. It is always the poorest people in society who have to pay the most in bribes as a proportion of their income. And growth that propagates inequality contains the seeds of its own destruction, as Klaus Schwab says. So, these were some of the key responses on pecuniary externalities; UNCTAD also had some quite interesting points on that.

This little graphic from *Oxfam* is quite striking:

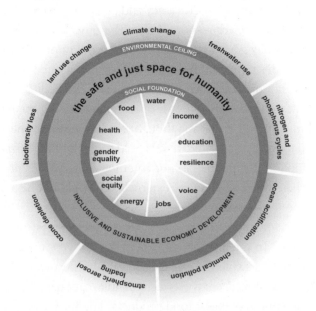

Oxfam has the idea of a doughnut, as they called it, with a social floor (the inside boundary), implying a minimum level of key goods from a social point of view, and then an environmental ceiling, which is the outer side of the doughnut. Within these bounds, we can develop an inclusive, sustainable economy.

36

VI. WELFARE AND THE ROLE OF CIVIL SOCIETY

Question six was concerned with whether civil society could have an active role in welfare or not. There was an almost universal yes in answer to this question. The following points are just details within what the OECD called an "enabling state that creates active citizens". *Oxfam* talked about the importance of a universal approach to health and education. The cooperative sector talked about the importance for them to understand communities and what communities need, through listening to NGOs and then working with them to make them more activist, more involved in confronting problems; social enterprise also came up. The FAO was quite interested in emphasizing the importance of social welfare for rural families because it helps them manage risk and avoid harmful coping strategies, like eating less or taking their children out of school when they are facing a crisis, and it supports them to invest in their own resilience. Here, we see the importance of historical background or the path-dependency of different countries or areas. Most of the people who wrote this questionnaire came from Italy, and in this country we do have a problem with a kind of "assistentialist" state and welfare system, tending to limit people's active participation in society. But, in a situation like the one FAO is dealing with, it's quite the opposite. Such welfare payments can actually help people to become much more actively involved in their communities and societies. We need fora to guide us in how to deal with our problems, such as the *World Economic Forum*. The *World Bank* talked about the need to develop a global partnership for social accountability, so that we can decide together how we measure our progress. And then Simona Beretta talked about the fact that we are always going to have sin in our systems; we are never going to be able to create a perfect system, and we need to keep that in mind when we are dealing with our proposals.

DIVERGENCE AND CONVERGENCE
AMONG THE RESPONSES

The discussion of divergence could be focused around the word *growth*. Take Vandana Shiva's very interesting proposal as a way of focusing some of the different points of view. One of the section titles in her submission says: "growth creates poverty". It was a very striking statement. We also had some interesting comments from Severine Deneulin in her paper where she was talking about how growth is a very rough measure, and we should be thinking about other kinds of indicators, at least alongside this. She talked about the happiness literature and related research. As an economist friend of mine once wrote: "much of US growth in the last twenty years is social decay under another name". As we know, there's a big debate about GDP, now. Wars, epidemics, and family breakdown all increase GDP, just as much as positive real, growth does, which is what Shiva means when she says: "growth creates poverty". At the same time, we also had other people saying yes but, as Griffiths said, "you know, when a prisoner looks out of his prison cell window through the bars, one sees mud and another sees stars", he's of course pointing at the fact that we have this complex situation where growth includes both, or at least GDP includes both positive and negative factors, so we don't want to forget that there is something positive there. UNIAPAC talked about people being lifted out of poverty by the opening up of economies, by participation in global economy, and actually used the phrase "this economy enables life", talking about life being saved as a result of this. Another point of divergence might be the market. Again, Vandana Shiva very strongly attacks the disembodied, decontextualized market. Certainly, if you look at any of the texts coming out of Catholic circles, very often you'll see this idea of finance having become self-referential, of having lost its purpose as something which supports the real economy. At the same time, many people mentioned the importance of markets, so one of the key issues is to discuss: what kinds of markets? Social markets and the civil economy, for instance, that came out in the UNIAPAC response. Vandana Shiva herself talked about the very lively bazaars in India, so the question of market again is another term which can crystallize some different points of view in a helpful way. Perhaps the divergence could be summarized by thinking about the strengths and weaknesses of capitalism, or if you want to put it in more apocalyptic terms: does this economy, that we are living in now, ultimately or fundamentally, nourish life or destroy it? A point of convergence is the idea of cooperation.

The various responses talked a lot about the need for a forum, a need for discussion, a need for international cooperation; the cooperative bank, of course, said a lot about this. The word "cooperation" kept coming up. It is an interesting word because it is a key theoretical idea in the existing thought about capitalism. We can think about Adam Smith or key thinkers in early economic thought, but also about new thinking about economics, with ideas of "co-opetition" and "wikinomics". These ideas re-emphasise cooperation as integral to economic life, along with competition, rebalancing the interaction between these two ways of behaving. Since we are here in a Pontifical Academy, it is appropriate to mention some Catholic moral theology. You can see this same idea in a different guise in the classical ideas of "primary" and "secondary" natural law, where "natural law" is an ancient idea in Catholic moral theology. On the primary level, we think about what a society would look like if it were fully developed, i.e. the ideal society. In some sense, everyone has a basic idea of what that kind of society would be like, since it relates to being human in a full sense. We could explain what the primary level is with a simple example: if today, you went out on to the streets of Rome or Calcutta or Rio de Janeiro and asked people: "if we could have an ideal economy, one where we don't have all the problems we have today, what would it look like? What would be in this economy? How would it work?" people would say a million different things, but there would be two main things you would find in most of the responses. The first one would be "everybody should be able to participate, nobody should be excluded from this economy", and the second one would be "we need a sustainable economy that is not going to destroy our planet, that's not going to destroy our environment." It relates to those two levels on the *Oxfam* limit that we saw on the doughnut, as well a social question and an environmental question. You can see here that a key word to sum up these two points could be "co-operation" – cooperation with each other and with nature. So that would be, in a classic way of thinking, the primary level of natural law, the ideal for us. But then, of course, we know that real life isn't like that and that systems that have tried to get there too directly tend to collapse. Those of us who are from the Christian religion – maybe the biblical scholars here might correct me a bit – know that we have in the Acts of the Apostles the story of the Jerusalem community, where everybody shared all their goods, but Saint Paul had to go around getting a collection to support them; they couldn't support themselves economically. We all know too that Communism, at least in its classical form, didn't work.

So, the secondary level of natural law involves thinking about a society that works for people the way they actually are, rather than what they could be ideally (which is what we saw on the first level). On the secondary level, we can see that actually we do need systems of private property, at least to some extent, in order to create wealth, and that competition is necessary to help us do that efficiently (without wasting resources) and to keep improving how we do that. Competition and private property, however, are "secondary"; they are "means" to help us get ever closer to our ideal, what we saw at the first or primary level of natural law. It's a secondary part of being human to need to own property and to compete, but it is only through using these means that we can get to a sharing, sustainable economy. Through this analysis from classical Catholic moral theology, we can arrive at similar ideas to those we were discussing above: competition and private property are important in a secondary way, and need to be based on cooperation, which is at the primary, ideal level of human existence. Severine Deneulin could have interesting things to say about that, given her paper on human agency. We have some practical examples, especially from the cooperative tradition, in the real economy. In the Anglo-Saxon worldview, however, I would say that cooperatives seem a bit staid, even if we have had some very dynamic cooperatives, including some that became too dynamic and collapsed, like the *Cooperative Bank* in UK. Anyway, normally a cooperative has a rather "staid" image, a sort of marginal part of the economy, not really a leading innovative force. Why couldn't that image change? Cooperatives have always been important in creating inclusion and helping vulnerable people to be part of the economic system. Perhaps they could become much more propositive and innovative in the future; especially if they can manage to link their, what we could call, more "classical" cooperation, which is richly relational and locally rooted, with the new forms of cooperation you can get through social networks, which are "thinly relational" but global. We have a different kind of cooperation emerging from modern technology which could perhaps be complementary to the more classical form.

We should have a discussion which is aimed more at the policy level than at dealing with a lot of analysis, combining engagement with current developments, trying to find what's good and what's going on and what's to be encouraged, and also providing a critique of what is bad, all the while being attentive to what the Holy Father is trying to do today, which is really to attack this "globalisation of indifference". There are so many things we could do, we know we could do, and we don't do them, because some key people just don't really take into their hands the power that they have to do something, or we as a community don't push enough for it. So, there is an urgency to confront the problems of today. The Pontifical Council for Justice and Peace, in conducting meetings like this, aims to help the Church in a sort of "aggiornamento", a sort of updating and continuing to keep up with current changes, in terms of its own teaching in relation to problems today.

We could conclude this opening session with a quote from *Evangelii Gaudium*, which was already mentioned by Cardinal Turkson. Pope Francis has a great devotion to an image of "Our Lady, the Untier of Knots". As we confront big and complex issues in this meeting, these "big knots" that we have to try to "untie", perhaps this text could give us hope: "The Holy Spirit can be said to possess an infinite creativity, proper to the divine mind, which knows how to loosen the knots of human affairs, even the most complex and inscrutable" (EG, 178).

OVERVIEW OF THE PRINCIPAL OBJECTIVES OF THE SEMINAR AND OF THE DISCUSSION PAPER PROVIDED PRIOR TO THE CONFERENCE

H. Exc. Msgr. Mario Toso, sdb
Secretary of the Pontifical Council for Justice and Peace

1. Introduction and context

Every historical moment experienced by humanity is in itself unique and valuable. Precisely for this reason, the principles, criteria and practical guidelines of the Social Doctrine of the Church (we can mention here as examples: the common good, the primacy of the person, the value and dignity of work, the preferential option for the least fortunate) must be applied in ever new forms, always taking into account the continuous changes taking place. With the exception of Benedict XVI's *Caritas in Veritate* and, in part, John Paul II's *Centesimus Annus*, previous encyclicals, for obvious reasons, had not yet had the opportunity to deliberate on the new challenges and opportunities that globalisation and the internet pose to the fulfilment of these principles, criteria and guidelines. At this precise moment in history it is the task of our generation to rise to the challenge.

The main objective of this seminar is to reflect with leading experts from the world of institutions, enterprises and academia, on the many aspects of development today, particularly from the perspective of anthropology and ethics. This requires that we place it in the particular historical context of today. The discussion paper and the research paper, provided to all participants, are intended to illustrate this by proposing a representation of the facts as a starting point and stimulus for discussion over the course of these two days.

We begin, then, with a brief description of the context and events. Today we live in an era that in some ways is remarkable. It reaps the fruits of technological progress that is consistent, rapid and following an almost exponential curve. It certainly is not linear. This progress is indisputable and in some respects irreversible. Once a scientific discovery in any field has become widespread and has produced its results, humanity cannot forget or give up the wealth of knowledge and tools related to it. The spread of the internet has enormously accelerated the speed of circulation of knowledge, giving us to understand that progress like this will continue to expand at this rate. Sages in ancient times had to travel for days in order to be able to transmit what they had discovered to other places. Today every member of the scientific community can instantly put the results of their work on the web and submit them to the judgment of their peers, thus contributing to research activity. Likewise, they can even initiate a discussion about their preliminary results with the global scientific community through social networking sites and discussion lists before they have them published. This extraordinary evolution allows us all to stand on the shoulders of a giant that continues to grow. Humanity has now solved the problem of aggregate production of goods and services. A spectacular example of this non-linearity of progress is the fact that 23% of this production, from the birth of Christ to the present, has happened since the start of this new millennium. The financial resources of the world are also considerable and sometimes overabundant, causing bubbles and crises. The key problem of today, therefore, is that of distribution.

Globalisation has set in motion a process of convergence between the average income of the poorest countries and the richest countries, but at the same time, it has increased the inequalities between different parts of the world population. The two phenomena are children of the same revolution. The market is becoming globalised while increasing the gaps in schooling levels, and by bringing about intense competition between low cost workers in low-income countries with workers with high wages in high-income countries. The convergence process that is in place is progressively improving income in emerging countries but it is causing difficulties for the rights acquired by workers in high-income countries. In the meantime, the mass media give more intense visibility to the contrast between the different levels of well-being, and this encourages the disinherited masses to abandon their land and to seek their fortune in rich countries.

We are therefore going through a long transition that is promising, although problematic and complex, which will hopefully lead from the old world, segmented within national borders, to a new world populated by a single human family. If current trends continue unchallenged, it is estimated that such a transition is likely to last 70-100 years. To date, one billion two hundred million people still live below the absolute poverty line and more than two billion 700 million people exist on less than two dollars a day. These people are unlikely to see this change come about in the course of their lifetimes.

Furthermore, it is known that the economic problem that economists have traditionally dealt with is only one of the dimensions of the problem. We have to ensure that the creation of economic value is environmentally sustainable (the environmental dimension), that it does not produce dramatic financial crises (the financial dimension) and that there is no disparity between GDP and well-being (the life satisfaction dimension) that will produce growing dissatisfaction and the loss of a sense of life, thus turning the rich countries into countries that are "satiated and desperate".

In a nutshell, the challenge ahead that is summed up between the lines of the discussion paper and the contributions contained in the research paper for which we thank professors Becchetti, Bruni, Habisch and Zamagni, is that we can do more, much more to accelerate the transition towards the transformation of humanity into a single family, where the four critical dimensions above are jointly transcended by: the defeat of poverty ('make poverty history' was chanted by an international campaign some time ago); the solution to the problem of environmental sustainability, by separating economic value creation from the destruction of natural resources; full reconciliation between the creation of economic value and social responsibility and the creation of regulations that are needed in order to avoid the risk of new relapses being caused by crippling financial crises.

2. *The main contents of the preparatory papers*

Pope Francis' apostolic exhortation *Evangelii Gaudium* contains some key messages for our reflection, especially in those sections devoted to the current economy, to ideological views of finance, to the idolisation of money, and to the consumer culture of indifference. Obviously, our reflections must be subjected to critical examination and be compared to the doctrines of today, with a view to their in-depth study, both cultural and conceptual.

The first message conveyed by the exhortation is that no positive determinism or automatic mechanisms can transform the sum of individual self-interest into good for everyone. It is very dangerous to think that "invisible hands" can replace both the hard work and the effort of all in promoting the civic virtues necessary for the market to function properly, and the system of regulations needed to put the strength of the economy at the service of each person. The recent global financial crisis has resoundingly refuted this unrealistic illusion. The *laissez faire* approach causes the regulators to sleep. When the market is made absolute and is abandoned to its spontaneous mechanisms, it will never produce a regime of perfect competition. It tends instead to create oligopolies of actors that are too big to fail. The very signals that the market transmits through the price system are either misinterpreted or, in any case, they fail to give advance notice of the danger of an approaching crisis or about bubbles that are about to burst. Precisely for this reason, after the latest crisis, economists have begun to seriously think about the "law of motion" which is capital and the civic virtues, the basic lifeline of the system and without which the market economy cannot survive.

The second message given by *Evangelii Gaudium* is that the social doctrine of the church (= SDC), can make a valuable contribution in breaking narrow mindsets and anthropological and ethical reductionism that diminish the human person, enterprise and moral values and neutralise their potential. The SDC, centred in Jesus Christ, the Redeemer of all humanity, of the whole person, proposes a new humanism that is open to transcendence. A person is more than goods and more than "a life to be discarded". Each person is a framework of relationships and not simply an acquirer of material goods. A business is not simply a corporation. It is, first of all, a "society of people" and an organisation that must aim to satisfy the well-being of various stakeholders who depend on its operation. The common good is not the same as GDP, although it includes, of course, the dimension of material well-being. The richness of the Church's social doctrine can ultimately provide important inspiration to help current socio-economic thinking understand that there are not only private, public or common goods, but that interpersonal and community relationships are key to the success and fertility of economic and social life. It should be recognised that while the great innovators of today (think of the inventors of social networks) have well understood the importance of relational goods, socioeconomic thought is finding it very hard to grasp fully the extent and the consequences both for markets and for the sustainable and inclusive development of countries.

A third and decisive message offered by *Evangelii Gaudium*, in view of the socio-economic growth of the family of nations, is related to fraternity, a good and value that is often forgotten. Until now, in the social sciences and political doctrines, reflection has been developed on the axes of only two of the three key words of the French Revolution, those of freedom (liberalism) and equality (socialism, equality of opportunity, redistributive policies). The SDC emphasises, however, the need for a third dimension. It is fellowship or fraternity, so that the full potential of living together in society can be developed. Fraternity is not a virtue to be confined to sacristies and churches.

It is the lubricant that makes relationships fertile, and it is the asymmetry of the gift that is able to initiate processes of reciprocity and make human interactions alive and vibrant.

The papers prepared for this seminar also emphasise that a decisive role can and should be carried out by organised forms of civil society, according to a polyarchic logic and in the implementation of the principle of subsidiarity. *Caritas in Veritate* had already discussed the fact that, in the dialectic between the only two poles of the public and the private profit maximisers, the economic system is likely to erode its own foundations and dry up the "law of motion" of the civic virtues. These virtues are essential for its smooth operation, such as compliance with covenants, trust and moral integrity. Today's financial crisis, from which we have not yet fully emerged, is, from this point of view, a typical situation in which all of this has happened. In the interests of pluralism and balance of powers, it is therefore necessary to stimulate the energies that come from the base, from civil society in its organised forms. In recent decades there has been significant spontaneous growth of these organisations that have often played a subsidiary role in producing public goods and services. The hybridisation of forms of enterprise is an important key to our future. The conference recently organised by the Pontifical Council for Justice and Peace on impact investing, which brought to Rome major global impact investors, informed us of what is now the highest ambition of a new generation of entrepreneurs. They are not content to increase earnings as compensation for their contribution to the creation of economic value but consider that the greatest ambition is to do something that can have a positive impact on society. Only in this way will they receive the highest gratitude, esteem and recognition from their peers.

The reflections prepared in advance of this Seminar also ask what regulations and institutions might facilitate the full development of the energies of civil society that are able to combine economic value creation and the creation of values and social capital, all necessary for the proper functioning of the economic system.

So, we ask how taxation, procurement rules, development of quality and of information intermediaries can help to increasingly turn globalisation into a path of growth, from the base upwards, from people's rights and from environmental sustainability, and not in a race to the bottom in each of these cases.

3. *The objectives of the Seminar*

On this basis it can be said that the aims of the seminar are condensed into one main goal that is, moreover, very ambitious. They are to develop a discernment process at the highest level, drawing on the wealth of experience and expertise of the participants, to understand how each of us, with our role and responsibilities, may do more and achieve *magis*, with a view to the activation of the processes of change that accelerate humanity's journey towards being a large global family and the conditions necessary for the achievement of our common good. Such a large goal involves two other more specific objectives: a) to overcome, as soon as possible, the great evils which afflict humanity today, such as the still huge proportion of people living below the threshold of absolute poverty, the environmental unsustainability of our development, and the lack of meaning in life and work for so many people; b) to move quickly towards an inclusive society, one in which the proportion of people able to find a reasonable meaning to their lives and their work is as high as possible.

The group of participants in this seminar is composite and heterogeneous. Precisely for this reason the work that lies ahead is promising. In a well-known story, some blind people ask a wise man to explain to them what an elephant is. The wise man suggests that they go and touch it and report to the others what they have experienced and perceived. Each of the blind people follows the advice of the wise man. By sharing their stories they come to get an idea of what an elephant is. The diversity of our lives and life experiences, as well as our professions and roles, is a great wealth. It allows us to put together the pieces of the puzzle and get a better view of the complexity of the problems and challenges that the human family is facing today. The synergies and complementarities that can be made between institutions, academia, the world of culture and businesses are very considerable. These are treasures that are within our reach and that these two days of joint reflection can help us to discover.

One method that could be adopted with the result of our work is Saint Ignatius Loyola's *Presupponendum*, a method certainly dear to Pope Francis, considering his spiritual family of origin. The Ignatian *Presupponendum* is like an open and positive preliminary ruling with regard to attitudes, words and sincere enquiry. It fosters dialogue among those concerned. It consists precisely in "being more willing to support a person's statement than to condemn it". In essence, the *Presupponendum* is a state of mind of departure. It is benevolent and avoids *a priori* prejudices and barriers that prevent us from enriching our lives through the sharing of that 'part' of truth that our interlocutor has discovered, by virtue of his or her original and particular life experience.

A prospect of a fruitful outcome that can guide us in our path is given by the striking illustration that Pope Francis proposed in *Evangelii Gaudium*. It is the principle of "time is greater than space". He says: "One of the faults which we occasionally observe in sociopolitical activity is that spaces and power are preferred to time and processes. Giving priority to space means madly attempting to keep everything together in the present, trying to possess all the spaces of power and of self-assertion; it is to crystallize processes and presume to hold them back. Giving priority to time means being concerned about initiating processes rather than possessing spaces. Time governs spaces, illumines them and makes them links in a constantly expanding chain, with no possibility of return. What we need, then, is to give priority to actions which generate new processes in society and engage other persons and groups who can develop them to the point where they bear fruit in significant historical events. Without anxiety, but with clear convictions and tenacity" (*Evangelii Gaudium,* 223).

Pope Francis does not intend to discourage anyone who assumes responsibility for organisational or policy management in an attitude of service. He is suggesting, rather, that we judge the *magis* of any policy action on the basis of its ability to generate positive processes that accelerate the pace of history. In view of this objective, it is not enough to have the important gift of being able to detect the line of progress one step ahead of others. It is not sufficient to indicate a goal well. It is more necessary and important to help humanity to chart paths that lead to it, living in the places where we build the new. In the passage above from *Evangelii Gaudium,* it is also very instructive to read the reference to the spiritual balance that those who are about to undertake an activity should possess. We must avoid falling into the anxiety of those who think that they have to solve the world's problems alone and are frustrated because they do not have the resources. If we are to proceed with clarity and tenacity in our mission, a necessary precondition is clear discernment of the situation, to be clear about how much each one of us can do in our own specific, original and precious life as we coordinate our efforts with those of others and develop synergies in initiatives. It is, as they say these days, to be a multi-stakeholder. It is to help this process of essential discernment that we are gathered here today, and everyone is invited to make their contribution.

4. Conclusion

As globalisation today has failed to totally resolve the issues of inequality and poverty – it has managed to deal with some problems but it created others like reducing the middle class – we can be permitted to ask some questions. Does a market economy really reject an inclusive economy as proposed by Pope Francis? Is it, perhaps, synonymous with centralised economy and finance that are totally planned? Would it be functional to an inclusive economy and democracy to have an economy and finance that are totally independent from policy and the common good? What concrete steps should be considered necessary in order to have international and supranational institutions that are commensurate with markets and global finance? Many scholars and politicians now believe that you need to accelerate the reform of the existing international institutions, as well as the creation of new democratic political entities, at least at the regional level, so that the global common good can rely on the contribution of, in addition to that of the United States of America, also that of the United States of Europe, Africa, Latin America and Asia. On these issues, the Pontifical Council for Justice and Peace, in our desire to practise the guidelines given in number 67 of *Caritas in Veritate*, have offered some proposals.[2]

With a view to victory over inequalities and poverty, is it necessary to return to the separation between commercial banks and investment banks? Must we maintain the view that work is marginal with respect to the production of national and global wealth? Is the market enough to create a sustainable and inclusive economy for all, to cultivate a welfare society? Should this be totally privatised or mercantilised?

It seems that the solution cannot be found in the radicalisation of the public economy against a private economy, or in neo-statism against neo-liberalism. It is to be found in a healthy flowering of forms of organisation that are present in a modern economy with entrepreneurship that has a wide range of values, democratically oriented towards the common good, through the logic of participation and gift, in the context of social justice.

---

[2] Pontificio Consiglio della Giustizia e della Pace, *Per una riforma del sistema finanziario e monetario internazionale nella prospettiva di un'autorità pubblica a competenza universale*, Libreria Editrice Vaticana, Città del Vaticano 2011, 3rd edition.

ANTHROPOLOGICAL AND SOCIAL REDUCTIONISM OF TODAY'S ECONOMIC THOUGHT AND ACTIVITIES: CHALLENGES TO CIVILIZING GLOBALIZATION

Luigino Bruni
Professor of Economics
LUMSA University - Rome

I'll try to be brief, although the issues are very complex and articulated. The two parts of our Discussion Paper are based on anthropological issues that can be, or maybe can appear more abstract than the first panel about general issues – distribution, inequality and so on. But maybe, it is also part of this moral framework that we are discussing now because economics, economy, business and policy are based on some idea of human being. Then, in our discussion paper we thought it would be important to discuss, in a critical way, the anthropological hypothesis behind the *Homo Oeconomicus Paradigm* that is so important in policy choices and policies.

1. The first anthropological reductionism is probably a very well used, popular word in English, reductionism, but it is a sort of philosophical expression that is a way of cutting the human being in a very peculiar way. As you know, any model, any scientific model requires some form of 'reductionism', but any reductionism is indifferent, neutral in terms of predictions and policies, and in particular in social sciences. The first is the idea of the views of man, of economic activities and their values. The first, as Sister Helen Alford said, is to see the human being, the human person as an economic agent driven primarily by self-interest or egoism.

Now, my introduction is to just add a few considerations for each of these three issues. Self-interest or egoism, as you know, may exist, as the people working on economic theories know very well. This idea that economics is based on self-interest, the economic principal is egoism and so on, is one of the 'charge sheets' to market economy coming from a huge part of virtue ethics and communitarianism, philosophy today. Because most of the critics of market economy said ok, markets depend on instrumental rationality and extrinsic motivation. Common good, virtue, and what is good in life requires internal value and intrinsic motivations. Therefore, markets tend to corrupt virtue or at least are not compatible and, by using the market as its central model, economics normalizes instrumentality and extrinsic motivation, and thus destroys virtue and common good, and maybe also common goods.

We are not against market economy, but we are not for the market as it is, because we are here for a criticism of the market in order to help market agents and the market economy to become closer to its vocation or its *telos* as the Greek philosophers said. Then our point: this criticism, and also the praise of market, depends on a peculiar idea of market nature, because there is no need to take self-interest as the economic principle. We know that the classics of economic science, like Smith or Ricardo, Edgeworth, Marshall, Keynes, and also contemporary anthropological, social and neuro sciences say that the basic principle of economic interactions is not self-interest, but reciprocity, mutual advantage, mutuality, or fraternity. There is no need to take self-interest as the economic principle, there is no need in Adam Smith, there is no need in Edgeworth, there is no need in contemporary social sciences, there is no need in our approach. Then, we claim that the market is not just a place for vices; there is a vocation or *telos* of the market to be also a place for virtues. Because if we don't rescue the market from the realm, the kingdom of vices, there is no hope, because we have just one option to condemn, to say there is no salvation for people working on market economy.

Our mission statement for the market is that it is an institution that promotes mutually advantageous transactions. Reciprocity or mutual assistance in the work of civil economy tradition is the *telos*, the purpose of the market, neither self-interest nor altruism or philanthropy. Mutuality: our vision, in particular my vision, but I think it's part of the document on market, is that mutuality, reciprocity, mutual advantage, is the vocation, the purpose of market. That means that any way of understanding market in a different way, like Zero-sum game or exploitation, is to deny the vocation of the market, it is to go against the nature of the market. For that reason, our approach is not just to call for a moral approach to market, but it is to discuss the nature of market and to call the market to its more human original vocation.

2. Then, the second reductionism is to see the subjects of economic activity as entities oriented towards simply producing goods and services or maximizing profit, or even rent, as most of you know the work of people like Piketty and others, rent as the disease of our capitalism. If this is true, that the *telos* of the market in general is not self-interest but mutual advantage, there is no need of understanding firms, business, as the realm of, how do you say, the maximization of profit, because the *telos* of the firm, the *telos* of business is even mutuality, mutual advantage. This is very important because business and firms are not necessarily against virtues and common good; there are pathologies of that, but any time that the firm and business go for Zero-sum game, for exploitation, they are going against the idea of market as mutual advantage. For that reason, for us the cooperative economy is the paradigm of productive inclusion, as the *telos* of the market. Productive inclusion is not an exception, not an accident of the market, but it is the nature of the market, because the market works and is for the common good when it takes people outside the society, brings people inside for common growth. For that reason, cooperative economy is one interesting paradigm.

Then, for instance, it is not enough to say, as Adam Smith said in the Wealth of Nations, that "the merchant who intends only his own gain and promotes an end that was no part of his intention." For us, the virtuous merchant, the virtuous trader intends that the transaction is a party to be beneficial to his trading partners, as well as to himself. There is the intention of common good. This is very important in order to be consistent with the virtue of the market. For that reason, when speculative finance, not all finance, when some part of speculative finance is as Zero-sum game, because it is just gambling, is a negation of market *telos*, because it is a Zero-sum game.

3. The third reductionism is the concept of value in economics. We mentioned also in some of your interventions today, the wealth of nations is not merely the flow of goods and services, GDP and so on. This is a very well-known, very discussed issue, I would just like to add something, to conclude my introduction. GDP is not enough, gambling and the all legal corruption is GDP against the poor. In Italy, we are the third economy in the world for gambling; our GDP grows for that, but it is against the common good, against the poor, just as an example. GDP is not the most important indicator for wellbeing, but GDP is important anyway. We cannot just say ok, don't think about GDP because we look for other indicators, of course. We need more indicators, because democracy needs a plurality of indicators, with equal dignity; just an example in the World Cup, not like what happens in football matches, where there are many indicators (ball possession, faults, shots) but what is really important is goals. In GDP this is not the case, we need more indicators of wealth with equal dignity.

In these indicators, as also Bishop Toso said, we would like to insert relational goods, right, and freedom. Value, according to us, is linked to the biodiversity of economic and financial forms. This is very important for us, because we are claiming for a biodiversity of economic, commercial, productive forms: the global capitalistic system has reduced the biodiversity of the economies. Twentieth century capitalism was much more "biodiverse" than twenty-first century one. There is a sort of tendency towards monophysitism of capitalism, form of firms and so on. We argue for more biodiversity, because without biodiversity there is no life, even economic life.

To conclude, in your document you also can read something about the role of time and the role of public happiness. Why? Virtues are matters of cultivation, virtues are to be cultivated, and cultivation, as in agriculture, requires time: the dimension of time is absent from our financial capitalism, that is more and more close to the novel of "Flatland," because the third dimension of time is missing. Institutions are not only high forms of commons, but they are also guardians or keepers of time. In the relay race of generations, when the race is over, institutions allow for yet another goal to be reached, ensuring that the rules of the game are respected and maintained. Institutions are guardians, keepers of time.

The idea of virtues related to happiness is very old; we are in Rome now, I would like to give you, just to conclude, very few pictures about the idea of *felicitas publica*, the idea of cultivation of virtues as the way for public happiness, *felicitas publica*, that in this classical tradition in Rome was very much related to cultivation of life, cultivation of the earth. For instance, this idea of *Felicia tempora* in the Roman coins, where you see children and tools of agriculture, the idea that happiness is not pleasure, but comes from cultivation, from time. *Felicia tempora*, happy times, and also the idea of women, pregnant women, life is ready to fecundity, *femina, ferax, felicitas*, the idea of *fecundus*, fecundity. Then, the child over the leviathan, the life that is fighting against death.

To conclude, I'm very much convinced that for a more sustainable, gender fair and moral society, we need a new idea of human excellence, virtue, *areté* means excellence. What we have to change is the very deep rooted idea in our society, that what matters in a successful human being is excelling in work only, that work is the only thing that matters. We need a new idea of human excellence;

everybody would be seen as a person that does work but also loves and is engaged in care work, in family and community. "Part-time work for all, part-time care for all." If we don't discuss really anthropologically this idea of what excellence means, it is very difficult to imagine a sustainable economy.

Is it possible to imagine a good or decent society trusting mainly on invisible hand mechanisms? How to stop the growing reduction of economic and financial biodiversity? Is economic inclusion the golden market virtue? We are convinced that most of the present economic and financial institutions are founded upon anthropological Hobbesian pessimistic and cynic hypotheses, that human beings are not capable of virtue. Then, we have to use incentives in order to align interests. But incentives develop only the self-interested side of human beings. We need also instruments, maybe awards, to develop the virtuous part of human beings.

FINANCE, TRADE, LABOUR, WORK, AND TAXATION

Leonardo Becchetti
Professor of Economics
University of Tor Vergata - Rome

When talking about finance, trade and work we need to incarnate our morality and ideal principles into the flesh and blood of the real life economic functioning with its potential and its constraints. First of all, some facts need to be acknowledged. We know that in presence of conditional convergence – we live in an era of conditional convergence – poor countries grow more than richer, higher-income countries. If we play the game of extrapolating this, for the future years (even though we know that things may change), we may calculate that it will take 70 to 100 years to achieve full convergence on GDP per capita. But looking at levels and growth of average country figures without considering its distribution and fiscal implications is not enough. Average values hide a lot of inequality. We know that the Asian countries and African countries will grow more, we know that a lot of GDP is created in these countries, but a lot of times taxation in these countries does not keep resources there due to evasion and dodging, and some people participating to this conference have contributed to a great extent to raise awareness on this issue. Absolute poverty is slowly falling, but this is also not enough, because we still have 2,700,000,000 people living below 2 dollars per day and, as the Pope said, many of these people will not see exit from poverty during their life. And we know that the socioeconomic problem of the world is not just mono-dimensional and related to poverty, but is multi-dimensional and related as well to environmental sustainability, financial crisis and the decoupling between life satisfaction and GDP growth. So we have at least four sides to tackle. We as well know that the problem is not the creation of wealth at aggregate level (the world GDP growth was sustained and positive in the last decades) but its distribution. From this point of view we also have been told that the 85 richest men in the world have the same aggregate wealth as the 3 billion poorest and that the top 1% owns 46% of the world wealth. Those who are smart are used to saying that what is more important is to make the right question. And the best question to pose when facing these data is – "Why inequality hasn't slowed with democracy ?" – which is the title of a paper that the economist Bonica published in the *Journal of Economic Perspectives*. In other terms, the puzzle is why, in a democratic one-person-one-vote system, the bottom 3 billion people do not win elections against the top 85 individuals and support policies which reduce inequality. The explanation is that the top 1% accounts for a much larger share of election funds and therefore has very strong power and control over politicians. One currently provided justification for laissez fair is that, by making the rich richer in any case, you create more wealth which, sooner or later, trickles down. However, as Stiglitz remembers, in the global economic system, tax evasion and tax dodging reduce a lot the potential of trickle-down since "Money that was meant to have trickled down has instead evaporated in the balmy climate of the Cayman Islands."

We are all aware of the damages that the financial crisis has generated, but we also know that finance has a tremendous potential. I always say that 1 Euro invested in guarantee funds for capitalising micro-finance institutions, which went bankrupt after the tsunami in Sri Lanka, produced up to 18 Euros of economic value, fostering investment projects and the inclusion of the poor. On the contrary 1 Euro can be wasted into the slot machine of high-frequency trading and, at best, not be harmful. It is impressive that thirty years ago the average holding period of a stock was 4 years while today it is just 22 seconds. So, finance has a tremendous potential, we can do much better with finance, and the global financial crisis is a clear example that laissez-faire did not work. Financial markets left to themselves produced too-big-to-fail banks and did not produce competition but rather oligopolies and vacancy of regulators and the prices of financial assets didn't give the right information before financial crises. That's a very important point, a very important market (and institutional) failure to which only the contribution of bottom-up action of concerned consumers and investors (and active citizens) may pose remedy.

As well, financial markets dominated by high-frequency trading have the natural tendency to create very large upward and downward trends around so-called fundamentals. For example, at the moment, the Italian government is very excited about the fact that the Bund-BTP spread is very low, but the volatility of financial markets may easily open the way to a new situation in which the spread will overshoot, moving upward even beyond the level consistent with the fundamentals of the two countries. We know that financial crises are very harmful for our capacity of doing welfare, serving the poor and providing public goods and services. A very good paper of Laeven and Valencia, of the IMF, shows the impact of past and current financial crises on the debt to DGP ratio, and this phenomenon equally hit high-income countries in the last global financial crisis as well as emerging countries in the previous crises.

The most urgent issue is to reform the financial system, to enable it to produce its maximum potential for the common good. I think there are four main issues under discussion. *The first one* actually is not very much under discussion but it is the most important. The deep root of the financial crisis is the distorted and asymmetric system of incentives of managers and traders. When the stock market goes up, managers and traders gain a lot with bonuses and stock options; when the stock market goes down, they don't pay the consequences and they can still paradoxically gain if they leave the company due to the golden parachutes. This asymmetry and lack of financial responsibility in the bad state of affairs is a big problem since it pushes them to risk much more than what should be safe for the company moving up to the upper side of the risk-return frontier thereby endangering survival of financial intermediaries.

The second reform which is urgently needed is the separation between commercial and investment banking (both 1929 and 2007 financial crisis occurred after the removal of the separation principle). This issue start being widely discussed in a moment in which Central Banks are putting a lot of money into the economy. But when this money goes to profit-maximising banks, how do they use it? Not in financing the real economy, because this is a low-return, high-risk activity in a highly competitive banking system. So the separation between commercial and investment banking is an important issue to force banks to do their work for the real economy, and we know that the US, the UK, Germany and France have done something in this direction, by pursuing either straightforward separation or ring-fencing.

Third: it is very important to tackle the problem of tax evasion and tax arbitrage in globalization. The advantage we have on this point is that both sovereign countries, international institutions such as OECD, and the civil society and NGOs all agree that this is the problem. I really think that the first step in this direction is that of creating a broader information base and exchange. A fundamental step is adopting country-by-country reporting – which we know is now compulsory only in some specific countries and industries such as the mining industry in the US. With country-by country reporting it will be easier to track within company transfers which are actually tax dodging practices. Once we have this information, NGOs like *Oxfam* can do the very nice job of stimulating people to vote with their mouse, or to vote with their click, with their computer, for companies which perform better in terms of fiscal responsibility as they did for social and environmental responsibility with the "Behind the brand" campaign on top world food companies.

The last point is very controversial, it is about financial transactions. When we regulate road circulation, what is the goal we want to achieve? Maximizing speed? No, I mean, if we wanted to maximize speed, we would remove all speed limits and all traffic lights. Of course, when you regulate road circulation, you want speed but you also want safety and things like these. That should be the same in financial markets. We cannot evaluate a reform of financial markets only on the basis of velocity of the market, because the velocity and the liquidity of the market is already too high. Actually, with an average holding period for a stock of 22 seconds, we do not need more velocity, we need on the contrary more patient capital. There is a very nice quote from Krugman, who remember that millions of dollars were spent to lay optic fiber on the bottom of the Ocean to reduce by some milliseconds the distance between London and New York Stock Exchange, while there was no money for the construction of a building which was an important physical transportation infrastructure in New York.

Financial biodiversity is very important as it has been acknowledged to make the financial system more resilient. There are different types of banks serving different purposes and all types of banks are important for different reasons. The financial system is like a forest, you need biodiversity, you need big giant trees and you also need smaller trees. Empirical evidence documents that cooperative banks have significantly higher net loan/total asset shares than non-cooperative banks. The rationale for this finding is simple. Profit maximizing banks prefer other financial activities to the traditional lending activity since the latter is not the best in terms of risk- adjusted returns, while cooperative banks who do not need to maximize profits are closer to their original mission of serving the real economy. In spite of it, even though cooperative banks do not maximize profits or shareholder wealth, they still end up being with higher equity than the systemic ones.

Meetings, exchange, and specialization (exploitation of comparative advantages) are very important when discussing trade, they determine efficiency gains and enable better use of resources, but I think the real important issue is that free trade is not a goal in itself, it is just a mean. If it becomes a goal to which we sacrifice social rights or environmental rights, that is a problem. So we must give to it the right role. The real issue here, I pose to you as a question, how far can we go in terms of putting a sort of "ethical" tax on procurement rules? This is very important because some value chains are more socially and environmentally responsible than others, as they promote more workers' rights and environmental rights. How should we use the tax system to award companies which do more in this direction? This is a crucial question that the European Union discussed in the Social Business Initiative, but that has been discussed everywhere. Tax advantages for socially or environmentally responsible product chains are already in the system in some cases, but we have to decide how much further we want to go in this, for procurement rules for example, where the government may "vote with the wallet". Should we rule out from the procurement "race" unsustainable companies? Should we give preferential points to companies or should we create rules, tendered in such a way that only socially responsible goods and services can be provided? That's a very important issue. Of course we must do this without falling into protectionism. So, the real issue is this one. We need to create bottom-up processes, bringing the poor to the rich level and not the other way around. We must bring the Rana Plaza workers to the level of workers' rights which are in the North and not the other way round. We have to transform tax and labour arbitrage from a top-down to a bottom-up convergence process. How can we do this? Rules can help a lot, but also the design of proper incentives for people action, that's what I will speak on now. And when doing so we must pay attention not to move in the opposite direction by signing treaties which make it easier for transnational corporations to sue sovereign states when the latter raise social and environmental standards (as it is likely to happen with the TTIP).

The fight against unemployment should be at the forefront of political economy as it is in the Christian Social Doctrine. Recent evidence from the life satisfaction literature confirms the dominance of the employment problem for human beings by showing that the strongest negative effects of life events on life satisfaction are those related to the loss of job and by documenting that the cost of unemployment exceeds the wage which is lost by the worker. An interesting case demonstrating this was when judges in Italy said to Fiat (top Italian car industry) that the company had to give back the work to laid-off workers. The answer of Fiat was "I give you the money but I won't get you the job" and the people were not happy. So the job loss is more than the wage lost, it is something that has to do with dignity.

With globalisation and conditional convergence the poor of low income countries successfully compete with their cheaper cost of labour with richer low skilled workers in high income countries. This transition is very painful, especially for the latter. I read on the questionnaire about ILO *General Agreement on Wages and Labour:* can we calculate PPP adjusted decent wages and use these in some kinds of these incentive schemes that we decided before? What is the role for responsible consumption, for pioneers and imitators, for changing the rules of the game? How can we increase, stimulate the market of information intermediaries? We have a lot of labelling companies, social rating companies. In terms of overcoming the value reductionism when looking at labour, we should not just look at employment/unemployment level but, as well, to the share of those who are satisfied of their job. The idea is that today within the employed there are large groups of working poor and workers who suffer from a sharp skill mismatch between their qualifications and their job characteristics. There's not just an unemployment problem, there's also a problem of whether the wage is good or not, and whether you find sense in the job.

To sum up what said above we must start from the awareness that the problems we face are multifaceted and interconnected. I resume this point symbolically with the image of the Hydra, the multiple head monster fought by Hercules in the myth. As in the case of the Hydra the problem is that, if you concentrate your effort only on one side of the problem fighting just one head, you risk the other heads becoming bigger: if you consume less to solve the environmental problem, you reduce aggregate demand and exacerbate the poverty problem, if you consume more to solve the poverty problem you exacerbate the environmental problem. The three sources of this multifaceted problem are the three reductionisms which are fuelling the hydra: the anthropological reductionism (human being intended as homo ecomomicus), the value reductionism (value intended as GDP and not as the stock of spiritual, cultural, economic, relational and environmental goods of which a community may enjoy) and the corporate reductionism (corporation intended as a merely profit maximizing entity). How can we work on that? I talk in terms of Ptolemaic and Copernican systems. The Ptolemaic system accepts the three reductionist views and is intrinsically unbalanced, because it is based on the idea that the sum of self-interested actions of consumers and companies is "magically" reconciled with common good by the heroic action of two hands, the invisible hands of the market and the visible hand of institutions. This system is unbalanced because it asks ethics only on the side of institutions. People in the private market are just selfish while, when they are in the institutions they must be heroes, they must be benevolent, they must be perfectly informed, they must not be captured by the companies, and that's really too much to be asking to them. The only way to solve the problem is to move from a two-hand to a four-hand system. We need two additional hands, we need the hands of concerned consumers and investors who vote with the wallet for good companies and the hand multi-stakeholder companies – many of them are here – cooperatives, for-profit companies which take seriously corporate social responsibility, micro-finance, not profit-maximizing micro-finance, ethical banks, sustainable banks.

The role of these not-for-profit pioneers is fundamental since they also trigger imitation on the side of profit-maximizing companies. We saw in the food industry, we saw in the banking industry, how many companies in the food industry introduce fair trade products, but we really need a hand from concerned citizens, consumers. I call them those who are socially responsible, those who vote with the wallet. What does voting with the wallet mean? It means that if, as a citizen you are self-interested in a long-sighted sound way, you should award companies which are at the vanguard of three-sided efficiency, creating economic value with social and environmental sustainability. This is your own interest, it's your own interest to buy a high environmental quality product for your health, it's your own interest to socially high quality product for your work. I think this is a very important point. Data is telling us that economy is slowly going in this direction. There was a Boston Consulting Group release just a few days ago, saying that 15% of products sold at grocery stores are either green or ethical, and 15% of investment funds in the US are ethical investment funds and not just conventional investment funds.

So my conclusion is the following. We have discussed a lot about morality versus technicalities. I don't think we should separate these two things because this would be against the principle of incarnation. We need new rules, but we also need to understand that morality is not created in a vacuum, it is not fixed across time. There is a lot of research on social capital and its law of motion. I like very much the quote of Muhammad Yunus, who said that human beings can be pro-social, reciprocal, or exactly the opposite, and that depends a lot on the rules of the game, and we are those who are making the rules of the game. Morality and social capital are stocks with their law of motion, what are the factors which affect them? History, intergenerational transmission of values in family, but also rules of the game and good practices. So, procurement rules, tax rules, competition rules and the vote with the wallet practices of citizens really matter.

I really think that if you want to overcome the current eclipse, you have to seriously think of that, you have to stimulate this new Copernican economy and the bottom-up energies of the civil society by creating incentives to stimulate civic virtues and social capital. This will be the more effective and the less expensive way to promote the common good.

TOWARDS THE GLOBAL FAMILY WITH NEW RULES AND INSTITUTIONAL DESIGN

Stefano Zamagni
Professor of Economics
University of Bologna -
Johns Hopkins University, SAIS Europe
Consultor of the Pontifical Council for Justice and Peace

1. It is certainly true that globalisation is a positive-sum game that increases aggregate wealth. However, it is also true that it exacerbates the contrast between winners and losers. This fact is linked to the emergence of a new form of competition, unknown until recently: positional competition, according to which the "winner takes all and the loser loses everything" – the so-called "superstar effect" as understood by Shermin Rose. Why is literature on the subject so hotly divided? A credible answer comes from a recent work by Branko Milanovic (*The haves and the have-not,* New York, Basic Book, 2011) who distinguishes between *world* and *international* inequality.

International inequality considers the differences in the average incomes of various countries, unweighted ("1st concept of inequality" according to Milanovic) and duly weighted to account for the size of the population ("2nd concept of inequality"). World inequality, on the contrary, also takes into account the inequalities in income distribution within the individual countries ("3rd concept of inequality"). Therefore, it is world or global inequality that is increasing as a consequence of globalisation. Indeed, in order to decrease the 3rd concept of inequality, two conditions must be met: i) poor and densely populated countries must grow at a faster rate than rich countries; ii) this must occur without showing an increase in inequality within these countries.

Now, while the first condition is more or less satisfied, the second condition is virtually absent. In fact, over the last quarter of a century, the growth rate of the poorest countries has been higher than that of the richest countries (4% versus 1.7%). So why should we be concerned about the growth of global inequality? It is because it is a principal cause of conflict and ultimately of civil war. Conflict can be defined as "trade gone awry". If a country's gains from trade are not as high as it thinks it should receive, this becomes a major determinant of conflict, which might in the end jeopardise peace itself. That is why the search for a system that integrates socially responsible trade, one that is also capable of taking into consideration the "pains from trade" (T. Verdier, "Socially responsible trade integration", NBER, Oct. 2005), is a duty from which those responsible must not escape.

A related aspect concerns the relationship between globalisation and poverty. Over the past two decades, poor countries have increased their participation in world trade, so much so that today they can be said to be more globalised than rich countries. Yet, there is very little evidence to prove this relationship and even the scanty evidence available only indirectly deals with the link between globalisation and poverty.

Three general propositions deserve special attention: a) contrary to the Heckscher-Ohlin theory of international trade, the poor in countries with a lot of unskilled labour do not typically gain from trade expansion; b) globalisation generates both winners and losers among the poor and this creates social instability to the extent that it destroys social capital: c) the poor segments of the population obtain the largest benefits from globalisation when national governments endeavour to enhance welfare policies aimed at improving the capabilities of life of their citizens, rather than merely their living conditions.

2. Humanise the market, don't demonise it: this is the slogan that describes the challenge confronting us to-day. That is why we cannot consider any solution to the many and grave problems now

70

afflicting our societies that would delegitimize the market as a social institution. If people continue to demonise the market, it really will become hell. Indeed, the real challenge is the humanisation of the market. CST will never be able to accept any step backwards in this regard. Those who cultivate the concept of time as *kairos*, and not merely as *chronos*, know that difficulties are surmounted by transforming visions of the future into reality – and not with operations that would wind back the clock of history. Although the temptation to return to times gone by is understandable, it certainly cannot be justified by those who fully embrace an anthropology based on the human person. While they reject individualism, they can never pass over to the opposite side of communitarianism. In both cases the final outcome would be nihilism.

Finance is a tool that has tremendous potential for the proper functioning of economic systems. Good finance allows savings to be pooled in order to use them efficiently and allocate them to the most profitable uses; it transfers the value of assets in space and in time; it implements insurance mechanisms that reduce exposure to risk; it allows those who have disposable income but not productive ideas to meet with those who, conversely, have productive ideas but no funding. Without this coming together, the creation of economic value of a community would remain in a state of potentiality.

Unfortunately, the finance with which we are dealing today has largely escaped from our control. Financial intermediaries often fund only those who already have money (as they can put up collateral equal to or greater than the amount of the loan requested). The vast majority of derivative instruments were constructed potentially to achieve insurance benefits, but instead they are bought and sold for very short-term speculative motives with the opposite result. Paradoxically, they put at risk the survival of the institutions that have them in their portfolio. Systems that use asymmetric incentives for managers and traders (with profit sharing, bonuses and stock options and no penalty in case of losses) are constructed in such a way that they encourage people to take excessive risks. This makes the organisations for which they work structurally fragile and at risk of failure. A further element of dangerous instability is given by the tendency of these organisations to aim for profit maximisation (which is not the same as seeking to attain lawful and reasonable profit) because they place the well-being of shareholders over that of all other stakeholders. Banks that maximise profit through distorted incentives will find it increasingly profitable to channel resources to the business of speculative trading or to activities whose rates of returns are greater than those in lending activities.

The evolution of finance in recent decades has made it clearer than ever before that markets, especially where the returns to scale are increasing, do not at all tend spontaneously towards competitiveness but towards oligopoly. Indeed, the gradual easing of rules and forms of control (such as that on the separation between investment banking and commercial banking), have gradually led to the creation of an oligopoly of intermediary banks too big to fail and too complex to be regulated. The illusion of regulators has therefore produced a serious problem of balance of power for democracy itself. The *Corporate Europe Observatory*[1] issued a report in 2014 that highlights the imbalance of power relations between the financial lobbies and those of civil society and NGOs: the finance lobby spends 30 times more than any other industrial pressure groups (according to conservative estimates, they spend 123,000,000 euro per year with about 1,700 lobbyists in the EU). The relationship between the representation of financial lobbies and the representation of NGOs or trade unions in consultation groups are 95 to 0 in the stakeholder group of the ECB and 62 to 0 in the *de Larosière Group on financial supervision in the European Union.*

---

[1] http://corporateeurope.org/sites/default/files/attachments/financial_lobby_report.pdf.

This dominance of finance not only in terms of lobbying power but also in ease of access to information, knowledge and technologies has enabled the managers of large financial oligopolies to appropriate huge revenues at the expense of all other stakeholders. In confirmation of how this all distorts the use of resources, there is the recent abandonment of infrastructure projects that would have enabled better mobility of vehicles and people. And, compared to this, the recent construction of a tunnel between New York and Chicago that cost hundreds of millions of dollars in order to reduce by three milliseconds the trading time of some operators that benefit from the laying of the cable to achieve an information advantage that is to the detriment of others.

The disasters produced by this kind of finance are obvious to all. In a recent working paper of the International Monetary Fund, (Fabian Valencia & Luc Laeven, 2012. "Systemic Banking Crises Database: An Update". IMF Working Papers 12/163) Laeven and Valencia calculate this effect, following the crisis of 2007, to be an increase in the debt / GDP ratio of 70 percentage points in Iceland and Ireland and more than 20 percentage points in Greece, Germany, UK, Belgium and the Netherlands. In Italy, the impact has been more limited (8%), but the risks are very high given the levels of the Italian public debt. It is also estimated that the financial crisis has caused a gap of 65 billion dollars in the budgets of low-income countries.[2] No one can have any doubt that this model of finance is largely ineffective as well as harmful (as evidenced by the authoritative reports by Vickers in the UK and Liikanen in the European Union).

The ultimate sense of the argument developed above is that the search for a way to humanize the economy contains a demand of relationality which one should carefully investigate and satisfy at best if one wants to dispel perverse effects of great magnitude.

[2] http://www.oxfam.org/en/policy/impact-global-financial-crisis-budgets-low-income-countries

Indeed, how good the performance of an economic system is depends also on whetter certain conceptions and ways of life have achieved dominance. As a growing number of economic scholars over the past couple of decades have tenaciously stressed, economic phenomena have a primary interpersonal dimension. Individual behaviours are embedded in a preexisting network of social relations which cannot be thought of as a mere constraint, as maintream economists continue to believe. Rather, they are one of the driving factors that prompt individual goals and motivations. It seems to me that the central problem in the current transition towards a post-Fordist society is to understand how to fare so that individuals may be at liberty to decide the procedures for the supply of the goods they demand. What is at stake here is not so much freedom to decide the overall *composition* of goods to be produced (more of private *versus* more of public goods; more merit *versus* more relational goods), but freedom to decide *how* that composition should be achieved. This is why one cannot advocate the efficiency principle in order to decide *what* and *how* to produce. Undiscriminating admirers of the market as a social institution seem to overlook the fact that it is the very hegemonic expansion of those relations that I called private economy, that will slowly but inexorably destroy the whole system of social norms and conventions which constitute a civil economy, thereby paving the way for the success of new forms of statism. Today it is urgent to admit that the hypertrophic growth of both State and private market is a major explanation of the many problems that embarrass our societies. Such being the situation, the solution cannot be found in the radicalization of the public economy *versus* private economy alternative, or neo-statism *versus* neo-liberalism, but in a healthy flourishing of those forms of organization that shape a modern civil economy.

The most obnoxious consequence of a narrow-minded (and obsolete) notion of market, still predominant to this day, is to lead us to believe that a behaviour inspired by values other than non-egocentric and opportunistic interests inexorably drives economy to disaster. By encouraging us to expect the worst of others, such vision eventually brings out the worst in us. Moreover, in the end it immensely hampers the exploitability of such inclinations as trust, benevolence, reciprocity, since that vision perceives these inclinations as merely inborn peculiarities of human nature, unrelated to the civilization process in progress in our societies. As A. Wolfe pointed out some time ago with great insight referring to the sphere of the relations that shape private economy: "... The problem with reliance on the [private] market as a moral code is that it fails to give moral credit to those whose sacrifices enable others to consider themselves freely choosing agents. By concentrating on the good news that we can improve our position, rather than the not-so-good, but socially necessary, news that one might consider the welfare of others as our direct concern, the market leaves us with no way to appreciate disinterest".(*Whose Keeper? Social Science and Moral Obligation*, Berkeley, University of California Press, 1989, p.102).

Since motivations sustaining the principle of reciprocity are motives whose fulfilment is at least as legitimate as the fulfilment of self-interested motives, a truly liberal society should not prevent beforehand - that is, at the level of institutional design – the growth and dissemination of the former to the detriment of the latter, as is foolishly happening today. In the absence of actual - not just virtual - competition among different subjects of supply of the various categories of goods, the citizen-consumer will be left with a reduced space of freedom. One might end up living in a more and more affluent society, more and more efficiently inundating us with commodities and services of all sorts, but more and more "indecent" and, ultimately, desperate. Indeed, the reduction of human experience to the "accountancy" dimension of utilitarian calculus is not just an act of intellectual arrogance; it is disclaimed by actual exprerience in the first place.

CST, at least since the times of the encyclical *Populorum Progressio* (1966) by pope Paul VI up to *EG* by pope Francis, is striving to avoid that such an anthropological reductionism should become a sort of benchmark in economic reasoning. This would be really disgraceful for a double set of reasons. On the one hand, because the discipline will prove to be unable to cope with the major problems of present-day societies –growing social inequalities; failure to tackle poverty; environmental degradation; conflicts of identity; etc. On the other hand, because the limited conception of personal well-being and integral human development is a major impediment to innovation of economic ideas and a dangerous shelter for mainstream thought from both factual criticism and competing scientific perspectives. What CST is urging social scientists to adhere to is the spirit of "scholarship of engagement" – in the sense of E.L. Boyer, *Bullettin of the American Academy Association*, XLIX, 7, 1996 – according to which moral commitment and cognitive interest should always be kept intertwined in order to reciprocally contaminate each other.

DISCUSSION OF THE POST-2015 DEVELOPMENT AGENDA AND SUSTAINABLE DEVELOPMENT GOALS. CHRISTIAN SOCIAL THOUGHT: A DRIVER OF SOCIAL INNOVATION

André Habisch
Professor of Christian Social Ethics and Society
Catholic University of Eichstätt-Ingolstadt

> ... et renovabis faciem terrae. Alleluia.
> ... and Thou shalt renew the face of the earth. Alleluia.
> (Psalm 104, 30)

Social Ethics and Social Innovation

Randomly ask passers-by today about Christian Social Thought – and (if they would know it at all) they would surely emphasize its 'conservative' character. Accordingly, basic social innovations of the modern world like human rights and democracy but also transparency, economic progress and social wellbeing are primarily perceived as secular achievements, which originate outside the realm of organized religion and their representing institutions.

A conservative flavour also dominates the corporate governance discussions. "Sticking to the rules" and refraining from opportunistic detours represents the main imperative, here: independently of whether it is formulated in the context of the traditional ten commandments, the ten principles of the Global compact, the OECD guidelines or the ILO principles. For many outsiders, morality may sometimes appear as a mere extension of national law in the international realm.

Given the regulatory void of the global markets, which became obvious in the financial crisis or in the disastrous conditions of textile production in Southern Asia, this 'call for order' has of course a right in its own and should not be denounced here. On the other hand, however, a complete reduction the of morality and ethics to a (conservative) imperative of 'law and order' severely neglects its crucial characteristic: the inherent focus on social innovation, on the striving for a better world, on a critical attitude towards prevailing social (dis-) order of human exploitation, environmental destruction and the culture of death. In this sense, during recent decades, research concerning social innovation emerged and influenced social ethical academic education programs in different respects.

For example, in 2011 the EU commission[1] (DG Enterprise and Industry) defined social innovation as "… about new ideas, that work to address pressing unmet needs. We simply describe it as innovations that are both social in their ends and in their means. Social innovations are new ideas (products, services and models) that simultaneously meet social needs (more effectively than alternatives) and create new social relationships or collaborations". Consequently, not only the corporate sector but also NGOs, religious groups, civil society and public institutions as cross-sectional partners are perceived as partners in this Social innovation project: "They are innovations that are not only good for society but also enhance society's capacity to act. Social innovations take place across boundaries between the public sector, the private sector, the third sector and the household."Best practices of social entrepreneurship, bottom-of-the-pyramid market cooperation, public-private partnerships, associative banking and organization etc. strengthened the perception in that perspective. Within the framework of this short intervention, we want to consider the Jewish-Christian tradition as well as Western Christian Social Thought as one (of many) historical roots of a genuine 'social innovation' ethical approach.

Social innovation in the history of Christian Social Thought

The progressive character of the Christian Gospel is expressed by its ethos of solidarity. For business entrepreneurs and NGO leaders, this is of special importance. Firstly, it is deeply ingrained

---

[1] See http://ec.europa.eu/enterprise/policies/innovation/policy/social-innovation/past-editions/definition_en.htm (29.06.15).

in the stories and admonishments of the Holy Bible; second, it is not primarily *restricting* but on the contrary *provoking, empowering and directing* Human action and innovativeness. Thereby, it corresponds to the Christian 'impatience' concerning prevailing "structures of sin" (John Paul II), injustices and discriminations in society, exploitation and neglect. Entrepreneurs and social entrepreneurs are eager to engage – and to involve others as well.

From the very beginning of the Jewish-Christian tradition, the idea of social innovation has been present. Abraham, whom the church calls 'our father in faith', marks the beginning of the history of God with His people (*Gen* 11,31). Abraham receives God's call to leave his city Haran in order to into walk the desert – only trusting the divine promise of a land that will be given to him and his progeny. What becomes obvious here is that God's call is not restricted to certain well-defined acts of 'religious duties', but requires a holistic dedication towards divine calling. It requires a leap of faith – and engagement to search for a better world, even if the exact structure of that alternative is not yet exactly known. What is needed here is to leave the traditional social order and to head towards an alternative one, which can only be discovered and more clearly elaborated in an attitude of faith and openness towards God's promise.

Later in the history of faith, Israel's covenant with God is characterized by an inseparable connection between religious bond and basic requirements of social justice. For God's chosen people, staying faithful towards His covenant necessarily implies to care for the poor, for widows, orphans and strangers (*Ex* 22, *Dtn* 24). On the contrary, if the poor have to live in misery, if entrusted power is abused and unjust laws are crafted, this regularly indicates that the people has left God's path (*Jes* 1, *Jer* 5). The inseparable link between God's covenant and the practice of social justice (and social reform) is symbolized by the charismatic figure of the prophet, who keeps himself regularly apart from the political and economic elite. The role of the prophet physically represents the critical attitude of the Jewish religious tradition towards the usual social injustices of the traditional political and economic order.

In the context of the New Testament, this traditional doctrine is even strengthened and re-emphasized: nobody can state that he loves God if he does hate his brother (*1 Joh* 4, 21); on the contrary, loving the neighbour and giving to those in need represents the human answer to God's preceding love. Therefore, the disciple of Jesus gives and helps because he sees Jesus in every needy person (*Mt* 25). This becomes tangible in the social practice of the first Christian communities in Jerusalem, from which the Scripture reports that they lived in a community of goods, in which the faithful continuously cared for each other (*Acts* 2,45). In the context of traditional society, a practice of continuous solidarity, that also includes strangers and reaches out beyond the natural bonds of family and kin, clearly represents a rather revolutionary social innovation.

Having said this, however, it also has to be stated that we do not see any genuine social ethical instruction in the documents of the New Testament. More precisely, we neither find the description of an ideal socio-economic order nor is there any genuine 'Christian' social or economic agenda developed. Interesting enough, the first symbol Jesus employed in his early appearance is a explicitly *social* one: the kingdom of God ('Basileia tou theou'); and this message clearly contained general principals guiding the organization of a human form of living together. However, neither Jesus himself nor the early Christian communities ever called for the crafting of certain political or economic institutions. Rather a differentiation between secular and religious order clearly prevented a politicization of faith as well as a clericalization of politics.[2] The social ethical restraint of the early Christian tradition has to do with its eschatological character: where God is felt so near that this earth seems

---

[2] See Franz-Josef Stegmann/ Peter Langhorst, *Geschichte der sozialen Ideen im Deutschen Katholizismus*. In: H. Grebing (Ed.), *Geschichte der Sozialen Ideen in Deutschland*, VS Verlag: Essen, S. 599-866, 608.

to come to an end soon, there is no need to waste time and effort for reflecting about a worldly socio-economic order. Moreover, until the closure of the biblical canon, early Christian communities represented social minorities, which generally did not hold any political or economic power. Therefore, they were neither inclined nor positioned to speculate about political or economic concepts.

This only changed during the 4th century, when Christianity became the official religion of the late Roman Empire. Therefore, it does not represent an occasional coincidence that early monasteries emerged precisely during this period, keeping the spirit of social innovation alive among the Christian communities (e.g. Benedict founding his community at Subiaco in 529). From now on and during medieval times, in the context of monastic communities, Christians lived together explicitly dedicated to God and renouncing to personal wealth and comfort. Moreover, many of these communities were caring for the poor and the marginalised. Representing a social innovation itself, monastic life at the same time also provided multiple impulses for innovative social practices. For example, as Harvard law professor Harold J. Berman has intriguingly shown, in early medieval times clerical lawyers constantly influenced the emerging western legal tradition against personal dependence of poor labourers in the context of feudalist serfdom; consequently, in their case law they continuously fostered contractual agreements and commercial law. Well-educated but nevertheless without any personal possessions, these monkish judges in a way represented something like the 'critical intellectuals' of medieval times.[3]

Other social innovations of the medieval society included the *montes pietatis*: early forms of charity and associational banking, which might be compared with today's microfinance associations. *Montes pietatis* consisted of lending out to the poor and disadvantaged against a (modest) payment of interest. These social inno-

[3] Harold H. Berman, *Law and Revolution. The Formation of the Western Legal Tradition*, Cambridge MA/ London: Harvard Univ. Press 1983.

vations were brought about by Franciscan monks, who took part in the *ordo fratrum minorum*, a foundation of St. Francis of Assisi (1181-1226), which became the symbol of a 'Church for the poor' during medieval times. However, even other monastic communities brought forward multiple social innovations, with their engagement for disintegrated groups in the pre-modern society. Moreover, religious movements and teachings in many parts of the world also influenced social practices and policies. In this sense, Latin America was not discovered by Christopher Columbus but by Bartholome de Las Casas, the Dominican friar who fought for the human rights of indigenous people in the Spanish colonies during the 16th century. The colonial ethics of the School of Salamanca generalized these experiences and was very influential for universalizing social ethical standards during early Modern times.

Industrialisation, Modernisation and the rise of Modern Catholic Social Thought

As Stanford economic historian Gregory Clark has shown,[4] the rise of the industrial age during the late 18th century in the United Kingdom and during the 19th century in many parts of Europe and North America, clearly represents the sharpest socio-economic transformation in the history of human civilization. In the wake of that process, economic productivity and mean income *per capita* rose sharply in many countries but declined in others, which did not take part in the transition processes. By far, it exceeds the possibilities of this short intervention to discuss the multiple economic, political, cultural and intellectual consequences of this 'modernization' process. For our purpose, we can limit ourselves to the enormous social and conceptual challenges, which modernization brought about for simple people of that time and which in different forms called for social innovations. The industrialisation and modernisa-

---

[4] See his book *A Farewell to Alms. A brief economic history of the World*, Princeton 2007.

tion represented – and still represents in many countries of the world! – a radical transition of the living conditions not only for a tiny elite minority, but also for the majority of poorly trained simple labourers. It is true that during the decades of the modernisation process, societies are able to increase their per capita income in an unprecedented way.[5] At the same time, however, with the emergence of the industrial world, living and working conditions regularly undergo a complete change. Intellectual, social and cultural transformations accompany the economic ones. They revolutionise the way in which the daily program is structured (now governed by the necessities of industrial production), it transforms the family life (separation of labour from the private space, segregation of sexes, lack of child care), how one perceives oneself as an individual in society (social mobility and the importance of education), and the interaction mode within the family (individualization) as well as with other people ('weak' ties in a modern city instead of strong ties in village life). Moreover, especially at the very beginning of that process, labourers and their families regularly find themselves in a very challenging economic, social and also spiritual situation. Lacking access to basic social security institutions, economic and social insecurity and the inability to feel at home at this new urban environment characterizes their situation.[6]

These challenging transition processes regularly raise a lot of critical objections and general skepticism. For many European observers during the 19th and early 20th century – lay people as well as clerics – industrialisation appeared as a wrong path, which in itself threat-

---

[5] In earlier times, such a large increase would have only been possible, if catastrophic events like wars or epidemics had seriously reduced the population size. With industrialization, however, the increase of income was rather accompanied by a population growth – in Germany, for example, inhabitants nearly doubled during the period 1870-1914.

[6] See Goldschmidt, Nils; Habisch, André: "Western religion, social ethics and public economics" in: Forte, Francesco; Mudambi, Ram; Navarra, Pietro (Hrsg.): *A handbook of Alternative Theories of Public Economics* - Cheltenham, GB : Elgar, 2014 - S. 198-226.

ened basic values in society. Therefore, many adhered to the principal opposition against the new system of market-based enterprises and industrialized production. For them, Christian values were only practicable in the context of the traditionally highly integrated social world. Consequently, in the perspective of these critics, those who wanted to remain faithful should refrain from entering into the newly emerging industrial cities but should stay in the village; criticism even continued when (with time passing-by) the socio-economic situation, living conditions, and cultural standards in the cities clearly dominated those of rural populations. Social innovation and Christian ethics even seemed to be in contrast with each other, here.

In this situation, two businesspersons played an import role as social entrepreneurs. The French textile entrepreneur Leon Harmel, born in 1829 at La Neuville-lès-Wasigny as a son of a wool entrepreneur, continued his father's company at Val-des-Bois. The German textile entrepreneur Franz Brandts was born in 1834 at Gladbach also in a family of entrepreneurs. After a short stay in Britain, Brandts in 1872 launched his private company. Together, Harmel and Brandts founded the "Arbeiterwohl" Association in 1880. Within that network, they tried to overcome the exploitation of workers and the atmosphere of conflict, which characterized the relationship between workers and firm owners during the late 19th century. Following his moral intuition as a dedicated Christian, Harmel paid a 'family wage' (well above the market wage), installed a factory council to strengthen the worker's voice, empowered Catholic worker circles and Christian trade unions, appointed a factory chaplain and even organized a factory pilgrimage to Rome. It was Harmel, who substantially influenced the first Papal Social Encyclical *Rerum Novarum* in 1891 and may therefore be called a driving force behind the Catholic Social Thought tradition.

On the other side of the Rhine, Franz Brandts was similarly active. He limited the working time in his factory while at the same time paying the highest salary in town; he founded health funds with obligatory membership for every worker, installed family insurance funds and pension plans (self-administered by worker's representatives). For empowering and strengthening the personal responsibility and the general skills of his employees, he installed an on-site chapel, a canteen and a sewing school, he founded an on-site music club, a library and saving clubs. All this was done in the situation of fierce competition among enterprises with similar products, in which higher costs of course also result in a competitive advantage. But the corporate culture of solidarity and community (Brandts and his family were even physically living amidst the workers), which resulted from these activities, nevertheless resulted in a higher productivity and reputation of the company and also strengthened its economic position.

Even though they were friends and working for the same goals for many years, when they died (Brandts at Gladbach in 1914, Harmel at Nice the following year) their countries fought against each other in the First World War. However, in their particular way, both Harmel and Brandts became important social innovators. Their influence on humanising working conditions was indirect but nevertheless lasting. Especially, with their 'Christian' leadership and management style, they provided evidence to their contemporaries that sticking to Christian values does not necessarily mean to keep oneself outside of the modern industrial sector. Rather they delivered the living proof that Christian social innovators could indeed make an important difference even for the program of 'civilising capitalism' (Oswald von Nell-Breuning), i.e. for the humanization of living conditions in the modern society. Moreover, beyond this indirect even a direct influence on social development resulted: in 1893 Brandts had appointed a factory chaplain, a priest named Dr. Franz Hitze, who later became the first professor for Christian Social Science at the university of Münster (1893). Subsequently, as an important member of the German Parliament (1894-1921) and a leading Catholic Social policy expert, Hitze actively participated in the social security legislation of the Bismarck era, which represents the first public insurance scheme in modern history.

In their way, these entrepreneurs – together with politicians, union representatives, journalists, academic teachers etc. – became front-runners of the Catholic Social Thought tradition. They helped to spelling out the Christian message even in the totally transformed context of the modern industrialized society.

It reflected these and other experiences of the Christian Social movement, when in 1891 Pope Leo XIII presented his first social Encyclical *Rerum Novarum*. This was a rather innovative type of Church document, which discussed topics like the rights and duties of employers and workers, pledged against socialism, emphasized the dignity of the person with a special focus on workplace relationships, called for a joint striving for the common good, participation and solidarity, and weighed the right of private property against the universal destination of goods. As we know, with *Rerum Novarum* Pope Leo XIII had only started a whole series of social encyclicals, in which the church continuously addressed contemporary social and economic issues. In 1931, Pope Pius XI (*Quadragesimo Anno*) entailed a justification of private property (against Marxism) and coined the term "subsidiarity". During the 1960s, Pope John XXIII in his *Pacem in Terris* (1963) laid the emphasis on peace and relations between nations. Only 4 years later Paul VI (*Populorum Progressio*) focused on global justice and development (1967). Pope John-Paul II deeply impacted the Social Encyclical tradition with no fewer than 3 documents: in his *Laborem Exercens* (1981) he depicted a (philosophically grounded) theology of labour and labour relations, in *Sollicitudo Rei Socialis* (1987) he dealt with issues of global justice thereby also mentioning the natural environment. In *Centesimus Annus* (1991) he provided a reflection on the decline of socialism but also emphasized the flaws of the capitalist system. Again, after a long silence, Benedict XVI in his *Caritas in Veritate* (2006) reflected the financialization and dehumanisation of companies, which became so obvious in the diverse crises of the young new century. Facing that decay in global business culture, *Caritas in Veritate* introduced the topic of gratuitouness[7] in business. However, Benedict XVI also did not hesitate to use new terms like corporate responsibility and socially responsible finance and investment, and he discussed topics of personal responsibility (like responsible consumption and lifestyle). Thus, the Pope emphasized the important role of civil society and calling for a new global social order and a transition towards a socially responsible globalisation.

Looking ahead

Within the framework of this short intervention, we could only shortly sketch the history of Catholic Social Thought as driver of social innovation. The main challenge for the continuation of that history into the 21st century is a re-formulation of the Global Development Goals Agenda (post 2015 process) from the perspective of the poor, i.e. maintaining a clear perception of *their* priorities. For example, self employed poor rural farmers, city dwellers, young start-up entrepreneurs – all need non-discriminatory access to their relevant markets in a fair and transparent process. Probably the most important prerequisite in that respect are political and administrative reforms in many countries around the globe – with the goal of implementing sound legal rules suitable to induce a widespread rule-following behaviour. For the different countries concrete steps in that direction would include tax reforms, which insure the participation of all national income groups (especially the more affluent one) in the provision of local public goods like education, infrastructure, health care etc. Moreover, promoting social innovation requires a fight against 'structures of sin', especially the combination of 'crony capitalism' with authoritarian and crony political governance structures. Administrators have to treat

[7] For the role of that notion for Social innovation, Habisch, A. Loza, A. Cristian R.: "Entrepreneurial Spirit and the Role of Gratuitousness for Innovation" in: Melé Carné, Domènec; Dierksmeier, Claus (Hrsg.): *Human Development in Business : Values and Humanistic Management in the Encyclical 'Caritas in Veritate'*. - Basingstoke u.a. : Palgrave Macmillan, 2012 - S. 217-236.

citizens with respect for their human dignity; they have to enforce legal and administrative rules internally in order to guarantee that. Independent lawyers and judges should rule impartially and transparently without any preference for their kin or certain powerful local groups; moreover, appeals against judicial decisions should be accessible even for poor people without high costs.

Economic entrepreneurs should concentrate on the value creation and avoid corruptive or discriminatory 'rent-seeking' behaviour.[8] They should respect the personal dignity of their 'stakeholders' (employees, costumers, suppliers etc.) acknowledging their legitimate claims towards the companies.

Media must report relevant decision making objectively and stick to their ethos of transparency. This does especially include not shying away from reporting potential abuse of power, discrimination of certain social groups as well as exploitative behaviour of all kinds. Civic alliances (including business representatives and politicians) have to promote common good oriented governance for economic and civic participation of the poor.

In that sense, common good oriented governance structures and institutional frameworks on the one hand and strong personal values of local political and civic leaders on the other are two sites of the same coin. Consequently, value-based schools and universities, newspapers and associations must strengthen moral character formation of young people. The (often implicit) depreciation of personal values as idealistic, old-fashioned or as an obstacle to reach personal goals must be corrected. At the same time, however, value-based politicians and managers also must not find themselves at a disadvantage compared with their ethically less sensible competitors: hence the importance of legal rules and institutions assuring transparency and procedural justice for example in filling leadership positions in political, administrative or organizational bodies.

---

[8] See the document, *Vocation of the Business Leader*, Pontifical Council for Justice and Peace, 2012.

Finally, education plays a crucial role in developing a more human society and in the attainment of social innovation and progress in the 21st century. This includes:

- Political education: people should be educated to take more informed decisions when casting their ballots in democratic elections: a 'culture of political attentiveness and participation' should be promoted already among young people for example in Catholic Schools and universities; this includes a discernment of spirits towards alternative groups and initiatives.

- Economic education: As the Encyclical *Caritas in Veritate* has also emphasized, persons should become mindful of the consequences of their economic activities – for example consumption, investment, environmental behaviour – on the poor. However, those 'caring' for the poor should not treat them as mere objects, but rather empower them to become subjects of their own development. It is a matter of dignity of the poor to recognize their own efforts to overcome their misery.

Social innovators play an important role as change agents for a more integrative economy. They develop and spread innovative solutions for long standing social and environmental problems on a regional and national level. This short intervention tried to show, that the current international discussion on social innovation is far from being novel for the tradition of Catholic Social Thought. Rather, from the very beginning of the Jewish-Christian tradition, following the divine calling has always implied an impatient fight against social discrimination, injustice and force. The spirituality of Jesus Christ has always included the search for 'making the world a better place'.

Moreover, our reflection on the tradition of Christian Social Thought brings about important implications for a secular and political-economic discourse about social innovation as well. For it demonstrates, that moral goals and a common good orientation, which is rooted in a spiritual world-view, accompanied the emergence of many social innovations throughout human history. Thus, religious ethics cannot be reduced to a conservative law-and-order orientation, which would prevent social progress and innovation from happening. Rather, in reality, many social innovations stem from persons and movements, which are inspired by religious spirituality of different origins. Positioning themselves in distance towards the worldly *status quo* of power and wealth thereby following their strong spiritual roots, for these witnesses resulted in openness towards innovative models and institutions. Therefore, religious spirituality can push in both directions – conservative as well as progressive.

In this sense, I would like to finish with a quote from the Encyclical *Sollicitudo Rei Socialis* of Pope John Paul II, which may orientate us in that struggle: Solidarity is not "a feeling of vague compassion or shallow distress at the misfortunes of so many people, both near and far", but rather "a firm and persevering determination to commit oneself to the common good; that is to say to the good of all and of each individual, because we are all really responsible for all" (SRS, 38).

CONCLUDING REMARKS

Stefano Zamagni

1. Pope Francis' message in *Evangelii Gaudium* is not a warning, but a heartfelt exhortation to reconsider the foundations of the market economy model now in vogue. It is therefore an invitation to quit the "night of worry" in which the crisis forces us to stay. Markets are not all the same, because they are the precipitate of cultural and political projects. One market reduces inequalities, while the other swells them. The first one is called civil, since it broadens the *civitas* with the aim of virtually including everyone; the second one is the uncivil market, because it tends to exclude and regenerate "existential peripheries". In the current phase of financial capitalism the second type of market has become dominant, and the results are plain to see: social inequalities increase to an unprecedented extent and the substantial, not formal freedoms of too many people decrease. To this situation and not to hypothetical realities, the Pope draws the attention of everyone, believers and non-believers.

The point is that the Pope's speech has a much more solid theoretical foundation than some mass-mediological vulgate is having us believe. Its code is that of historical realism: to reconnect knowledge and experience of reality; to turn thinking into life practice. Thus, according to Pope Francis, Christianity can't be reduced either to mere orthodoxy – this is the risk of rationalistic intellectualism – or to mere orthopraxis, and a sort of spiritual pathos. Actually, this implies that besides *factum*, what man does, there is *faciendum*, what man can do in view of a new historical project.

2. The "trickle-down" theory, also known in economic literature as "trickle-down effect", is effectively expressed by the aph-

orism – apparently used for the first time by American economist Alan Blinder – according to which "a rising tide lifts all boats". Neo-liberal thinking has believed in it for a long time: therefore, there is no need to worry over the distribution of income and wealth as everyone will then be better off. The important thing is to increase the size of the pie (GDP) without worrying about the cutting of individual slices. This embodies the foundation of the well-known adage of conservatives: "we do not worry about the poor because for every rich person more there is a poor one less". Well, the Pope tells us that in the current historical conditions (market globalization and economy financialization) the trickle-down effect is no longer possible, as those who are not blinded by preconceived positions well know (the famous "Kuznets curve" is no longer valid today).

Thus, the Social Doctrine of the Church (SDC) has solid foundations from the scientific perspective. The truth is that it demonstrates an understanding of what too many observers and scholars pretend not to see, namely that poverty (absolute) and inequality are substantially different phenomena. Consequently, fighting strategies are different: while fighting absolute poverty just requires changing redistributive mechanisms, addressing the latter front requires acting on the very moment in which wealth is produced. And this really irks a great many!

3. Capitalism is one, but it has several varieties which change in relation to both the cultural background prevailing in the various societies and the characteristics of the historical period in question. There is nothing irreversible in capitalism, as well as in other socio-economic systems. Another important point to be noted is the distinction between market economy and capitalist economy. The first one anticipates the coming of the second one by at least a couple of centuries. This is to confirm that markets are not all the same. For example, the civil market economy – so called from Antonio Genovesi (1753) onwards – does not accept what J. Schum-

peter (1912) defined as the engine of capitalism, namely "creative destruction": the capitalist market must "destroy", or expel enterprises and people that are not (or less) productive to create something new, thus expanding indefinitely. This version of Social Darwinism ends up reducing economic relationships between people to relationships between things and things to goods. According to the SDC, this specific model of capitalism, typical of the current historical period, is no longer sustainable today.

This does not at all mean condemning wealth as such. It means, instead, that the *ways* in which wealth is generated and the *criteria* by which it is distributed among the members of the human family are necessarily submitted by Christians to their moral judgment, since they are not merely technical matter. The crisis of 1929 was the first major crisis of capitalism and it too, like the current one, originated in the sector of finance. Let us look at the situation today. As is known, in 1980 global financial assets were equal to global GDP (27 trillion US Dollars). In 2007 – on the eve of the outbreak of the crisis – they had grown to 240 trillion compared to 60 trillion of global GDP – four times as much. That ratio has now increased even more. In the same period, the labour income share of GDP has fallen in most countries by over nine points, increasing that of financial income. I do not think one can remain indifferent or, worse still, accommodating towards such phenomena.

4. How could all this have happened? What is the deep root? The answer to this question requires a clarification that is never made. In October 1829, renowned professor of economics at the University of Oxford Richard Whately first enunciated the principle of NOMA (*Non overlapping magisteria*): if economics wants to be a science it has to cut relationships with politics and ethics. Roles are divided as follows: politics is the realm of the aims that the society intends to pursue; ethics is the realm of the values that should guide human behaviour; economics is the realm of the most effective means to achieve those aims respecting those values: therefore,

economics has no need to maintain relations with the other two spheres. The entire subsequent economic thinking – with very few exceptions – has accepted the principle of NOMA *et pour cause*. Since the advent of globalisation (late seventies of the last century) a radical role reversal has gradually materialised: economics has become the realm of aims and politics the realm of means. That is why, as all observers do not fail to notice, democracy is today at the service of the market. The influential president of Bundesbank, Hans Tietmeyer, had understood it ahead of time, when in 1996 he wrote: "I have sometimes the impression that most politicians about it are still not aware of how much they are under the control of the financial markets today, and even be dominated by these". Need we say more? (Today, even Alan Greenspan, who was chairman of the Federal Reserve for many years, expresses the same concept in his book published in 2013 *The Map and the Territory*).

Well, the SDC cannot accept such a "division of roles". Politics must once again be the realm of aims and there must be a cooperative, systematic and non-extemporary relationship between the three abovementioned spheres. There must be autonomy and not separation between them. It should always be noted that Catholic ethics is based on the principle (Aristotelian-Thomistic) of the supremacy of good over right. Justice makes sense if it is aimed at good; otherwise, it risks becoming justicialism. As we know, post-modernity does not accept this vision. It considers rules and laws as originating only from the consent of the parties involved, which are not required to refer to some conception of good life. The economic action is therefore based on the principle that *consensus facit iustum*, just as required by the currently leading structure of libertarian individualism.

5. It is so obvious that private property cannot be considered an absolute right that even great John Locke John Locke (second half of the seventeenth century) admitted it. Instead, what should be clear is the distinction between common good and total good

– terms that are too often taken as equivalent. If common good is the product of individual goods, total good is the sum thereof. The meaning of the metaphor is clear: by the logic of common good we cannot undo someone's wealth to increase, no matter how much, someone else's wealth: the product would be zero all the same. This would not happen with a summation. Moreover, common good is the good of *all* men – even those who are not very efficient – and of *the whole* man in his three dimensions: material, socio-relational, spiritual. Total good is the typical expression of utilitarianism, while common good is one of the four pillars that support the SDC.

In the current historical climate, the practical repercussions of the teaching of the SDC imply the recovery of important pieces of that tradition of thought, established during the eighteenth century in Naples and Milan, which is civil economy. On the one hand, it is a matter of redesigning the rules of the game, namely institutions, especially economic ones, which are still largely extractive – to use the fitting expression of D. Acemoglu and J. Robinson (2013) – and therefore exclude, instead of including citizens. On the other hand, it is necessary to insert the principle of gift as gratuitousness – and not as a present – in the economic discourse and practice, undertaking all those economic initiatives whose regulating principle is reciprocity. Think of social enterprises, productive associations, the so-called ethical finance, voting by wallet, the institutional facilities of the *corporate governance* that include *positive* worker participation rights, and so on. It is highly encouraging to note that the paradigm of civil economy is now gaining support almost everywhere. We can understand why if we consider that we cannot continue with the suffocating dichotomy that sees on one side the neo-liberal thesis according to which markets almost always work well – and therefore there is no need to demand special regulatory interventions – and on the other side the neo-statist thesis according to which markets almost always fail – and therefore it is necessary to rely on the visible hand of the state. On the contrary, just because markets – which are necessary – often do not work well, it is urgent to act on the causes of the many malfunctions, above all in the financial sector, rather than to merely correct their effects. This is the way that is supported by those who fit in the context of civil market economy.

The market is not only an efficient mechanism of trade regulation. It is, above all, an ethos that induces deep changes in human relationships and in the character of men living in society. Hence the insistence of the SDC on the principle of fraternity that must find a proper place *within* the action of the market and not without it, as required by "compassionate capitalism."

6. The other great peculiarity of civil economy is to recognize that the principle of gift as gratuitousness has a place within the economic discourse and practice. This means that the person-principle is introduced in economy as a decisive factor, so that the focus shifts from the mere traded object to the trading subjects and the relationship established by such trading. This way, we would find out that reciprocity as such is the principle of social organization, able to solve the problem of social order in a credible manner. A long tradition of thinking has improvidently taught that social order can be established only through a cross-reference between two poles: the pole of force (violence, fight, competition) and the pole of law (social contract). However, let us consider the case of "perfect strangers". If two perfect strangers meet, they cannot sign an agreement because they do not even have a common language. Therefore, as it seems, they necessarily have to fight, or not. One may decide to make a gift, as it happens in the apologue – unfortunately little known – of the eleven camels, and find out that social order ensues.

Why then do we keep thinking that power is only the one founded either on law or on force? Because Western civilization has always been under the indiscreet spell of calculative thinking, often deriding thoughtful thinking. In his diagnosis of the cultural degeneration in Germany in the thirties and forties, Dietrich Bonhoeffer talked about *Dummheit*, i.e. stupidity, specifying that it "is not an intellectual defect but a human one" (*Resistance and surrender*, 1988, p. 65).

The intellect can calculate, but it is only the person's humanity that can produce thoughtful thinking. Thus, this is today's great challenge, the challenge that the SDC is called on to take up (and win if possible).

REFLECTIONS

FINANCE AS A TOOL FOR INCLUSIVE GROWTH

Personal reflection

Bertrand Badré
Managing Director and CFO
World Bank Group

Finance can be highly disruptive and destructive.[1] This was borne out by the 2007-2008 global financial crisis, where excessive borrowing, risky investments, and lack of transparency brought significant hardship to yet more families worldwide. However, we must also concede the reverse – finance can be an immeasurably powerful tool for good. Flow of capital into emerging markets and developing economies for infrastructure increases the availability of basic services of a community, resulting in increased access to water, electricity, and sanitation, more hospitals, schools and roads and stimulation of entrepreneurship, trade and prosperity. However, if we are to help the neediest in our communities, we must build an inclusive financial system that is more robust, principled and well governed to attract more flows.

The scale of poverty in our 21st century world is reprehensible: today, in a population of over seven billion, more than one billion still live in extreme poverty – living on less than \$1.25 a day. There is no room for negligence in financial reform with the welfare of so many at stake. We must be, at the same time, prophetic and practical in resolution.

Re-establishing Ethics

If finance is again to serve the common good, we must begin by revisiting the ethics of the individuals and organizations

---

[1] *1 Timothy 6:10 "For the love of money is the root of all evil".*

involved and the system in which they operate. Retrospection into the actions that sparked the financial crisis should have given us pause to avoid a repeat of past behavior. Yet, already we see that risks are increasing and misbehavior is recurring.

Improving the lives of the poorest people of our world must be the driver for our growth and development work; it should not be for profit. Questioning our relationship to money, addressing weaknesses in the system – both are needed. We must show tangibly that if we do finance well and honestly, it can be useful and successful, from the perspectives of both financier and beneficiary.

Responsible behavior by financial service providers and improved ability of users of financial services to protect their interests will lead to economic empowerment of the population and facilitate the smooth functioning of financial markets and the economy. Financial literacy and increased access to basic financial services, such as savings accounts or remittances, will help poor families afford essential services like water, health care or housing. Moreover, small businesses will be able to grow and create new jobs.

Many countries, such as Zambia and Rwanda, are investing in financial inclusion strategies to address their particular circumstances. Just this year, for instance, Rwanda became the first country in Sub-Saharan Africa to benefit from the Financial Inclusion Support Framework (FISF). This US$2.25 million trust fund, executed by the World Bank Group and financed by the Dutch Government, will focus on improving access, usage and quality of financial services, for those at most risk in rural areas and low-income segments.

Financial integrity, however, goes beyond individual or country-specific action.

As we continue to move into a new growth and development context, with new economic geography and expectations, it is incumbent upon citizens, corporations, governments, non-profits and others collectively to rebalance the framework. And, we must think outside the box with a humanitarian lens if we are to rebuild public trust in the good of finance as a tool for inclusive development and growth. The world community today needs a new, daring, altruistic financial and governance system.

Visionary System

With various economies at different stages of maturity and countries facing different social challenges, it is important to develop a heterogeneous yet cooperative approach. It is troubling then that many voices in our multi-polar world are not fully reflected at the epicenter of policy discussions, although each has an interest in the integrity of a future system. We must shift even further away from protective self-interest and unilateralism if we are to serve the common good. Building strong partnerships and listening to all voices has become increasingly important if we are to overcome global and local obstacles to address longer-term development goals.

We must be prophetic in order to achieve transformative global financial governance. It is time to step back and ask ourselves, what is the system that the world needs? How can it be governed equitably? Where can citizens, corporations and governments collaborate? And more.

On a practical level, we have made remarkable progress over the past four years. Emergency and short-term measures were successful in stopping the damaging trend. The results of international and regulatory responses, however, are mixed: Basel III acts as a cornerstone and the efforts of the Financial Stability Board continue to move us in the right direction. Yet, concerns linger around the lack of fundamental changes in banking and financial markets and the burden that regulators face, many of whom are unprepared for the complexities involved. In response, the Bank Group continues it work with national financial sector regulatory and supervisory authorities, such as the recently approved US$500 million Financial Sector Reform and Modernization Development Policy Loan for Indonesia, to help build strong and efficient financial systems.

National level work is necessary, but a multilateral global regulatory framework with international standards that can be applied to diverse countries and organizations is challenging to define and implement. Can we set aside decades of diverging opinion? We must if we are to avoid a repeat of past crises; strong, equitable financial consumer protection laws, regulations, supervisory and oversight structures are needed, created with all in mind. The World Bank Group is particularly concerned about the potential unintended short-term and longer-term consequences on emerging markets and developing economies if only a few vocal advanced economies sway opinion and drive reforms.

Collective voices provide unparalleled creativity, depth of experience and real-life perspective. Forging new, broader partnerships is imperative if we are to move away from systems forged by isolationist or sectarian views. Therefore, it is encouraging seeing a new financing paradigm in play with greater and more alliances between the public and private sector.

New Financing Paradigm

While the 1979-2007 financing model was effective during its time, the new financing paradigm will shape the future and speed of economic growth. Development banks are reaching their limits; commercial banks are pulling back from long-term finance. To address this reduction, the World Bank Group and other multilateral banks are taking steps to increase their infrastructure financing. In fact, the Bank Group estimates that its annual capacity will grow from US$45 to US$50 billion a year now to more than $70 billion.

With the private sector playing an ever-increasing role in markets traditionally the jurisdiction of the public sector, we see new and innovative transactions to help countries offset environmental and regulatory risks and the fiscal repercussions of natural disasters. This new model offers astonishing financing capacity that can make a significant difference to economic growth and development problems.

The decline in private long-term infrastructure investment in emerging markets is particularly worrisome though; in 2013, amounts were down from US$186 billion in 2012 to US$147 billion. This is nowhere near enough if we are to bridge the current estimated infrastructure gap. For emerging markets alone, the estimate is US$1 to 1.5 trillion more annually until 2020, plus another US$170-200 billion every year to spend on creating low-carbon, livable cities. We must mobilize untapped sources of finance, such as commercial banks and institutional investors.

The World Bank Group recognizes that new public private partnerships, new coalitions, are perhaps the most important feature of a future financing structure. This is where the Global Infrastructure Facility (GIF), an open global platform that will facilitate preparation and structuring of complex infrastructure public private partnerships in emerging markets and developing economies will be beneficial. The criticality of infrastructure to support economic growth and end extreme poverty cannot be understated. Financing solutions to challenges such as social stability, rapid urbanization, climate change adaptation and migration, natural disasters and food and energy security will take a communal effort on a scale we have not seen or experienced before.

The GIF will help coordinate the efforts of multilateral development banks, national development banks, private sector investors and financiers, and governments interested in infrastructure investment. The result? Better coordination, increased collaboration and effective collective action on complex projects that no single institution could realize alone, with a pipeline of bankable projects that will attract a greater variety of investors.

Conclusion

Where do we go from here? Extreme poverty in the 21st century is diminishing. In 1990 there were 1.91 billion people living on less than US$1.25 a day, whereas in 2010 there were 1.22 billion.[2]

---

[2] http://www.worldbank.org/en/topic/poverty/overview

However, there is more we can do. It is time to aspire to a new financial system, one that is inclusive, that rebuilds trust in finance. We cannot repeat the previous failures in financial regulation and supervision, corporate governance and risk management. As a single solution will not suit everyone, future financial governance should be transparent and promote the right incentives, allowing for adaptation based on national circumstances.

The moral imperative to aid the poorest of our populations is one that underpins the work of the World Bank Group. By 2030, the Group's aim is to reduce extreme poverty to 3% or less and improve prosperity for the bottom 40 percent of the world's population. Yet, we must not underestimate the complexity of achieving those goals, particularly as we plan for sustainable development. It will take significant effort to reform the system, readjust the moral compass of individuals and organizations and rededicate ourselves to correcting the imbalance around profit versus common good. Let's start with the foundation and make sure we do not build on sand. Finance was and can be again a positive tool for development impact.

"THE GLOBAL COMMON GOOD: TOWARDS A MORE INCLUSIVE ECONOMY"

Personal reflection

Simona Beretta

Professor of Economics
Catholic University of the Sacred Heart, Milan
Consultor of the Pontifical Council for Justice and Peace

Eradicating poverty and addressing inequality are key to the global common good – the good of each and all persons (*Populorum Progressio*). Each person's inclusion in social, economic and political life is the ultimate criterion by which to assess how inclusive is the whole system: both micro (personal) responsibility for the good of one's neighbour and macro system of rules and institutions are at stake.

The Seminar offered a unique opportunity of dialogue among many scholarly, professional, and institutional perspectives on the global public good, at the very special time of preparing for the post-2015 SDGs.

What is at stake in moving from 2000 MDGs to post 2015 SDGs? Is the global community simply striving to find the consensus on a new, more complete, "book of dreams" for its own future? Are individual agencies simply **mapping the space** so that each agency's particular agenda can be adequately represented in the overall emerging consensus? We can hope and work for more than that.

The effort to finding a consensus can become a true possibility of human dialogue, aimed at rebalancing the relationship between human beings and nature. *Christifideles laici* have a special contribution to offer to this process, announcing and practicing the social teachings of the Church and entering the debate with realistic and practical proposals. That is, **initiating a process** - following the criterion that time is superior to space (*Evangelii Gaudium,* 220).

My reflections will develop three points:

1. **Eradicating poverty: human dignity as an intrinsically relational notion** – speaking the language of human dignity (a gift from above) is key in eradicating poverty, realizing justice (there is something due to man because he is a man, JPII) and peace (development is the new name of peace, Paul VI) in the one human family we actually are called to be. This calls for an explicitly relational perspective.

2. **Addressing inequality: power asymmetries and the universal destination of material and non-material goods** – we are one family entrusted with the wealth of creation, and with the wealth of technical and cultural awareness previous generations bestowed us. Addressing inequality is a process of addressing power asymmetries that tend to exclude persons and peoples from this common inheritance of humanity.

3. **Global common good: the primary goal is realizing the good of living-together** (the good of the all-of-us, Benedict XVI, CV 7). Within this basic common good, all specific common material goods (land, water, air, natural resources), human common goods (food security, health, education, technical knowledge and cultural traditions) can find their appropriate setting. Even the debate on the respective roles of states, civil society organization, and markets in providing those common goods can become more fruitful and less ideological

4. I will conclude on the relation between time and space, that is **on the importance of activating processes.**

1. Eradicating poverty: human dignity as an intrinsically relational notion

"... a new trajectory of thinking is needed in order to arrive at a better understanding of the implications of our being one family ... so that integration can signify solidarity rather than marginalization. Thinking of this kind requires a deeper critical evaluation of the category of relation. This is a task that cannot be undertaken by the social sciences alone... As a spiritual being, the human creature is

defined through interpersonal relations. The more authentically he or she lives these relations, the more his or her own personal identity matures. It is not by isolation that man establishes his worth, but by placing himself in relation with others and with God. Hence these relations take on fundamental importance." (CV, 53)

While mentioning the centrality of the person and human dignity is common in a variety of milieus, there is a special contribution *christifideles laici* can give. They experience in their life what it means that Christ reveals man to man – hence in their everyday life the expression 'human dignity' assumes a fullness of meaning that can only be approached with a mix of baldness and humility. Baldness in announcing the gift of the Gospel to any fellow human being; humility in proposing and realizing practical initiatives, and in critically highlighting which are the (often reduced) anthropological perspectives driving development policies and projects to eradicate poverty. Dignity is the inalienable God-given right of each and every person; hence, preparation for the post-2015 SDGs can greatly benefit from exploring the meaning and the practical implications of basing development policies on human dignity – thus contributing to purifying the (ambivalent) language of human rights.

The language of human dignity helped to forge consensus in the immediate post-WWII international debate, thus becoming the theoretical pillar of the 1948 Declaration of Human Rights. The practical implication of the notion of human dignity are usefully clarified in the words of a crucial character of that period, Eleanor Roosevelt:

> *"Where, after all, do universal human rights begin? In small places, close to home—so close and so small that they cannot be seen on any map of the world. Yet they are the world of the individual person: the neighborhood he lives in; the school or college he attends; the factory, farm or office where he works. Such are the places where every man, woman, and child seeks equal justice, equal opportunity, equal dignity without discrimination. Unless these rights have meaning there, they have little meaning anywhere".* [1]

---

[1] E. ROOSEVELT, "In Our Hands" (March 27, 1958, speech delivered to the United Nations Assembly on the tenth anniversary of the Universal Declaration of Human Rights).

The person lives in the network of her meaningful relations; more in depth, her inner self is relational intrinsically: the person flourishes in fully living her constitutive tensions between the individual and the community. Each individual person – in the network of her relevant relations, from family up to the economic, social and political structures from local to global – is to be protagonist of her life.

The **intrinsically relational nature of being human** is especially significant when the dignity of women is considered. This is a very sensitive issue, for two reasons: one, women are disproportionally represented among the poor and marginalized; second, technological changes – from 'modern' contraception to techno-sciences applied to human reproduction – bring with them unprecedented transformations in the social role of women, that requires time and wisdom to be fully appreciated. Women's dignity is at stake, well beyond women's empowerment as such. The relational nature of dignity calls for a relational perspective in gender studies, which is mostly missing. Most information we have on the situation of women and girls are 'attributional', not relational, in nature: school/university enrollment, adolescent pregnancies-motherhoods, number of children, gender wage gaps with respect male workers, and so on. We do collect some relational data, which typically refer to access to economic resources (access to land, access to credit); but women's dignity goes beyond material empowerment. Say, access to modern contraception (or to free abortion practices) may reduce the numerical incidence of adolescent motherhoods – but cannot restore any violated girl's personality; technocratic intervention may succeed in reducing measurable 'evils' – with no necessary correlation with enhancing human dignity.[2] As a self-evident illustration,

---

[2] There is an urgent need to expand 'relational' gender studies, where human dignity are at the core of research. For a very provisional outline of possible research directions, S. BERETTA, "What do we know about the economic situation of women, and what does it mean for a just economy?", IN FINN D., *The True Wealth of Nations*, Cambridge University Press, 2010.

these same techniques greatly contributed to the phenomenon of 'missing girls' in demographic patterns.

The relational nature of being human finds a counterpart in the intrinsically relational nature of the common existence of the humankind, including material dimensions such as production, consumption, growth. Economic development itself is not meaningfully represented by any quantitative expansion of a given material entity – no matter how inclusive and sophisticated. The important and fruitful debate tending to move 'beyond GDP' makes a lot of sense, but remains a partial effort if it simply ends up including in the calculations other 'good things' (say, acres of forests) and subtracting 'bad things' (say, pollution indicators). **Development itself occurs in crucial relations**: with nature; with one's contemporaries; with one's own cultural and religious tradition; ever more frequently, in relations with other tradition, since each of us can experience the 'plural' world in one's own neighborhood; last but not least, development occurs in relationships of care for future generations. Development is a dynamic process occurring here and now, not an expected outcome set in the future; it consists in a change 'for the better' in the relational dynamics described above; it is the path itself, not the destination.

As relations matter in development, the experience of being poor consists not only in deprivation of material means, but in relational and symbolic deprivations. One can clearly see it when poor people are asked to define poverty.[3] Hence, addressing poverty is more than solving (urgent and complex) issues of material

---

[3] Here are some quotes from *Voices of the Poor*. "Poverty is humiliation, the sense of being dependent on them, and of being forced to accept rudeness, insults, and indifference when we seek help". (Latvia 1998); "Poverty is lack of freedom, enslaved by crushing daily burden, by depression and fear of what the future will bring." (Georgia 1997) "Poverty is pain; it feels like a disease. It attacks a person not only materially but also morally. It eats away one's dignity and drives one into total despair". (Moldova 1997). See D. NARAYAN, WITH R. PATEL, K. SCHAFFT, A. RADEMACHER & S. KOCH-SCHULTE, *Voices of the Poor: Can Anyone Hear Us?* The World Bank, Washington D.C., 2000.

deprivation; it also involves essential relational issues, where meaning and purpose are at stake. The relational nature of addressing poverty can be summarized by two elements: one is the need for poor people to be protagonist of their own progress; the other is the need for finding reliable partners in this effort.

First, poor people are to be dignified and feel **protagonist** in eradicating poverty. The poor themselves know what they need to eradicate their own poverty, and their dignity demands that are in charge of their own flourishing (development is a right and a duty, says *Populorum progressio*). This is a necessary condition for true sustainability of development, as opposed to assistentialist redistribution initiatives.

It is true that poor communities' empowerment can achieve what individuals never could; they can, but seldom alone. Here comes the second element: **partnership** is key in development, as social and economic progress occurs within meaningful relations. The essence of partnership consists in building personalized and durable relationships that foster community life and reciprocal support. Partnership relate to the most difficult part of any development policy: namely, who will actually cover the "last mile", reaching out to the least privileged.[4]

---

[4] Partnering is an operational principle that can actually make the difference in policy design and implementation, and in dramatically improving the cost effectiveness of development policies. As a powerful example, let me mention the experience of Stop TB, a WHO initiative about which I developed an on-going research project titled: *Love Matters in Policy Making: The Stop TB Partnering Process.* Love for persons, community participation and social justice are the inspirations and motivations behind the launch of the Stop TB Partnership in 2008; they are explicitly elaborated and communicated in official documents (see WHO, *Community Involvement in Tuberculosis Care and Prevention – Towards Partnership for Health,* 2008, especially pp.11-16, http://www.who.int/rpc/guidelines/9789241596404/en/index.html. The recently approved Global TB Strategy (2015-2035), for the first time addresses the issue of social determinants of the TB disease – clearly connecting the medical issue with issues of poverty and exclusion. Partnerships will be key for forging national and local alliances across different agents and institutions as a necessary precondition to venture out from the strictly medical/public health field into the domain of social work with other partners and institutions.

Empirical evidence, anecdotal evidence and even simple self-observation show that durable relations, in closed proximity to partners, effectively foster sustainable development in disadvantaged areas. Despite insufficient research, each of us can recall examples of long-term commitment that translated into friendship, local empowerment, and sustainable development partnerships. Durable relations also provide (un-planned) opportunities to deal with emergencies, especially in conflict-torn situations.

In the words of the Catholic social tradition, we can say that truly generative partnerships rely on three pillars. One is human dignity – the innate and inestimable dignity of each person, origin of both rights and duties; a second is subsidiarity – trusting that poor people can be protagonist of their development, when they are empowered to exercise their rights and responsibilities. The third is solidarity – awareness of interdependence, *"sensed as a system determining relationships in the contemporary world, in its economic, cultural, political and religious elements, and accepted as a moral category"* (*Sollicitudo Rei Socialis,* 38).

There are some remarkable features in partnerships that are worth mentioning. Partnering is a humble process: no 'optimal solution' is expected to hold in all situations, no one size fits all! There is no presumption of solving each and all problems; there is no easy 'code of conduct' to be applied, as no mechanistic ethics can substitute for personal responsible agency. The expression 'process' has become prominent in the Catholic social discourse, as Pope Francis has repeatedly used it with reference to the common good and peace in society (*Evangelii Gaudium,* 223-224). Partnering is an open-ended adventure. We value the path we are treading with our peers, at least as much as we value the final destination we intend to reach – a destination which remains clouded in uncertainty, but we know at least that we are trying to take distance from injustice and disrespect of human dignity, subsidiarity and solidarity.

2. Addressing inequality: power asymmetries and the universal destination of material and non-material goods

The sharp rise in inequality (especially within-countries inequality) the world experienced as either a cause and/or a consequence of the recent crisis, prompted a new awareness of inequality's role in curtailing development, both in the broad sense of hindering human flourishing and in the narrow sense of producing significant economic costs.

Dealing with inequality means much more than addressing unequal outcomes in a remedial way. It requires as a starting point the awareness of how interdependence connects all members of the human family. Interdependence is a practical reality, with enormous moral significance; hence, the appropriate method for dealing with inequality begins by concretely understanding the link between power asymmetries and inequality. Power asymmetries of all kind are key to injustice, so addressing power asymmetries can be an effective path towards addressing distributional and social justice issues.

We observe asymmetries of power due to the **role** of different agents: creditors and debtors, for example – one cannot exist without the other, but debtors bear a disproportional share of costs when distress comes. We also face asymmetries of **economic power** (between national entities , and/or between economic actors); and asymmetries in **access** (institutional and social constraints in access to food, to land ownership and use, to health and education, in access to financial markets and insurance opportunities; last but not least, in access to information). With a self-reinforcing circular causation mechanism, the above asymmetries tend to weaken the weakest – one possible manifestation of how 'structures of sin' become embedded in social, economic and political institutions. Think about smallholder farmers, for example. The world food supply mainly depends on their efforts, yet the lack of access to financial credit and insurance deeply undermines their attempts to increase their capability to cope with uncertainty, smoothing their access to goods and services across periods of plenty and scarcity, and allowing them to realize productivity-enhancing investments.

From an economic point of view, power asymmetries are manifest in pricing processes (especially in pricing financial assets, setting wages, pricing primary products and international trade flows) represent a very relevant dimension of inequality. The more asymmetric are the power conditions across economic and social actors, the more likely it is that actual prices will deviate from "just" prices (and much effort – both theoretical and practical – is continuously required to explore what a "just" price is, in any given circumstance). Unjust actual prices may be 'market' prices, but they may as well be internal transfer prices whenever we face offshoring some stages of the supply chain – a process that produces burgeoning amounts of international trades flows, which are in facts cross-border intra-firm trades. In the last decades number of transnational corporations have de facto become "global systemically important enterprises"; many of these enterprises provide services which are essential for the normal functioning of the world (merchandise and passenger transport, telecommunications, media, financial services, internet operations). Many of them use complex legal structures with clear intentions to minimize the tax burden by generating their highest profits in tax havens – in consequence, important proportions of world economic activity unjustly avoid taxation. Justice (social justice at the global level) requires matching power with responsibilities: 'big' players obviously need to comply with rules of justice, but also to creatively decide to face their 'big' responsibilities and to find ways for realizing cooperation among unequal partners.

On the political side, power asymmetries seep in and shape local and national policies. Moreover, power asymmetries provide a terrific inertia in policy making, so that inequality becomes ever more deeply structurally built in those societies where only lip service is offered to human dignity (and on the contrary we observe all sorts of manifestations of that *"culture of discard"* Pope Francis often mentions[5]). This is why addressing inequality needs a movement, affirming God-given human dignity and defending each and every human person (*Centesimus Annus*[6] describes the Catholic social tradition as being exactly such a movement).

At the deepest anthropological and moral level, power asymmetries are a challenge to the fact that all human beings are equal in dignity, with their multifaceted, irreducible individual being. Equal in dignity, as stated in the first article of the Universal Declaration of Human Rights and as mysteriously and perfectly revealed in Jesus Christ, teaching us to pray "Our Father". Each and all of us form one human family entrusted with the wealth of God-given creation, and also with the wealth of technical and cultural knowledge previous generations bestowed on us. Addressing inequality can thus be seen also as a process of addressing power asymmetries that tend to exclude persons and peoples form this common inheritance of humanity.

In the language of the Catholic social tradition, we speak of the universal destination of all goods, material and immaterial (including knowledge). Through human work, human beings receive and circulate the goods of the Earth and the fruit of previous human

[5] "Human beings are themselves considered consumer goods to be used and then discarded. We have created a "throw away" culture which is now spreading. It is no longer simply about exploitation and oppression, but something new. Exclusion ultimately has to do with what it means to be a part of the society in which we live; those excluded are no longer society's underside or its fringes or its disenfranchised – they are no longer even a part of it. The excluded are not the "exploited" but the outcast, the "leftovers" ", (*Evangelii Gaudium*, 54).

[6] "(T)he great outpouring of the Church's Tradition ... (includes) the fruitful activity of many millions of people, who, spurred on by the social Magisterium, have sought to make that teaching the inspiration for their involvement in the world. Acting either as individuals or joined together in various groups, associations and organisations, these people represent *a great movement for the defence of the human person* and the safeguarding of human dignity. Amid changing historical circumstances, this movement has contributed to the building up of a more just society or at least to the curbing of injustice." (*Centesimus Annus*, 3)

work: this activity is in fact the key driver of wealth creation and innovation of all kinds – including political innovation aimed at addressing inequality. In this global world, which is so obviously lacking appropriate global governance procedures, we need innovative solutions to deal with the different dimensions of interdependence (real/financial, environmental/social, local/global, material/non-material dimensions) so that inequality is addressed and the fundamental common good of living together is pursued.

Innovative solutions require an untiring effort where even imagination can play a role. Any intuition we have of possible solutions for bettering the institutional, political and social frame where the common life of the human family occurs is both a gift we receive and a responsibility we have. Any such intuition calls for opening a practical dialogue, aimed at shaping political consensus. Each person, each generation is called to participate in this process.

3. Global common good: the primary goal is realizing the good of living-together

Realizing the good of living-together is the basic common good, where all specific common goods find their appropriate place: material goods (land, water, air, natural resources), and human common goods (food security, health, education, technical knowledge and cultural traditions).

Living together in a 'plural', interdependent world is both tremendously difficult to realize, and badly needed. Finding ways for realizing the good of the all-of-us living together requires a common grammar for human encounter, starting from recognizing what we, as human beings, have already in common. Hence, the roots of ethical dialogue are in sound anthropology, one that resonate with elemental human experience.

No matter how 'plural' the world is, we have in common the experience of being human – that is, the 'incandescent nucleus' of our inner self. This nucleus is totally personal, and at the same time common to each human being; it makes it possible for each of us to profoundly meet the inner self of other persons from all ages, all latitudes and longitudes. *"Homo sum, humani nihil a me alienum puto" (Publio Terenzio Afro, 1ˢᵗ century a.d.).*

The Christian social tradition is deeply attached to the elemental, common experience of humanity – the human heart, to use the powerful expression of the Old and New Testament. This tradition is keen on reaching each person in the concrete space of her relevant relations, since *"... man is ... the fundamental way for the Church";*[7] and the basic grammar of being human is about love and truth *(Caritas in Veritate).* Hence, no grand design on the one side, no detailed governance structure on the other side make sense if we are not ready to openly talk about love, and truth – despite the fact that these words are almost unspeakable in today's world. Even more clearly, then, we are called to witness our humble belonging to Love and Truth, that is, to the Person of Jesus. The need to witness Jesus as the most reasonable answer to the elemental, common experience of being human is not to downplay the fact that we also need both grand designs and detailed governance structures. We need to find solutions that are capable of highlighting and addressing asymmetric structures of power. We need solutions that are both realistic, and practical - in other words, incarnated: "Realities are greater than ideas".[8]

---

[7] "Man in the full truth of his existence, of his personal being and also of his community and social being - in the sphere of his own family, in the sphere of society and very diverse contexts, in the sphere of his own nation or people (perhaps still only that of his clan or tribe), and in the sphere of the whole of mankind - this man is the primary route that the Church must travel in fulfilling her mission: he is the primary and fundamental way for the Church, the way traced out by Christ himself" *(Redemptor Hominis,* 14).

[8] "The principle of reality, of a word already made flesh and constantly striving to take flesh anew, is essential to evangelization. It helps us to see that the Church's history is a history of salvation, to be mindful of those saints who enculturated the Gospel in the life of our peoples and to reap the fruits of the Church's rich bi-millennial tradition, without pretending to come up with a system of thought detached from this treasury, as if we wanted to reinvent the Gospel." *(Evangelii Gaudium,* 233).

We often hear a saying that goes: 'the devil is in the details'. This expression conveys a useful message, yet it can be quite misleading. What *christifideles laici* know for sure is that the transcendent, the sacred, the ultimate meaning – in a word: Jesus – is the ultimate fabric of all reality, details included. His presence is the only reasonable reason for never giving up hoping and striving for human dignity and for justice. *Christifideles laici*'s contribution to shaping to post-2015 SDGs agenda for the international community is both very demanding and very simple. We are called to be, here and now, that "*movement for the defense of the human person* and the safeguarding of human dignity" mentioned in *Centesimus Annus*, 3. We just need to move along this path, with our brothers and sisters, shaping the social economic and political life with our work, rooted in gratitude and driven by the reasonable hope that we are not alone. He is with us, and – as He says – we can do nothing without Him.

4. Time and space, or the priority of activating processes

Benedict XVI, in analysing the movement leading to re-shaping political institutions for the common good, uses the interesting category of 'moral consensus' (Benedict XVI, Aparecida Address, 2007;[9] *Spe Salvi*, 24-25[10]); Pope Francis speaks of the 'processes

---

[9] "In truth, just structures are a condition without which a just order in society is not possible. But how do they arise? How do they function? ... Just structures ...neither arise nor function without a moral consensus in society on fundamental values, and on the need to live these values with the necessary sacrifices, even if this goes against personal interest ... (J)ust structures must be sought and elaborated... with the full engagement of political, economic and social reasoning. They are a question of *recta ratio* ... in different cultural and political situations, amid constant developments ... adequate answers must be sought in a rational manner, and a consensus must be created... (J)ust structures will never be complete in a definitive way. As history continues to evolve, they must be constantly renewed and updated " (Benedict XVI, *Aparecida Address* 2007).

[10] "... (I)n fundamental decisions, every person and every generation is a new beginning. ... (T)he right state of human affairs, the moral well-being of the world can never be guaranteed simply through structures alone, however good they are. Such structures are not only important, but necessary; yet they cannot

of people-building', beyond citizenship (*Evangelii Gaudium*, 224).[11] These two expressions are particularly interesting, and quite complementary.

Moral consensus, when applied to political organization, broadens our perspectives beyond both overlapping consensus (the minimum common ground – which can be so minimum that it amounts to the empty set), and democratic consensus (the majority rule, which may contradict the basic grammar of elemental human experience – love and truth). Moral consensus requires human encounter and dialogue within societies, which are characterised by a plurality of ethnicities, cultures, political options. In all this plurality, there remains a common core, the common 'incandescent nucleus' we have in common with all human beings.

Pope Francis describes the processes of people-building as "*an ongoing process in which every new generation must take part: a slow and arduous effort calling for a desire for integration and a willingness to achieve this through the growth of a peaceful and multifaceted culture of encounter*". This process of encountering works deeper and moves forward, beyond citizenship as such.

Both achieving moral consensus and people-building need persons freely engaging their energy in activating processes, as "time

and must not marginalize human freedom. Even the best structures function only when the community is animated by convictions capable of motivating people to assent freely to the social order. Freedom requires conviction; conviction does not exist on its own, but must always be gained anew by the community. ... (E)very generation has the task of engaging anew in the arduous search for the right way to order human affairs; this task is never simply completed. Yet every generation must also make its own contribution to establishing convincing structures of freedom and of good, which can help the following generation as a guideline for the proper use of human freedom (*Spe Salvi*, 24-25).

[11] "(R)esponsible citizenship is a virtue, and participation in political life is a moral obligation. Yet becoming a people demands something more. It is an ongoing process in which every new generation must take part: a slow and arduous effort calling for a desire for integration and a willingness to achieve this through the growth of a peaceful and multifaceted culture of encounter". (Francis, *Evangelii Gaudium*, 220).

prevails over space" (*Evangelii Gaudium,* 223).[12] The prevalence of such process over the 'mapping' of spaces obviously does not mean that mapping in unimportant. An important contribution to achieving moral consensus comes from being aware of each institution and agent's specific role in possibly promoting the good of the human family. Technocratic approaches may be very dangerous, when based on presumptions of self-sufficiency; conversely, the plurality of institutions and institutional diversity itself may, up to a certain point, be useful. Even apparent duplications may be conducive to virtuous processes in a diverse and changing world – just like biodiversity is fundamental for preserving life. Each institution and organization has different sources of power and legitimacy – there are many layers that intersect. For an inclusive, global common good, indeed, "the model is not the sphere" (*Evangelii Gaudium,* 236).[13]

---

[12] "One of the faults which we occasionally observe in sociopolitical activity is that spaces and power are preferred to time and processes. Giving priority to space means madly attempting to keep everything together in the present, trying to possess all the spaces of power and of self-assertion; it is to crystallise processes and presume to hold them back. Giving priority to time means being concerned about initiating processes rather than possessing spaces. Time governs spaces, illumines them and makes them links in a constantly expanding chain, with no possibility of return. What we need, then, is to give priority to actions which generate new processes in society and engage other persons and groups who can develop them to the point where they bear fruit in significant historical events. Without anxiety, but with clear convictions and tenacity." (Francis, *Evangelii Gaudium*, 223).

[13] "The whole is greater than the part, but it is also greater than the sum of its parts. There is no need, then, to be overly obsessed with limited and particular questions. We constantly have to broaden our horizons and see the greater good which will benefit us all. But this has to be done without evasion or uprooting. We need to sink our roots deeper into the fertile soil and history of our native place, which is a gift of God. We can work on a small scale, in our own neighbourhood, but with a larger perspective. Nor do people who wholeheartedly enter into the life of a community need to lose their individualism or hide their identity; instead, they receive new impulses to personal growth. The global need not stifle, nor the particular prove barren. Here our model is not the sphere, which is no greater than its parts, where every point is equidistant from the centre, and there are no

121

There is no single recipe for creating just institutions, and existing structures require continuous re-generation. Encounter and dialogue are processes conducive to a 'decent' state of world's political and economic relations. Dialogue must be engaged at all levels: within nation states and across nations (in multilateral institutions, in regional institutions, in self-aggregating groups such as G7/8, G20…); but also within other crucial global players (firms and institutions which hold economic and financial power; but also scientific and technical power; agents that hold communication power). Non-strictly-political forms of power, in today's world, play a huge role, and are to be involved within the process of achieving moral consensus over global governance issues.

I am convinced the Church has a unique role/responsibility in people-building and promoting moral consensus in our complex, plural societies, as its 'catholic' nature empowers her with the capacity to address the basic, elementary human experience (Jesus Christ, Love and Truth, fully reveals what it is to be human).

differences between them. Instead, it is the polyhedron, which reflects the convergence of all its parts, each of which preserves its distinctiveness. Pastoral and political activity alike seek to gather in this polyhedron the best of each. There is a place for the poor and their culture, their aspirations and their potential. Even people who can be considered dubious on account of their errors have something to offer which must not be overlooked. It is the convergence of peoples who, within the universal order, maintain their own individuality; it is the sum total of persons within a society which pursues the common good, which truly has a place for everyone". (*Evangelii Gaudium*, 235 -236).

INCLUSIVE CAPITALISM: CREATING A SENSE OF THE SYSTEMIC

Personal reflection

Mark J. Carney

Chairman of the G20's Financial Stability Board

Introduction

Inclusive capitalism is fundamentally about delivering a basic social contract comprised of relative equality of outcomes; equality of opportunity; and fairness across generations. Different societies will place different weights on these elements but few would omit any of them.

Societies aspire to this trinity of distributive justice, social equity and intergenerational equity for at least three reasons. First, there is growing evidence that relative equality is good for growth.[1] At a minimum, few would disagree that a society that provides opportunity to all of its citizens is more likely to thrive than one which favours an elite, however defined. Second, research suggests that inequality is one of the most important determinants of relative happiness and that a sense of community – itself a form of inclusion – is a critical determinant of well-being.[2] Third, they appeal to a fundamental sense of justice.[3] Who behind a Rawlsian veil of ignorance – not knowing their future talents and circumstances – wouldn't want to maximise the welfare of the least well off?

---

[1] See Ostry, Berg and Tsangarides (2014).
[2] See Alesina, Di Tella and MacCulloch (2004); Wilkinson and Pickett (2009).
[3] In 31 of the 39 countries surveyed by Pew Research in 2013, half or more of the population believed inequality to be a "very big problem" in their societies (Pew Research Center, 2013).

The problem: the growing exclusivity of capitalism

This gathering and similar ones in recent years have been prompted by a sense that this basic social contract is breaking down. That unease is backed up by hard data. At a global level, there has been convergence of opportunities and outcomes, but this is only because the gap between advanced and emerging economies has narrowed. Within societies, virtually without exception, inequality of outcomes both within and across generations has demonstrably increased.[4]

The big drivers of globalisation and technology *are* magnifying market distributions. [5] Moreover, returns in a globalised world are amplifying the rewards of the superstar and, though few of them would be inclined to admit it, the lucky.[6]

Now is the time to be famous or fortunate.

There is also disturbing evidence that equality of opportunity has fallen, with the potential to reinforce cultural and economic divides. For example, social mobility has declined in the US undercutting the sense of fairness at the heart of American society.[7]

---

[4] The Gini coefficient pertaining to household disposable income rose from 0.26 in 1961 to 0.36 in 2008 in the UK, and from 0.39 to 0.46 over the same period in the US, according to data collected by Atkinson and Morelli (2014). Those data show this to be a common pattern across many advanced economies. In emerging markets, Gini coefficients remain high relative to the average for OECD countries, and rose between the 1990s and 2000s for India, China and the Russian Federation, though falling for Brazil (OECD, 2011a). The share of income received by the top 1 per cent of the population has also risen since the 1980s across many industrialised countries, including Australia, Canada, the United Kingdom and the United States (Atkinson and Morelli, 2014).

[5] See Autor, Katz and Krueger (1998) and Autor, Katz and Kearney (2008). For example the last 60 years have seen US returns to education rise despite a large increase in the supply of more educated workers. And there is evidence that increases in the employment of more skilled workers between the 1970s and the 1990s were greater in more computer intensive industries.

[6] As Michael Lewis has remarked, "Success is always rationalised. People really don't like to hear success explained away as luck – especially successful people. Lucky [to] live in the richest society the world has ever seen, in a time when no one actually expects you to sacrifice your interests to anything." Lewis (2012).

[7] See for example Corak (2013), who finds that the elasticity of a son's adult

Intergenerational equity is similarly strained across the advanced world. Social welfare systems designed and enjoyed by previous generations may prove, absent reform, unaffordable for future ones.[8] And environmental degradation remains unaddressed, a tragic embarrassment now seldom mentioned in either polite society or at the G20.

To maintain the balance of an inclusive social contract, it is necessary to recognise the importance of values and beliefs in economic life. Economic and political philosophers from Adam Smith (1759) to Hayek (1960) have long recognised that beliefs are part of inherited social capital, which provides the social framework for the free market.

Social capital refers to the links, shared values, and beliefs in a society which encourage individuals not only to take responsibility for themselves and their families but also to trust each other and work collaboratively to support each other.[9]

So what values and beliefs are the foundations of inclusive capitalism?[10] Clearly to succeed in the global economy, *dynamism* is essential. To align incentives across generations, a *long-term perspective* is required. For markets to sustain their legitimacy, they need to be not only effective but also *fair*. Nowhere is that need more acute than in financial markets; finance has to be *trusted*. And to value others demands *engaged citizens,* who recognise their obligations to each other. In short, there needs to be a sense of society.

---

earnings with respect to his parents' earnings – the "intergenerational elasticity" – rose from 0.3 to around 0.55 between 1950 and 2000 in the US, indicative of a decline in social mobility. Corak has also shown that the intergenerational earnings elasticity tends to be higher in more unequal countries; a phenomenon termed the "Great Gatsby Curve" by Alan Krueger (2012).

[8] Government spending has increased in most countries around the world since the 1960s, reflecting increased spending on social protection, education and healthcare (IMF, 2014). And, looking forward, all OECD countries face increased budgetary pressure due to expected increases in age-related healthcare, long-term care and pensions (OECD, 2011b, Table 1.1). Merola and Sutherland (2012) analyse long-run fiscal sustainability in the context of these budgetary pressures.

[9] E.g. Putnam (2001).

[10] For a similar list see Shanmugaratnam (2013).

Social capital has been eroded

These beliefs and values are not necessarily fixed; they need to be nurtured. My core point is that, just as any revolution eats its children, unchecked market fundamentalism can devour the social capital essential for the long-term dynamism of capitalism itself. To counteract this tendency, individuals and their firms must have a sense of their responsibilities for the broader system.

All ideologies are prone to extremes. Capitalism loses its sense of moderation when the belief in the power of the market enters the realm of faith. In the decades prior to the crisis, such radicalism came to dominate economic ideas and became a pattern of social behaviour.[11] As Michael Sandel argued, we moved from a market economy to a market society.[12]

Market fundamentalism – in the form of light-touch regulation, the belief that bubbles cannot be identified and that markets always clear – contributed directly to the financial crisis and the associated erosion of social capital.

Ensuing events have further strained trust in the financial system. Many supposedly rugged markets were revealed to be cosseted:

- major banks were too-big-to fail: operating in a privileged heads-I-win-tails-you-lose bubble;
- there was widespread rigging of benchmarks for personal gain; and
- equity markets demonstrated a perverse sense of fairness, blatantly favouring the technologically empowered over the retail investor.[13]

Such practices widen the gap between insider and outsider returns and challenge distributive justice. More fundamentally, the resulting mistrust in market mechanisms reduces both happiness and social capital.

[11] Padoa-Schioppa (2010).
[12] Sandel (2012).
[13] See Martin (2012), also Lewis (2014).

We simply cannot take the capitalist system, which produces such plenty and so many solutions, for granted. Prosperity requires not just investment in economic capital, but investment in social capital.

It is necessary to rebuild social capital to make markets work. This is not an abstract issue or a naive aspiration. I will argue that we have already made a start with financial reform and that by completing the job, by returning to true markets, we can make capitalism more inclusive.

What then must be done?

There are a wide range of policies to promote inclusive capitalism from early childhood education, training and the importance of differentiated pathways and mixed-income neighbourhoods. These are all fundamentally political issues.

The Bank of England's mission "to promote the good of the people of the UK by maintaining monetary and financial stability" suggests that central banks have an important role to play in supporting social welfare.

Central banks can contribute in two areas. First, our core macroeconomic objectives promote social welfare. Second, we can help to create an environment in which financial market participants are encouraged to think of their roles as part of a broader system. By building a sense of responsibility for the system, individuals will act in ways that reinforce the bonds of social capital and inclusive capitalism.

Some of this is straightforward. Inflation hurts the poor the most and the real costs of financial instability – unemployment and the seizure of credit – are likely to be felt most acutely by the poor.[14] Conversely, monetary and financial stability are corner-

[14] For example, using data on over 30,000 households in 38 countries, Easterly and Fischer (2001) find that the poor are more likely than the rich to mention inflation as a top national concern. Moreover, higher inflation is associated with greater income inequality in cross-country data (Albanesi, 2007). Financial crises in developing countries are associated with an increase in poverty and, in some cases, income inequality – see for example Baldacci, de Mello and Inchauste

127

stones of strong, sustainable and balanced growth and therefore directly affect distributive justice.

Some is more nuanced. While to not have acted would have been catastrophic for all, the distributional consequences of the response to the financial crisis have been significant. Extraordinary monetary stimulus – both conventional, through low short-term interest rates, and unconventional, through large scale purchases of assets – raised a range of asset prices, benefiting their owners, and lowered yields, benefiting borrowers at the expense of savers.[15]

Central banks are not blind to these issues. Rather we recognise that decisions to redistribute wealth are rightly political, as are most policies that promote social mobility. It is only in extreme circumstances, such as in the wake of a financial crisis, that we can have some limited influence on social mobility and intergenerational equity.

That is because the depth and duration of recessions can profoundly affect the opportunities over the rest of the lives of affected workers. For example, a rise in unemployment by 5 percentage points is estimated to imply an average initial loss of earnings for new college graduates of around 9%, an effect which is estimated to fade only after a decade.[16] The persistent effects from adverse labour market conditions are much larger for individuals in the first year of their careers than for those with a few years of experience.

(2002). OECD (2013) documents an increase in market income inequality over the period 20072010 across developed countries, and reports with respect to the top and bottom 10% of the income distribution that "lower income households either lost more from income falls or benefitted less from the often sluggish recovery." In general it is likely that adverse income and employment shocks hurt the poor the most, for example because they lack the ability to hedge against these shocks and may lack access to credit markets to smooth them. Even if crises have a neutral effect on income inequality, the poor are much less able to absorb a cut in income (Honohan 2005).

[15] For an assessment of the distributional effects of the Bank of England's asset purchases, see http://www.bankofengland.co.uk/publications/Documents/news/2012/nr073.pdf.

[16] See Oreopoulos, von Wachter and Heisz (2012).

And losses are magnified for those whose earnings are predicted to be lower, based on their college major. The current situation in many advanced economies is very challenging: over 40% of recent graduates in US are underemployed[17] and youth unemployment is around 50% in the worst affected countries in the Euro area.

With clear risks of a misplaced if not lost generation, to the extent appropriate under our mandates, the monetary policy response has represented a race against long-term (or hysteretic) unemployment. As Janet Yellen remarked, "the risk that continued high unemployment could eventually lead to more-persistent structural problems underscores the case for maintaining a highly accommodative stance of monetary policy."[18]

In Britain at least, these risks have been sharply reduced. The Bank of England has used a range of policies first to stimulate and then to secure the recovery. These have helped support the strongest job growth on record including record-high transitions back into employment by the longer-term unemployed. Longer-term social mobility will benefit from this track record.

Looking ahead, improvements in policy frameworks should help to reduce – but not eliminate – the incidence of financial crises. A core lesson of the recent episode is the need to think of the system as a whole. That is now reflected in the Bank of England's responsibility to bring a macroprudential perspective to financial stability policy.

Financial reform and rebuilding social capital

Central banks' greatest contribution to inclusive capitalism may be driving financial reforms that are helping to re-build the necessary social capital.

In doing so, we need to recognise the tension between pure free market capitalism, which reinforces the primacy of the individu-

---

[17] See Abel, Deitz and Su (2014).
[18] Yellen (2012).

al at the expense of the system, and social capital which requires from individuals a broader sense of responsibility for the system. A sense of self must be accompanied by a sense of the systemic.

Consider four financial reforms that are helping to create this sense of the systemic and thereby rebuild trust in the system.

First, ending Too-Big-To-Fail

Perhaps the most severe blow to public trust was the revelation that there were scores of too-big-to-fail institutions operating at the heart of finance. Bankers made enormous sums in the run-up to the crisis and were often well compensated after it hit. In turn, taxpayers picked up the tab for their failures. That unjust sharing of risk and reward contributed directly to inequality but – more importantly – has had a corrosive effect on the broader social fabric of which finance is part and on which it relies.

By replacing such implicit privilege with the full discipline of the market, social capital can be rebuilt and economic dynamism increased.

The leaders of the G20 have endorsed measures to restore capitalism to the capitalists by ending too-big-to-fail and, in response, the *Financial Stability Board* (FSB) has identified systemically important institutions; made them subject to higher standards of resilience; and developed a range of tools to ensure that, if they do fail, they can be resolved without severe disruption to the financial system and without exposing the taxpayer to loss.

This is the year to complete that job. Governments must introduce legislative reforms to make all systemically important companies, including banks, resolvable. Jurisdictions must also empower supervisors to reach agreements for credible cross-border resolution plans. The FSB is developing proposals, for the G20 summit in Brisbane, on total loss absorbing capacity for institutions, so that private creditors stand in front of taxpayers when banks fail. In addition, we are working with industry to change derivative contracts so that all counterparties stay in while resolution of a failing firm is underway.

Second, creating fair and effective markets

In recent years, a host of scandals in fixed income, currency and commodity markets have been exposed. Merely prosecuting the guilty to the full extent of the law will not be sufficient to address the issues raised. Authorities and market participants must also act to re-create fair and effective markets.

In the Bank of England's view, changes to both the hard and soft infrastructure of markets will be required. Examples of the former include reforming the calculations of benchmarks such as Libor or the daily foreign exchange fixes. The upcoming FSB report on these issues, co-chaired by the Financial Conduct Authority's (FCA) Martin Wheatley and the Fed's Jeremy Stein, will be decisive in this regard. Consideration should also be given to increasing pre- and post-trade transparency in a host of fixed income markets and accelerating the G20 pledge to move the trading of all standardised derivatives onto electronic exchanges and platforms.

Such changes are vital, but they cannot anticipate every contingency or discipline every miscreant.

The scandals highlight a malaise in corners of finance that must be remedied. Many banks have rightly developed codes of ethics or business principles, but have all their traders absorbed their meaning? A first step to restore trust in markets might be to rely on traders' intuitive understanding of what makes a true market. Consideration should be given to developing principles of fair markets, codes of conduct for specific markets, and even regulatory obligations within this framework. There should be clear consequences including professional ostracism for failing to meet these standards.

The basic point is that all market participants, large and small, should recognise that market integrity is essential to fair financial capitalism. Confidence in the integrity of those markets needs to be reinforced alongside genuine competition to ensure that the needs of end customers are properly and effectively served. Doing so will

131

reinforce the City's well-deserved reputation as the world's leading financial centre, with the most effective and efficient markets.

Third, reforming compensation

Dominic Barton and Mark Wiseman (2014) have detailed the need for long-term thinking by concentrating on shareholder incentives. A related lesson of the crisis was that compensation schemes that delivered large bonuses for short-term returns encouraged individuals to take on too much long-term and tail risk. In short, the present was overvalued and the future heavily discounted.

To align better incentives with the long-term interests of the firm – and, more broadly, society – major changes are underway. At the request of G20 Leaders, the FSB has developed the principles for sound compensation practices to align incentives with long-term risks. In the UK, the Bank of England has adopted a new code for banks prescribing deferred variable performance payments, introducing the ability to reduce deferred bonuses when subsequent performance reveals them not to have been fully deserved, and paying bonuses in stock rather than cash.

The deferral of bonuses awarded today allows them to be reduced before they are paid if evidence emerges of employee misconduct, error, failure of risk management or unexpectedly poor financial performance by the individual, their team or company.

We are continuing to refine our approach. The Bank has just completed a consultation on a requirement for variable remuneration to be clawed back *after* payment and will consult later in the year on new standards for bonus deferrals.

These provisions will apply not only to employees who are judged culpable directly, but also to others who could reasonably have been expected to identify and manage risks or misconduct but did not take steps to do so, and senior executives who could reasonably be deemed responsible by establishing the culture and strategy of the organisation. Where problems of performance or risk management are pervasive, bonuses should be adjusted for whole groups of employees.

Of course, no compensation package can fully internalise the impact of individual actions on systemic risks, including on trust in the system.[19] To do so, market participants need to become true stakeholders. That is, they must recognise that their actions do not merely affect their personal rewards, but also the legitimacy of the system in which they operate.

Fourth, building a sense of vocation and responsibility

To build this sense of the systemic, business ultimately needs to be seen as a vocation, an activity with high ethical standards, which in turn conveys certain responsibilities.

It can begin by asking the right questions. Who does finance serve? Itself? The real economy? Society? And to whom is the financier responsible? Herself? His business? Their system?

The answers start from recognising that financial capitalism is not an end in itself, but a means to promote investment, innovation, growth and prosperity. Banking is fundamentally about intermediation – connecting borrowers and savers in the real economy.

In the run-up to the crisis, banking became about banks not businesses; transactions not relations; counterparties not clients. New instruments originally designed to meet the credit and hedging needs of businesses quickly morphed into ways to amplify bets on financial outcomes.

When bankers become detached from end-users, their only reward becomes money. Purely financial compensation ignores the non-pecuniary rewards to employment, such as the satisfaction from helping a client or colleague succeed.

This reductionist view of the human condition is a poor foundation for ethical financial institutions needed to support long-term prosperity. To help rebuild that foundation, financiers, like all of us,

---

[19] More fundamentally, to think that compensation arrangements can ensure virtue is to miss the point entirely. Integrity cannot be legislated, and it certainly cannot be bought. It must come from within. See Carney (2013).

need to avoid compartmentalisation – the division of our lives into different realms, each with its own set of rules. Home is distinct from work; ethics from law; the individual from the system.[20]

This process begins with boards and senior management defining clearly the purpose of their organisations and promoting a culture of ethical business throughout them. Employees must be grounded in strong connections to their clients and their communities. To move to a world that once again values the future, bankers need to see themselves as custodians of their institutions, improving them before passing them along to their successors.

In the UK, two important initiatives are in train to help accomplish these ends.

The first is a new regime for regulating the senior-most managers of banks. That regime, proposed by the Parliamentary Commission on Banking Standards and now being established by the Bank of England seeks to reverse the blurring of the link between seniority and accountability that has developed over the years.

Its underlying principles are relevant across the financial sector. People who run major firms should have clearly defined responsibilities and behave with integrity, honesty and skill regardless of whether they work for global investment banks, regional building societies or insurance companies.

We are now considering a similar regime for senior persons in the insurance sector. This does not mean applying the banking regime indiscriminately. For one thing there is no statutory provision for applying a "reverse burden of proof" in insurance. For another, *Solvency II* requires us to monitor the fitness and propriety of a broader range of staff than in banks. In coming months we will build on the provisions of legislation to produce a regime that in

---

[20] As the CEO of TD Bank, Ed Clark, observed, "Bank leaders created cultures around a simple principle: if it's legal and others are doing it, we should do it too if it makes money. It didn't matter if it was the right thing to do for the customer, community or country." See Clark (2012).

spirit is aligned with the standards to which we hold bankers, but that in practice is a tailored approach for insurers. It will combine accountability with efficiency.

Ultimately, of course, social capital is not contractual; integrity can neither be bought nor regulated. Even with the best possible framework of codes, principles, compensation schemes and market discipline, financiers must constantly challenge themselves to the standards they uphold.

A meaningful change in the culture of banking will require a true commitment from the industry. That is why a second initiative, the creation of the *Banking Standards Review Council* (BSRC), is particularly welcome.[21] This new independent body, again proposed by the Parliamentary Commission, is designed to create a sense of vocation in banking by promoting high standards of competence and behaviour across the UK industry.

The BSRC will complement the work of regulators by setting out a single principles-based code of practice, based on the high-level principles now being considered by the Prudential Regulation Authority and FCA. Among other things, this should aim to guide behaviour in the face of conflicts of interest or of moral ambiguity. It will also identify activities where voluntary standards of good practice would be in the public interest, and work with industry to develop them. And it will engage with banks to establish good practice in developing the competence and training requirements of staff covered by the Certified Persons regime.

A prime objective of the BSRC will be to help individual banks and building societies to drive up standards of behaviour and competence through a process of internal and external assessment. It will work with banks to encourage a process of continuous im-

---

[21] Sir Richard Lambert's Review was commissioned by the Chairmen of Barclays, HSBC, Lloyds, Nationwide, RBS, Santander and Standard Chartered in response to the recommendations of the Parliamentary Commission on Banking Standards. See http://www.bankingstandardsreview.org.uk/

provement, and regularly assess and disclose the performance of each bank under the three broad headings of culture, competence and development of the workforce, and outcomes for customers.

The BSRC is an important sign of banks' recognition of the need for change. Its impact over time will be a crucial test of the industry's commitment to that change.

Conclusion

By encouraging enterprise and rewarding individual initiative, market-based economies provide the essential conditions for economic progress. But social capital must be maintained for that progress to be consistently delivered.

The combination of unbridled faith in financial markets prior to the crisis and the recent demonstrations of corruption in some of these markets has eroded social capital. When combined with the longer-term pressures of globalisation and technology on the basic social contract, an unstable dynamic of declining trust in the financial system and growing exclusivity of capitalism threatens.

To counter this, rebuilding social capital is paramount.

Financial reform is now helping. Globally systemic banks are simplifying and downsizing. Some are deemphasising high-profile but risky businesses that benefited employees more than shareholders and society. Authorities are working feverishly to end too-big-to-fail. The structure of compensation is being reformed so that horizons are longer and rewards match risk. Regulation is hard-wiring the responsibilities of senior management. And new codes are seeking to re-establish finance as a true profession, with broader societal obligations. A welcome addition to these initiatives would be changes to the hard and soft infrastructure of financial markets to make them dynamic and fair.

Through all of these measures, finance can help to deliver a more trustworthy, inclusive capitalism – one which embeds a sense of the systemic and in which individual virtue and collective prosperity can flourish.

References

Abel, J, Deitz, R and Su, Y (2014), "Are recent college graduates finding goods jobs?", *Federal Reserve Bank of New York Current Issues in Economics and Finance*, 20(1).

Albanesi, S (2007), "Inflation and inequality", *Journal of Monetary Economics*, 54(4), May, pages 1088-114.

Alesina, A, Di Tella, R and MacCulloch, R (2004), "Inequality and happiness: are Europeans and Americans different?", *Journal of Public Economics*, 88(9-10), pages 2009-42.

Atkinson, A and Morelli, S, (2014), "Chartbook of Economic Inequality", *ECINEQ Working Paper* 324.

Autor, D, Katz, L and Krueger, A (1998), "Computing inequality: have computers changed the labour market?" *Quarterly Journal of Economics*, 113(4), pages 1,169-213.

Autor, D, Katz, L and Kearney, M (2008), "Trends in US wage inequality: revising the revisionists", *Review of Economics and Statistics*, 90(2), May.

Baldacci, E, L de Mello, and G Inchauste (2002), "Financial Crises, Poverty, and Income Distribution", Working Paper 02/4, International Monetary Fund, Washington, DC.

Barton, D and Wiseman, M (2014), "Focusing capital on the long term", *Harvard Business Review*, JanuaryFebruary.

Carney, M (2013), "Rebuilding Trust in Global Banking", Speech at the Richard Ivey School of Business, 25 February. Available at http://www.bankofcanada.ca/2013/02/rebuilding-trust-global-banking/

Clark, E (2012), Remarks delivered at the Bank of Canada Annual Economic Conference, "Financial Intermediation and Vulnerabilities," Ottawa, 2 October 2012.

Corak, M (2013), "Income inequality, equality of opportunity, and intergenerational mobility", *Journal of Economic Perspectives*, 27(3), Summer.

Easterly, W and Fischer, S (2001), "Inflation and the poor", *Journal of Money, Credit and Banking*, 33(2), May.

IMF (2014), *Fiscal monitor April 2014: public expenditure reform – making difficult choices. Available at* http://www.imf.org/external/pubs/ft/fm/2014/01/pdf/fm1401.pdf

Hayek, F (1960), *The Constitution of Liberty*, Routledge.

Honohan, P (2005), "Banking sector crises and inequality", *World Bank Policy Research Working Paper* 3659, July.

Krueger, A (2012), "The rise and consequences of inequality in the United States", *mimeo*.

Lewis, M (2012), "Don't Eat Fortune's Cookie", remarks at Princeton University, June 3.

Lewis, M (2014), *Flash boys: a Wall Street revolt,* W. W. Norton & Company.

Martin, R (2012), "The Gaming of Games & the Principle of Principles", Keynote Address to the Global Peter Drucker Forum, Vienna, November 15.

Merola, R and Sutherland, D (2012), "Fiscal Consolidation: Part 3. Long-Run Projections and Fiscal Gap Calculations", *OECD Economics Department Working Papers,* No. 934.

OECD (2011a), "Divided we stand: why inequality keeps rising. Special focus: inequality in emerging economies". Available at http://www.oecd.org/els/soc/49170475.pdf

OECD (2011b), *Restoring public finances: Special Issue of the OECD Journal on Budgeting,* Volume 2011/12. Available at http://www.oecd.org/governance/budgeting/47558957.pdf

OECD (2013), "Crisis squeezes income and puts pressure on inequality and poverty". Available at http://www.oecd.org/els/soc/OECD2013-Inequality-and-Poverty-8p.pdf

Oreopoulos, P, von Wachter, T and Heisz, A (2012), "The short- and long-term career effects of graduating in a recession", *American Economic Journal: Applied Economics,* 4(1), pages 1-29.

Ostry, J, Berg, A and Tsangarides, C (2014), "Redistribution, Inequality, and Growth", *IMF Staff Discussion Note* 14/02.

Padoa-Schioppa, T (2010), "Markets and government before, during and after the 2007-20xx crisis", The Per Jacobsson Lecture, June.

Pew Research Center (2013), "Economies of emerging markets better rated during difficult times; global downturn takes heavy toll; inequality seen as rising", May. Available at http://www.pewglobal.org/files/2013/05/Pew-Global-Attitudes-Economic-Report-FINAL-May-23-20131.pdf

Putnam, R (2001), "Social capital: measurement and consequences", mimeo.

Sandel, M (2012), *What Money Can't Buy: The Moral Limits of Markets,* Macmillan

Shanmugaratnam, T (2013) "The Invisible Hand of Social Culture", 6th S Rajaratnam Lecture, December.

Smith, A (1759), *The Theory of Moral Sentiments.*

Wilkinson, R and Pickett, K (2009), *The Spirit Level: Why more equal societies almost always do better,* Penguin.

Yellen, J (2012), "The economic outlook for monetary policy", Speech to the Money Marketeers of New York University, April. Available at http://www.federalreserve.gov/newsevents/speech/yellen20120411a.htm

THE GLOBAL COMMON GOOD TOWARDS A MORE INCLUSIVE GLOBAL ECONOMY

Personal reflection

Brian Griffiths

Vice-Chairman
Goldman Sachs International

The Discussion Paper is an excellent document and makes some points very well and very strongly. I also thought that the presentations and discussions we had at the conference itself drew out important themes. However, I am delighted to offer my personal reflections in response to your request.

1. Where does wealth creation fit into the Global Common Good?

At various places in the Discussion Paper there are insights into what constitutes the common good: greater inclusion in economic life, less inequality in living standards between and within countries, a culture of reciprocity rather than materialistic possessive individualism, preserving and improving the environment for future generations and so on.

However, what about wealth creation itself? Is wealth creation one element of the common good along with inclusion and equality? If it is, then, wealth creation seems to receive less attention in the document than other aspects of the common good.

I believe there is a strong case for wealth creation being a part of the common good. First, the creation of wealth is based on human anthropology. Man is created *imago dei*, purposeful, enterprising and having authority, but not autonomy, in the physical world. It is this which enables humanity to fulfil the divine mandate. Second, for all its weakness as a measure of economic well- being, GDP does include measures of basic commodities such as food, clothing, housing, education and health. Even if inequality remains at current levels, an increase in these for all in society is surely a good thing?

Is there not a case for having an explicit reference to wealth creation as being one aspect of the common good in a revised Discussion Paper?

2. Finance (section 4.1)

This section makes some excellent points – both positive and critical – which need saying.

However it is important, as Mark Carney said in the discussion in Rome, to recognise the progress which has been made in the international banking system since 2008.

(a) All major countries established extensive reviews of the problem and the need for reform of regulation in the banking sector. Some (e.g. UK) have set up new institutions. All have passed new legislation (e.g. Dodd Frank in US, Financial Services Banking Reform UK, CRD4 European Union)

(b) The G-20 set up the Financial Stability Board which has played a key role in coordinating reforms in different countries.

(c) The Basel Accord is a voluntary, global, regulatory standard among countries regarding the capital, liquidity, leverage of their banks and the stress testing of these. In the light of the financial crisis 2008, Basel (III) has imposed tough new measures to ensure taxpayers will not have to bail out banks in a future crisis and that future crisis are less likely.

Taken together, these reforms have (I) made banks hold much more capital and liquidity, (II) forced them to divest certain risky businesses (e.g. propriety trading), the Volcker rule (III) required them to change the structure of compensation (deferred payment, payment in shares not cash of up to 7 years, claw back arrangements if performance fails to match expectations) and set limits to bonus payments, (European Union - Brussels) (IV) offered greater security to depositors through compulsory deposit insurance and ring fencing of retail banking activities and (V) required them to make "living wills" of how they would respond to a future financial shock. Regulators have also been given powers to take over failing banks.

As the same time, the supervision of banks has become more specific, more intense and more extensive. Large banks can now expect regulators to be on their premises or in conversation with some part of their organisation on a daily basis. This is a sea-change from the pre-crisis level of supervision. It has already led to major investigations into price fixing in LIBOR markets, foreign exchange markets, and the gold market.

The comment therefore in Section 5 "the global financial architecture has to be rethought" is frankly redundant. It has been.

As a result of all of this activity regulators have until now, and the process is not finished, fined banks a total of $150billion – an extraordinary figure, which would have seemed inconceivable in 2007.

All of this should be recognised in a final version of the Discussion Paper.

In addition, all large banks have conducted major internal reviews of the way they do business which has resulted in major changes. Perhaps best summed up by asking two questions regarding a new piece of business. "Can we do this? Should we do this?" It is asking the second question which is making the difference.

3. Diversity of Business Ownership Structures

One of the attractions of a market economy is that it includes many different types of business firms: self-employment, partnerships, private companies, not-for-profit enterprises, publicly quoted companies, mutuals, cooperatives, and so on.

I believe there is a great advantage in ensuring that such diversity remains an important feature of a modern market economy because different ownership structures suit the needs and preferences of different people, not least with respect to risk taking.

In some countries (the UK is one example), the enthusiasm over privatisation and deregulation in the 1980's led to the decline of mutual organisations (insurance companies, building societies, Trustee Savings Bank) with the result that today this part of the structure of the financial system is seriously weakened.

The Discussion Paper should also state the case for employee owned firms, greater participation of employees in the ownership of the companies for which they work (even if they are publically traded companies) and social enterprises.

4. A Greater Role for Business (Sections 3, 4.3, 4.4)

I like the idea of the "constructive synthesis" of wealth creation, civil society and redistribution (section 3); the challenge to competitive labour markets (section 4.3, first para) and the human dignity associated with work (hence the scourge of unemployment) and the challenges associated with rapidly changing technology and the governance of business firms (section 4.4).

However, I believe the potential which firms can play in the "constructive synthesis" is much greater than this.

The business firm has emerged as a dominant institution in the modern world. It is widely accepted even in countries with very different government philosophies, that well-managed companies operating in competitive markets are the key to wealth creation, the growth of jobs, innovation and the advance of knowledge.

More than that, business has emerged across the globe as a significant social institution in all societies. The mission statements, business principles and objectives set out by companies are important statements of values in their own right. Companies are carriers of value. They set standards. They inspire people. They provide a framework within which people seek meaning and fulfilment in their work, and not just financial compensation. At a time when the traditional institutions which were the source of values in our society – especially the family and religious institutions – have either been weakened or have abrogated their leadership in the West, the business firm has become a significant source and carrier of values. This is the challenge which should be given to business leaders and set out more explicitly than it is in the current Discussion Paper.

5. From Micro-Finance to Social Impact Investing

I think it would be a shame to issue a document on the Global Common Good without some reference to the benefits which have accrued to "the poor" from micro-finance, while recognising at the same time its limitations.

It is because of the limitations that social impact investing has grown up and is getting stronger. The objective is to create companies which aim to make a profit but have not just a single but a triple bottom line namely profit, social impact and environmental sustainability. Such a firm will be run on commercial lines but the rate of return which investors would seek on their investments would be less than that offered in private markets.

6. Credit Markets for Low Income Families

The ability of low income families to borrow funds is also a significant issue in high income countries. In our discussion in Rome, Mr. Yunus suggested that we need to create new institutions to meet the credit needs of low income families. I agree with him strongly. My conclusion is the result of my personal involvement in micro-finance since 1971 and in chairing a commission on the subject of debt, credit markets and low income families. I believe the following general conclusions can be supported with evidence.

- Low income families/the poor need credit as much as any other income group.
- The existing retail banking system in most countries does not find lending in this area an attractive return.
- As a result, specialised institutions have developed (credit unions, community finance initiatives, pay day loans, savings banks).

– Many of these institutions are either not viable without continued government support, or if they are viable charges exorbitant interest rates.

As a result, the challenge for public policy is how to create institutions which offer loans at competitive prices to fill the gap. This is where reciprocity/ profit/ government involvement meet.

7. Whatever became of "the poor"

One of the great strengths of *Evangelii Gaudium* is its repeated emphasis on the challenge of the poor, to everyone but especially for Christians. It is one of the most singularly important aspects of Pope Francis' vision for the Global Common Good (EG, 186-216) – "Each individual Christian and every community is called to be an instrument of God for the liberation and promotion of the poor…", "God's heart has a special place for the poor, so much that he himself 'became poor… the option for the poor'… none of us can think we are exempt from concern for the poor and social justice".

It is because of statements such as these that the Apostolic Exhortation is so challenging. If, however, its concerns are translated into terms such as inclusion, inequality, social justice, social construction and reductionism then, frankly, it loses its power and appeal. I realise that *Evangelii Gaudium* and the Global Common Good are different kinds of documents and that the appeal to commentators, bankers, corporate executives, international public servants and politicians should be measured as they may be people of other faiths or no faith. However, the occasional reference to Jesus and his teaching, who is after all one of the world's greatest leaders, would not go amiss.

SOME OBSERVATIONS ON INEQUALITY AND INCLUSIVENESS

Personal reflection

Kalpana Kochhar

Deputy Director
Strategy, Policy and Review
International Monetary Fund (IMF)

Six themes

- Globalization is generally a "good" but some aspects of it need coordination and cooperation.
- Inequality has a very different complexion in advanced markets and developing countries, and requires different interventions.
- Finance can be a force for good when properly regulated.
- Gender is an important element of inequality and needs specific interventions.
- Redistribution need not be inimical to growth and efficiency.
- The global financial and economic cooperation architecture may need to be strengthened to deal with some consequences of globalization.

Theme 1. Globalization can be a global common good

- In most cases, globalization improves productivity, technological absorption, knowledge transfer, etc.
- And contributes to reduction in poverty and a rise in living standards.
- Globalisation is a concern when it causes a race to the bottom. Of special concern in this regard:
- – Taxation
- – Labor protections
- – Wages

Theme 1.1 Global inequality has fallen

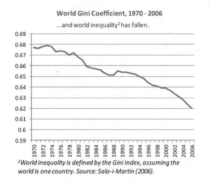

World Gini Coefficient, 1970 - 2006

...and world inequality[2] has fallen.

[2]World inequality is defined by the Gini Index, assuming the world is one country. Source: Sala-i-Martin (2006).

Income Inequality in the 1980s and 2000s

Nevertheless, within-country inequality has risen in the majority of countries, particularly in advanced ones.

- Advanced Economies
- Emerging Markets
- Low Income Countries

Source: Solt (2009)

Theme 1.2 Taxation: A race to the bottom?

- Taxation. Work by the IMF published in 2014 finds that spillovers effect on corporate income tax bases are significant and sizable for developing countries.

- Both base effects and strategic (policy) spillovers are large.

- Base spillovers arise from profit shifting and the effect on real activities.

- It finds that there is pressure to lower tax rates especially in resource-rich countries in Africa where there is also a need to raise revenues for redistribution.

- Changes are needed in the architecture of taxation— minimum domestic taxation, worldwide income taxation, base apportionment.

- But it is very difficult to achieve coordination.

Theme 1.3 A Race to the Bottom?

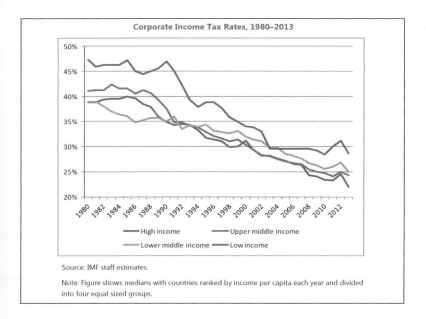

Theme 1.4 Declining shares of revenues

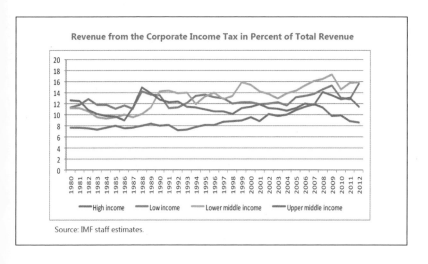

Theme 2. Inequality in AM's and DC's is very different

- Inequality has a very different nature in advanced and developing countries.

- In developing countries, poverty is still the biggest challenge.

- Vast inequality of opportunities.

- Recent attention to inequality in advanced markets should not divert attention from this point.

- Tackling inequalities in developing countries requires a somewhat different set of policies than in AMs.

- The "globalisation of indifference" should be avoided, but the good news is that people do care about inequality (Pew Surveys).

Theme 2.1 Poverty and inequality

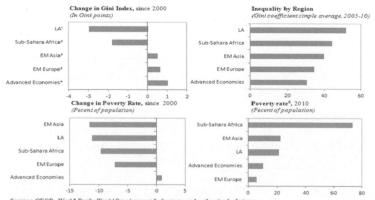

Developments in Inequality and Poverty since 2000

Sources: OECD; World Bank, *World Development Indicators*; and authors' calculations.
[1] Includes Argentina, Belize, Bolivia, Brazil, Chile, Colombia, Ecuador, Guatemala, Honduras, Mexico, Nicaragua, Panama, Paraguay, Peru, Uruguay and Venezuela R.B.
[2] Includes Burkina Faso, Burundi, Cameroon, Central African Republic, Chad, Comoros, Congo, Dem. Rep., Congo, Rep., Cote d'Ivoire, Ethiopia, Gabon, Ghana, Guinea, Kenya, Liberia, Madagascar, Malawi, Mali, Mozambique, Namibia, Niger, Nigeria, Rwanda, Senegal, Seychelles, South Africa, Swaziland, Tanzania, Uganda, and Zambia.
[3] Includes China, India, Indonesia, Philippines, Malaysia, Singapore, and Thailand.
[4] Includes Australia, Austria, Belgium, Canada, Denmark, Finland, France, Germany, Greece, Iceland, Ireland, Israel, Italy, Japan, Repub of Korea, Luxembourg, Malta, Netherlands, Norway, Portugal, Spain, Sweden, Switzerland, United Kingdom, and United States.
[5] Includes Bulgaria, Croatia, Estonia, Georgia, Hungary, Latvia, Lithuania, Poland, Romania, Turkey, and Ukraine.
[6] National coverage of poverty headcount (% of population living in households with consumption or income per person below the povert line of $76 per month ($2.5 per day)).

Theme 2.2 Inequality of opportunities

Inequality in Health Services and Outcomes, 2005-11
(in percent, unless otherwise stated)

Under-five mortality rate situation by place of residence
(Deaths per thousand live births)

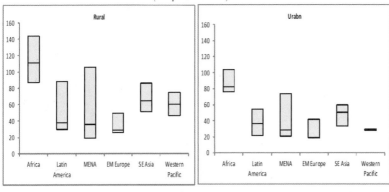

Theme 2.3 Inequality in AMs

- Caused by rising shares of income at the top and declining shares at the bottom.

- Tax structures become less progressive.

- Declining in collective bargaining and other labor market institutions.

- International tax competition.

Theme 3. We need a fin(ance) balance

- Finance is the lifeblood of business. Finance has three main activities-credit intermediation, insurance and risk management, and other finance (securities, commodities, private equity, investment banking, etc.).

- Inclusive finance is found to increase welfare and is often cited as a key to reducing poverty.

- But unregulated or poorly regulated finance is very dangerous from a financial stability point of view (see Philippon and Reshef, 2009).

149

- But also because it has tended to unleash strong forces contributing to inequality of income.

Relative Financial Wage and Financial Deregulation

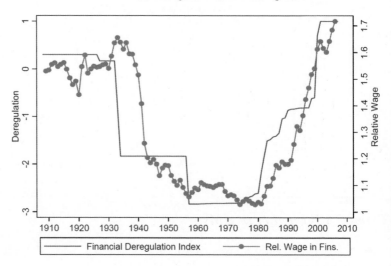

Notes: Wages are computed from the Industry Accounts of the U.S., from Kuznets (1941), and from Martin (1939). The relative wage is the ratio of Fins to Non Farm Private wages. See the text for the definition of the deregulation index.

Wages Relative to Non Farm Private Sector

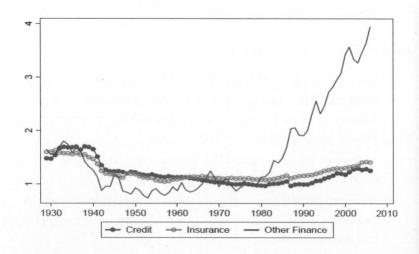

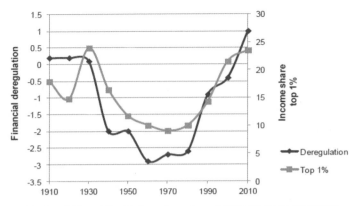

The relationship between financial deregulation and inequality in the US

Source data: Financial Deregulation, http://www.nber.org/papers/w14644.pdf; Income share: Piketty and Saez (2003, 2012).

Theme 4. Gender gaps are an important facet of inequality

- Women and girls make up 70 percent of the 1 billion people living on less than $1 a day.

- The share of women of working age who are employed is 48 percent compared with nearly 73 percent for men.

- There is a concentration of women in sectors that are generally characterized by low pay.

- Women dominate the informal sector, characterized by unstable earnings, vulnerability in employment status, and low degree of social protection. Part-time work is a predominantly female domain and part-time work is paid at a significantly lower rate than full-time work.

- Gender wage differentials are present in all occupations and across all skill bases. Even controlling for education levels and hours worked, there is a significant gap between male and female median wages. There is also evidence that the income gap for women has worsened over time. For example, in the U.S., the 90-10 income ratio (the ratio of wages in the

151

90th and 10th percentiles) has increased by twice as much for women as it did for men.

- Low incomes earned by women can have significant implications for intergenerational equity.

- Women are more likely to spend on health and education of their children, thus building human capital to fuel future growth. Women invest up to 90 percent of their earnings in their families and communities, compared with 30-40 percent for men.

Theme 5. Inequality, growth and redistribution

- Research at the IMF (Berg, Ostry and Tsangarides) shows that inequality is a robust and powerful determinant of the pace and sustainability of economic growth.

- Redistribution appears generally benign in terms of its impact on growth.

- Redistributive efforts (through taxes and subsidies) that are not extreme (too high or too low) are associated with higher and more durable growth.

Theme 6. The global cooperation architecture could be made more effective

- The IMF is the institution which has the expertise and the closest mandate for multilateral cooperation on economic policies.

- The ISD is a new stronger legal framework that came into effect in 2013.

- What does the ISD do?

- It provides the basis for the Fund to discuss a large range of global spillovers from domestic policies.

- It encourages members to be mindful of the impact of their domestic policies on global stability.

- It provides a framework for tackling global issues requiring collective action and global coordination.

BUT

- It does not change the scope of member countries' obligations. Such changes could only be done by amending the IMF's Articles of Agreement.
- The ISD continues to emphasize the collaborative nature of surveillance, the importance of dialogue and persuasion, the need for candor and evenhandedness, and the importance of paying due regard to country circumstances.

Final thoughts

- Capital market imperfections are at the root of the relationship between inequality and growth.
- Education is the key to social and economic mobility.
- Transfers and subsidies to those who are most vulnerable are the best option. Even better if these are used to increase access to education.
- Globalization can make inequality worse and raising skill levels can mitigate that effect (Maskin, 2014).

A LIFE OF DIGNITY FOR ALL: ACCELERATING PROGRESS TOWARDS THE MILLENNIUM DEVELOPMENT GOALS AND ADVANCING THE UNITED NATIONS DEVELOPMENT AGENDA BEYOND 2015[1]

Personal reflection

Amina J. Mohammed

UN *Assistant Secretary General;* UN *Secretary-General's Special Adviser on the Post-2015 Development Agenda*

Introduction

The world's quest for dignity, peace, prosperity, justice, sustainability and an end to poverty has reached an unprecedented moment of urgency.

In 2000, the States Members of the United Nations agreed on a bold vision for the future that reaffirmed the fundamental values of freedom, equality, solidarity, tolerance, respect for the planet and shared responsibility.

That vision, enshrined in the Millennium Declaration (General Assembly resolution 55/2) and rooted in the Charter of the United Nations, recognized the need to pool efforts as never before and to advance on three fronts simultaneously: development, peace and security, and human rights. Global challenges, local solutions; shared burden, shared gain: this remains the credo of international action for our collective well-being.

---

[1] This is an abridged and updated version of the Report of the Secretary-General A/68/202, *A Life of Dignity for All*. This version is submitted as a contribution to the upcoming publication of the Pontifical Council for Justice and Peace on the theme "The Global Common Good: Towards a more inclusive Economy," following from the seminar conducted at the Vatican on the 11th and 12th of July 2014.

Among the promises made in the Millennium Declaration was a compelling pledge to spare no effort to free all women, men, girls and boys from the abject and dehumanizing conditions of poverty. The call itself was not new; the commitment to better standards of living is part of the purposes and principles of the United Nations. But what was new was the sense of possibility — the conviction that through a combination of targets, tangible investments, genuine action and political will, countries and people working together could end poverty in all its forms.

The Millennium Development Goals gave expression to this resolve. Since their adoption, Governments, partners and an inspiring constellation of groups and individuals around the world have mobilized to tackle the many dimensions of poverty. Those efforts have generated unprecedented advances in human development.

There has been substantial progress in achieving the Millennium Development Goals and several successes in reaching specific targets globally and in individual countries. However, the prospects for achieving all of the Goals differ sharply across and within countries and regions. More than a billion people still live in extreme poverty. Far too many people face serious deprivation in health and education, with progress hampered by significant inequality related to income, gender, ethnicity, disability, age and location. The prolonged global economic downturn and violent conflicts in recent years have exacerbated poverty, inequality and exclusion. Biodiversity loss, the degradation of water, drylands and forests and the intensifying risks of climate change threaten to reverse our achievements to date and undermine any future gains.

We must do everything we can to achieve the Millennium Development Goals by the end of 2015. That work is unfinished and must continue in order to secure the well-being, dignity and rights of those still on the margins today, as well as for future generations. By meeting our existing commitments, we will be in the best possible position from which to agree upon and implement a universal agenda for sustainable development after 2015.

At the same time, the world has changed radically since the turn of the millennium. New economic powers have emerged, new technologies are reshaping our societies and new patterns of human settlement and activity are heightening the pressures on our planet. Inequality is rising in rich and poor countries alike.

A new era demands a new vision and a responsive framework. Sustainable development, enabled by the integration of economic growth, social justice and environmental stewardship, must become our global guiding principle and operational standard. This framework can bring together the full range of human aspirations and needs. It offers a template for mutually reinforcing approaches to global challenges. Sustainable development is, in short, the pathway to the future.

So the challenge remains, even as it has taken on new complexity and increased in scale: we must fulfil our promises and meet the aspirations of the world's peoples, and we must summon the unity to realize the dream of the Charter and the Millennium Declaration. Ours is the first generation with the resources and know-how to end extreme poverty and put our planet on a sustainable course before it is too late.

The transition to sustainable development must not mean any diminishment whatsoever in the commitment to ending poverty. As underscored in the outcome document of the United Nations Conference on Sustainable Development, held in Rio de Janeiro, Brazil, in 2012 (General Assembly resolution 66/288), poverty eradication is an indispensable requirement for sustainable development. This is a matter of basic justice and human rights. It is also a historic opportunity. If ours is the generation that can end poverty, there should be no deferring this essential mission, no shrinking away from the task. In a world of great wealth and technological advances, no person anywhere should be left behind. No person should go hungry, lack shelter or clean water and sanitation, face social and economic exclusion or live without access to basic health services and education. These are human rights, and form the foundations for a decent life.

Nor can progress be achieved or sustained amid armed conflict, violence, insecurity and injustice. These ills often have roots in social and economic deprivation and inequality. In the same vein, poverty can be a precursor and breeding ground of instability. We know that upholding human rights and freeing people from fear and want are inseparable; it is imperative that we do more to act on this basic truth.

The emerging outlines of a new sustainable development agenda include the following characteristics: universal in nature yet responsive to the complexities, needs and capacities of individual countries and regions; bold in ambition but simple in design; combining the economic, social and environmental dimensions while putting the highest priority on ending poverty and reducing inequality; protective of the planet, its biodiversity, water and land; rights-based, with particular emphasis on women, young people and marginalized groups; eager for new and innovative partnerships; and supported by pioneering approaches to data and rigorous accountability mechanisms. Guided by this far-reaching vision, a limited set of goals with sustainable development at the core, as called for at the United Nations Conference on Sustainable Development, could be constructed to encapsulate current challenges and the priorities of the new agenda and to guide the transformation we need.

We are all aware of the vulnerabilities and perils that define daily life across the world. But there is also simultaneously a sense of wondrous potential made possible in part by science and technology but even more by our own hard work and devotion to common progress. Collectively, we have the leadership, conviction and courage to address short-term uncertainties while seizing the opportunity for long-term change.

1. Achieving the Millennium Development Goals and the transition to a new agenda

The Millennium Development Goals are our promise to the world's poorest and most vulnerable. They have succeeded in placing people at the centre of the development agenda.

We have made remarkable progress. Many countries — including some of the poorest — have aligned their policies and resources with the Goals to make unparalleled gains. Several critical targets have already been met or will be met by the end of 2015, both at the aggregate level and in individual countries. Sizable gains have occurred in even the poorest countries.

However, progress has been insufficient and highly uneven. Rural areas and marginalized groups continue to lag behind on virtually all goals and targets. Countries in or emerging from conflict, disaster or instability face significant challenges. In addition, the economic and financial crisis has complicated efforts, including by putting pressure on official development assistance.

Yet progress continues. In the *Millennium Development Goals Report 2014*, it is stressed that despite challenges and gaps, the agenda embodied by the Goals retains great power in engendering collective action for faster results.

Fulfilling our existing commitments and promises on the Millennium Development Goals must remain our foremost priority. Member States, with the continued support of development agencies, civil society and the private sector, should and can take bolder action to accelerate progress.

Together, we need to focus on those Goals that are most off-track and on countries that face particular development challenges, including the least developed countries, landlocked developing countries, small island developing States and countries affected by or recovering from conflicts or disasters. In so doing, we must pay particular attention to the needs and rights of the most vulnerable and excluded, such as women, children, the elderly, indigenous people, refugees and displaced families, as well as people with disabilities and those living in poor rural areas and urban slums.

Multi-stakeholder arrangements have proven successful because they expand on traditional partnerships by significantly increasing available resources, improving the effectiveness of their use and increasing policy and operational coherence. To build on those advantages, I have put forward a proposal to Member States for a new United Nations Partnership Facility, which would aim to enhance the Organization's ability to facilitate delivery at scale at both the global and country levels.

The adoption of the Millennium Development Goals represented a major shift in galvanizing global political will for poverty eradication. The Goals focused the world's attention on halving extreme poverty and promoting human development by setting priorities, goals and targets. Yet the Goals represent only the halfway mark towards the aim of tackling poverty in all its forms. United Nations projections for 2015 indicate that almost 1 billion people will still live in extreme poverty, mothers will continue to die needlessly in childbirth and children will suffer and die from hunger, malnutrition, preventable diseases and a lack of clean water and sanitation.

The job we started with the Millennium Development Goals therefore needs to be finished. Careful attention will be needed as we make the transition to an agenda that embraces the three dimensions of sustainable development yet ensures that poverty eradication is its highest priority and that extreme poverty is ended within a generation.

Since the Millennium Development Goals were devised, major new challenges have emerged, while existing ones have been exacerbated. Inequality has deepened. Environmental degradation has increased, threatening our common future. People across the world are demanding more responsive governments and better governance and rights at all levels. Migration challenges have grown, and young people in many countries face poor prospects for decent jobs or livelihoods. Conflicts and instability have halted or reversed progress in many countries, affecting primarily women and children. Organized crime, including trafficking in people and drugs, violates human rights and undermines development. The deepening ways in which the lives of people and countries are linked demand a universal agenda addressing the world's most pressing challenges and seizing the opportunities of a new era.

2. Advancing the United Nations development agenda beyond 2015

a. Vision and transformative actions of the agenda

The articulation of a post-2015 development agenda provides an opportunity to place sustainable development where it should be: at the core of humankind's pursuit of shared progress. With a new sustainable development agenda, the world can make many historic achievements: eradicating extreme poverty by 2030, protecting the environment and promoting social inclusion and economic opportunities for all. Ultimately, the aspiration of the development agenda beyond 2015 is to create a just and prosperous world where all people realize their rights and live with dignity and hope.

As agreed at the United Nations Conference on Sustainable Development, the framework for sustainable development reflects our commitment to three interconnected objectives: economic development, social inclusion and environmental sustainability. Each of these dimensions contributes to the others and all are necessary for the well-being of individuals and societies. Together, they are meant to enable people to fulfil their potential within the finite resources of our planet.

For such a sustainable development agenda to take root, four building blocks need to be agreed upon: (a) a far-reaching vision of the future firmly anchored in human rights and universally accepted values and principles, including those encapsulated in the Charter, the Universal Declaration of Human Rights and the Millennium Declaration; (b) a set of concise goals and targets aimed at realizing the priorities of the agenda; (c) a global partnership for development to mobilize means of implementation; and (d) a participatory monitoring framework for tracking progress and mutual accountability mechanisms for all stakeholders.

Decisions on the shape of the next agenda rest with Member States. To support their deliberations, the Secretary-General put in motion an inclusive and transparent process to hear from all stakeholders. Through the efforts of the United Nations Development Group and others, consultations were held in over 100 countries, in addition to global thematic consultations on 11 issue areas and a global online conversation and "My World" survey. These efforts have reached more than three million people. A large number of civil society organizations and academic institutions worldwide have also actively participated in the discussions.

In addition, the High-level Panel of Eminent Persons on the Post-2015 Development Agenda provided critical proposals (see A/67/890, annex). Their report is an important contribution to this process.

The expertise of the science and technology community came through the Sustainable Development Solutions Network. The contributions of the private sector around the world were conveyed through the Global Compact. The United Nations System Task Team, comprising more than 60 agencies and international organizations, conveyed the knowledge and experience of the Organization, while regional perspectives were provided by the regional commissions.

The common ground in the findings of these processes is encouraging. Discussions point to the importance of arriving at a single and coherent development agenda centred on sustainable development, applicable to all countries while taking into account regional, national and local circumstances and priorities.

The key elements of the emerging vision for the development agenda beyond 2015 include: (a) universality, to mobilize all developed and developing countries and leave no one behind; (b) sustainable development, to tackle the interlinked challenges facing the world, including a clear focus on ending extreme poverty in all its forms; (c) inclusive economic transformations ensuring decent jobs, backed by sustainable technologies, to shift to sustainable patterns of consumption and production; (d) peace and governance, as key outcomes and enablers of development; (e) a new global partnership, recognizing shared interests, different needs and mutual responsibilities, to ensure commitment to and means of implementing the new vision; and (f) being "fit for purpose", to ensure that the international community is equipped with the right institutions and tools for addressing the challenges of implementing the sustainable development agenda at the national level.

Bringing this vision to life will require a number of transformative and mutually reinforcing actions that apply to all countries.

Eradicate poverty in all its forms. Poverty has many manifestations and is aggravated by discrimination, insecurity, inequality and environmental and disaster risks. Therefore, the eradication of poverty calls for a multifaceted approach, encapsulated in the concept of sustainable development, focusing on both immediate and underlying causes.

Tackle exclusion and inequality. In order to leave no one behind and bring everyone forward, actions are needed to promote equality of opportunity. This implies inclusive economies in which men and women have access to decent employment, legal identification, financial services, infrastructure and social protection, as well as societies where all people can contribute and participate in national and local governance.

Empower women and girls. The new agenda must ensure the equal rights of women and girls, their full participation in the political, economic and public spheres and zero tolerance for violence against or exploitation of women and girls. The practice of child marriage must be ended everywhere. Women and girls must have equal access to financial services, infrastructure, the full range of health services, including in the area of sexual and reproductive health and reproductive rights, and water and sanitation; the right to own land and other assets; a safe environment in which to learn and apply their knowledge and skills; and an end to discrimination so they can receive equal pay for equal work and have an equal voice in decision-making.

Provide quality education and lifelong learning. Young people should be able to receive high-quality education and learning, from early childhood development to post-primary schooling, including not only formal schooling but also life skills and vocational education and training.

Improve health. Address universal health-care coverage, access and affordability; end preventable maternal and child deaths; realize women's reproductive health and rights; increase immunization coverage; eradicate malaria and realize the vision of a future free of AIDS and tuberculosis; reduce the burden of non-communicable diseases, including mental illness, and road accidents; and promote healthy behaviours, including those related to water, sanitation and hygiene.

Address climate change. The international community must reconcile the challenges of mitigating and adapting to climate change while supporting the growth of developing countries. While the worst effects of climate change can still be averted by building the resilience of and investing in those communities and nations most vulnerable to disasters risk, those efforts will require a greatly stepped-up response, in keeping with the principle of common but differentiated responsibilities and respective capabilities. A successful outcome to the intergovernmental climate change negotiations is critical. Every effort must be made to arrive at a legally binding agreement by the end of 2015, as decided in Durban, South Africa, in 2011.

Address environmental challenges. Environmental change has compounded problems worldwide, especially in vulnerable countries, reducing their capacity to cope and limiting their options for addressing development challenges. Managing the natural resources base — fisheries, forests, freshwater resources, oceans, soil — is essential for sustainable development. So too is building the resilience of and investing in those communities and nations most vulnerable to disasters, especially in the least developed countries and small island developing States.

Promote inclusive and sustainable growth and decent employment. This can be achieved by economic diversification, financial inclusion, efficient infrastructure, productivity gains, trade, sustainable energy, relevant education and skills training. Labour market policies should focus in particular on young people, women and people with disabilities.

End hunger and malnutrition. Addressing hunger, malnutrition, stunting and food insecurity in a world experiencing rapid population growth will require a combination of stable and adequate incomes for all, improvements in agricultural productivity and sustainability, child and maternal care and strengthened social protection for vulnerable populations.

Address demographic challenges. While the population of developed countries is projected to remain unchanged at around 1.3 billion, the population of developing countries is projected to increase from 5.9 billion in 2013 to 8.2 billion in 2050. Countries with a high rate of population growth are generally on a path of falling fertility, especially as education for girls and sexual and reproductive health services become more widely available. Progress in these areas would enable many households to slow fertility rates, with consequent benefits for health, education, sustainability and the demographic dividend for economic growth. Countries with a high proportion of young people need to offer education and opportunities for decent work. Countries with an ageing population need policy responses to support the elderly so as to remove barriers to their full participation in society while protecting their rights and dignity.

Enhance the positive contribution of migrants. More than a billion people rely on international and domestic migration to improve the income, health and education of their families, escape poverty and conflict and adapt to environmental and economic shocks. Countries receiving migrants can also benefit significantly. Yet many barriers limit the positive effects of migration, including possible large economic and social gains. Discrimination is widespread and the human rights of migrants are often denied at different points in the migration process. The scourge of human trafficking, an unacceptable dimension of migration, must be ended.

Meet the challenges of urbanization. Some 70 per cent of the world's population will live in cities by 2050. Urbanization poses the challenge of providing city dwellers with employment, food, income, housing, transportation, clean water and sanitation, social services and cultural amenities. At the same time, living in cities creates opportunities for the more efficient delivery and use of physical facilities and amenities. Rural prosperity, land management and secure ecosystem services should form an integral part of sustainable urbanization and economic transformation.

Build peace and effective governance based on the rule of law and sound institutions. Peace and stability, human rights and effective governance based on the rule of law and transparent institutions are outcomes and enablers of development. There can be no peace without development and no development without peace. Lasting peace and sustainable development cannot be fully realized without respect for human rights and the rule of law. Transparency and accountability are powerful tools for ensuring citizens' involvement in policymaking and their oversight of the use of public resources, including to prevent waste and corruption. Legal empowerment, access to justice and an independent judiciary and universal legal identification can also be critical for gaining access to public services.

Foster a renewed global partnership. The Millennium Development Goals, in particular Goal 8, on the global partnership for development, speak to the importance of our common humanity and the values of equity, solidarity and human rights. The post-2015 development agenda will need to be supported by a renewed global partnership grounded on such values. As noted in the report of my High-level Panel, "the partnership should capture, and will depend on, a spirit of mutual respect and mutual benefit."

The global partnership should finish the job started with Goal 8, including meeting the assistance objective of 0.7 per cent of gross national income, as well as other existing and future intergovernmental agreements, such as the Millennium Declaration, the

Monterrey Consensus of the International Conference on Financing for Development, the Principles set out in the Rio Declaration on Environment and Development, the Johannesburg Plan of Implementation and the Istanbul Programme of Action, as well as the outcome of the Ad Hoc Working Group of the Durban Platform for Enhanced Action. All partners should deliver on past commitments, particularly those on official development assistance, climate finance and domestic resource mobilization.

The transformative actions of the post-2015 development agenda should be supported by multi-stakeholder partnerships that respond to the sustainable development agenda. These should include not only governments but also businesses, private philanthropic foundations, international organizations, civil society, volunteer groups, local authorities, parliaments, trade unions, research institutes and academia. Such partnerships can channel commitments and actions from a wider set of actors, and their success depends on assigning roles, responsibilities and clear accountability.

Official development assistance will remain crucial, including for leveraging other finance, particularly for the least developed countries, landlocked developing countries and small island developing States, many countries in Africa and countries emerging from conflict and disasters. In addition to delivering on past commitments, it will be critical for donors to establish a timetable for meeting official development assistance targets and enhancing development effectiveness, including through the principles and actions set out in the Busan Partnership for Effective Development Cooperation. The impact of official development assistance can be magnified by other sources of finance, including innovative sources.

A universal development agenda beyond 2015 will require a robust framework for sustainable development finance including both private and public funding. International efforts are needed to create an environment conducive to business and thus channel capital flows and portfolio investments to the sustainable development agenda, to eliminate illicit financial flows, to enhance the regulation of secrecy jurisdictions and to promote asset recovery. Multilateral development banks have an important role to play in identifying novel sources of sustainable development financing.

At the same time, the financing framework for the post-2015 period will require the mobilization of domestic resources, including by broadening the tax base and improving tax administration, including in developing countries, and improving corporate and public governance of extractive industries in resource-rich countries. In addition, the financing framework will require commitment by the public and private scientific and research communities to develop new and transformative technologies. Harnessing science, technology and innovative methods will be central in areas ranging from information and communications technology to transportation, the environment and life-saving medicines.

South-South and triangular cooperation will also play a key role. This has increased significantly in recent years and has taken various forms, including infrastructure investment, technical cooperation, joint research and investment and information-sharing.

The report of the Intergovernmental Committee of Experts on Sustainable Development Financing, will propose options on a strategy to facilitate the mobilization of resources and their effective use. The biennial high-level Development Cooperation Forum and the Third International Conference on Financing for Development in Addis Ababa, Ethiopia in July 2015 will also provide important opportunities for charting a way forward.

Strengthen the international development cooperation framework. In order to respond to the challenges of funding and implementing a sustainable development agenda, both national and international institutions need to be strengthened to overcome the institutional and operational separation between economic, social and environmental responsibilities. To this effect, Member States of the United Nations have established the high-level political forum on sustainable development. There is broad agreement that the forum should bring political support at the highest level to the coordination, coherence, implementation and monitoring of the commitments in a universal sustainable development agenda.

b. Monitoring and accountability

Strong monitoring and accountability will be crucial for the implementation of the post-2015 development agenda. Governments, especially parliaments, will play a central role. The monitoring and accountability framework can be strengthened through the direct engagement of citizens and responsible businesses making use of new technologies to expand coverage, to disaggregate data and to reduce costs.

The availability of information has improved during the implementation of the Millennium Development Goals. Still, there is an urgent need to further improve data collection, dissemination and analysis. Better baseline data and statistics are needed, especially because the post-2015 development agenda will involve measuring a broader range of indicators, requiring new and disaggregated data to capture gaps within and between population groups. Assessing the quality of outcomes should also feature more prominently in a results-based framework. As suggested by my High-level Panel, targets will be considered to have been achieved only if they are met for all relevant income and social groups.

In this context, the advances in information technology over the past decade provide an opportunity for a "data revolution", which should enable countries to strengthen existing data sources and develop new and participatory sources of information. Many developing countries will require technical and financial support to build solid statistical systems and capacity so as to take advantage of these new opportunities.

c. Setting goals for the agenda

Experience with the Millennium Development Goals shows us that goals can be a powerful way of mobilizing common action. To be effective, they need to be limited in number, measurable, easy to communicate and adaptable to both global and local settings.

168

At the United Nations Conference on Sustainable Development, Member States agreed that the sustainable development goals, "should be coherent with and integrated into the United Nations development agenda beyond 2015." The many consultations and reports suggest that a single, balanced and comprehensive set of goals, universal to all nations, which aims to eradicate all forms of poverty and integrate sustainable development in all its dimensions, should form the core of the agenda.

The framing of the set of goals for sustainable development will inevitably need to be broader than that of the Millennium Development Goals in order to reflect new challenges. Illustrative goals and targets have been proposed in a range of reports, including those of the High-level Panel, the Sustainable Development Solutions Network and the Global Compact, and in several initiatives from the research community.

Goals and targets should take into account cross-cutting issues such as gender, disability, age and other factors leading to inequality, human rights, demographics, migration and partnerships. The new goals should embrace the emphasis on human well-being and include the use of metrics that go beyond standard income measures, such as surveys of subjective well-being and happiness, as introduced by many countries and the Organization for Economic Cooperation and Development.

The Open Working Group on Sustainable Development Goals has recently issued its proposal for sustainable development goals. This is a unique and first-of-its-kind outcome, both in terms of what was discussed and how the discussions were conducted.

The breadth and depth of the proposed set of goals is unprecedented. Taken in their totality, they reflect an integrated, universal and transformative agenda, which builds and expands on the lessons learned from the MDGs to address the many and interlinked challenges the world faces today. In a remarkable shift to a universal agenda, goal 1 commits countries to eradicate extreme poverty for everyone everywhere, with special attention to those living with

169

disabilities, the aged and our youth. In addition to reinforcing the commitment to the human development agenda of the unfinished work of the MDGs, the report breaks new ground with goals on inequalities, economic growth, jobs, urbanization, energy, and sustainable consumption and production, including a target to address fossil fuel subsidies. Filling a notable gap in the MDG framework, the environmental dimension of the agenda is properly articulated in goals on oceans and marine resources, and on ecosystems and biodiversity. Against the expectations of many, the report also includes a goal on climate change –while avoiding to interfere with the separate ongoing UNFCCC negotiations. Finally the framework is underpinned with a goal on promoting peace, justice and institutions and another on global partnerships for the means of implementation of a sustainable development agenda.

Equally important was the way the discussions were conducted, and who took part. Unlike the MDGs, the sustainable development goals emerged from an open and inclusive consultative process. It is to the credit of the Open Working Group and its Co-Chairs that all stakeholders including Civil Society Organizations, the private sector and the scientific and academic communities, and notably the youth among others, all had a voice in the discussion and were able to participate actively, including in the formal sessions of the Group.

As expected in view of the number and nature of the issues considered, not all was agreed. Many contentious issues remain for further discussion as the intergovernmental process begins later in the year. But already the outcome of the Open Working Group and its proposed set of ambitious goals and targets is a success. Much political capital and expertise were injected in the discussions and reflected in the proposed set. Much common ground was found, even when starting positions appeared irreconcilable. At a time of widespread international crises and growing conflicts, this outcome of the Open Working Groups offers a hopeful sign that multilateralism is as vibrant and productive on some fronts as we need it to be on others, and that it is still possible, through courageous leadership and open dialogue amongst all parties, to aspire to a better world, for people and the planet.

Conclusion

Acting upon our common challenges demands a renewed commitment to international cooperation. Multilateralism is being tested. The United Nations, as a global beacon of solidarity, must do its part to strengthen collaboration and show that it can be effective in building the just, prosperous and sustainable world that people want and have a right to expect. Defining the post-2015 development agenda is thus a daunting yet inspiring and historic task for the United Nations and its Member States.

In so doing we must continue to listen to and involve the peoples of the world. We have heard their calls for peace and justice, eradicating poverty, realizing rights, eliminating inequality, enhancing accountability and preserving our planet. The world's nations must unite behind a common programme to act on those aspirations. No one must be left behind. We must continue to build a future of justice and hope, a life of dignity for all.

THE GLOBAL COMMON GOOD: TOWARDS A MORE INCLUSIVE ECONOMY

Speaking Points

Organisation for Economic Co-operation and Development (OECD)

ANTHROPOLOGICAL AND SOCIAL REDUCTIONISM OF TODAY'S ECONOMIC THOUGHT AND ACTIVITIES: CHALLENGES TO CIVILIZING GLOBALISATION

OECD work is critical to moving beyond the reduction of people to economic agents driven only by self-interest, and expanding the reductionist concept of 'value' in economic discourse.

- The OECD's *How's life?* framework puts a broader notion of people at the centre of its work, and stresses the multidimensional nature of human well-being (11 dimensions: i.e. jobs, education, environment etc.). The framework also recognises the importance of different types of capital (economic, natural, human and social) for achieving sustainability.

- The importance of considering people's motivation beyond self-interest is one that is increasingly present in the OECD's work: reflected in behavioural approaches across a number of policy-fields: from tax-compliance to competition-policy, from financial-market to healthy-life styles.

- But, we must recognise that most economic and policy analysis (e.g. on how to design benefit-systems, to avoid 'disincentives' effects) is still predicted on the notion of self-interested economic agents.

- The challenge of creating models based on more realistic foundations of what people value and how they behave has yet to be met by economists and policy analysts.

- OECD work on statistics has aimed to re-orient the statistical community towards measuring performance based on a more comprehensive concept of value which moves beyond-GDP.

- Broadening the concept of value in economic discourse requires looking beyond the National Statistical Organisations production and asset boundaries. It means confronting issues of valuation for non-market flows and stocks, and considering the limits of market-prices as metrics for value (due to the importance of externalities, mispriced risks, missing markets).

- At the core of our work on inequalities is the notion that each person matters. Our recent work has begun to look not just *"beyond GDP"*, but also *beyond the statistical bogeyman: Mr. Average*. By examining how policies affect different parts of the income distribution we get a better picture of how the economy is performing for all citizens.

- Developing better metrics of people's lives is not an end in itself, but a means to changing policies. The OECD has started to implement this broader approach to its policy-advice through its work on the *New Approaches to Economic Challenges* (NAEC) initiative, which was launched in 2012 as an organisation-wide reflection on the causes and lessons from the crisis.

Moving Towards a More Inclusive Economy Calls for More Inclusive Growth

- Creating a more inclusive people-centred economy cannot be achieved without an emphasis on growth. Without growth living standards stagnate and well-being declines.

- In the same vein, growth needs to be more Inclusive: Growing unequally bears a cost on growth. We calculated that on average, an increase in income inequality by 1 Gini point lowers yearly GDP per capita growth by around 0.2 percentage point.[1]

- Addressing inequalities is not merely a matter of redistribution. Inclusiveness should be at the core of a growth agenda!

- Inclusive Growth is the OECD's response to rising inequality and we see it as part of a growth agenda. The average income of richest 10% in the OECD is now around 9.5 times that of poorest 10%, up 30% on 25 years ago. Inequality also affects emerging economies and is soaring in India, Indonesia, and South Africa.

- The effects of inequality extend far beyond income and affect opportunities. Take the case of health: Data from 14 OECD countries showed that at the age of 30, people with the highest educational attainment levels could expect to live, on average, 6 years longer than their worst educated peers.

- The OECD's approach to Inclusive Growth takes account of the multidimensional nature of inequality, considering not only income, but also outcomes in health, education, employment, and many other dimensions that matter for people's wellbeing

- It also emphasises the distributional element going beyond the average to consider how different policies affect different social groups.

- Our analysis shows that in most OECD countries, income growth does make citizens better-off materially and improves well-being; however, this is not the case for all segments of society! In most OECD countries, multidimensional living

[1] F. Cingano, "Inequality, social mobility and growth – Evidence from OECD countries", forthcoming.

174

standards have risen faster for the average income household than for the median and poor households.

- The aim of the OECD's approach is to provide policy makers with an actionable tool to identify win-win strategies, which can foster *both* growth and equity: There is not necessarily a trade-off between treating people well and the productivity and profitability for companies.

Ensuring Inclusive Economies by Promoting International Governance

- The recent global financial crisis highlighted the extent to which our countries and economies are interconnected and interdependent. Today, we have the ability to move capital between financial centres almost instantaneously, and the production of goods today is fragmented across the world.

- This increase in interdependence calls for strengthened leadership, enhanced cooperation, and policy co-ordination among countries and international organisations to help countries take full advantage of the opportunities this dependence offers and assist countries in avoiding the potential negative consequences.

    o **Opportunity:** Dependence can improve efficiency, maximise wealth, and reduce poverty. Global Value Chains (GVCs) are making this opportunity a reality. The results are truly remarkable: Value added trade contributes to 30% of the GDP of developing countries (18% for developed countries) — emerging economies such as China and South Africa have benefited immensely from GVCs.

    o **Negative consequences:** Dependence can also result in as loss of autonomy and increased vulnerability to external shocks; instability and accumulation of global imbalances; and over-intensify competition, which can trigger races to the bottom in many domains and provoke adverse effects that cross borders: e.g. labour rights, taxation policies (Base Erosion Profit Sharing), environmental regulations (climate change).

- As part of our work programme, the OECD is undertaking research to identify policy challenges for the next 50 years, not only regarding growth but also inequality and the environment. Some of the preliminary results suggest that increased global integration and reliance on innovation for growth raise the potential benefits of international coordination and co-operation on the provision of certain public goods.

  - **R&D:** Cooperation can enhance investment in R&D as national incentives to invest and spend in this area decrease from (1) cross-country technological spill-overs, and (2) slower innovation and technology diffusion rates as a result of inconsistent legislation of intellectual property rights across countries.

  - **Taxation:** Cooperation in the area of taxation can limit excessive global tax competition related to increasingly mobile tax bases.

  - **Environment:** Global cooperation in emission reducing policies will help to reduce the high economic costs of climate change that are projected over the next few decades.

- To re-establish a stable equilibrium and restore confidence in globalisation, we must promote best practices at the international level and foster convergence towards global standards.

- The OECD is a global platform for best practices, benchmarking and standard-setting, supports the pursuit of this objective. It is leading the charge in many areas, in particular Global Value Chains, Base Erosion Profit Sharing, and Climate Change, and regulatory co-operation.

- In the field of global governance, the OECD worked on the *Recommendation of the Council on Regulatory Policy and Gov-*

ernance to support cooperation in the design, implementation and enforcement of rules. To carry this work forward, we launched a dialogue with 16 other international organisations (April 2014) to exchange information on the ways, means and impacts of IO rule-making activities in support of global governance.

FINANCE, TRADE, LABOUR, WORK AND TAXATION

FINANCE – Policy Makers Need to Adapt the Incentive Structures of Financial Activities to Promote Long-Term Sustainability

- A well-functioning financial system, based on sound and well-aligned economic incentives, serving intermediate savers and investors, is essential for Inclusive Growth and long-term sustainability.

- This is currently not the case! Increased sophistication of financial markets and products makes individual financial decisions i.e. saving for retirement, more challenging.

- Financial risks are being transferred onto individuals unequipped to bear them, while benefits of financial intermediation go disproportionately to high-income households.

- We need to recognise that access to finance is central to growth and job creation; yet the rewards from the operations of the financial markets are often distributed unequally. An increasingly complex financial sector puts small savers and investors at a disadvantage.

- At the OECD we have been very active in pushing for reforms to the financial system.
  - We have stressed that: **sound corporate governance and vibrant capital markets are key elements**. We call

for the structure of bank compensation to be well-aligned with long-term objectives, discouraging short-term risk strategies that are not socially optimal.

o We have acknowledged that: **effective and comprehensive financial regulation is fundamental**. We should recognise the FSB's considerable efforts to build a more resilient and transparent financial system, but more is needed – with a focus on the mispricing of risk capital arising from implicit government guarantees.

o We have called for: **business model reforms separating high-risk activities from deposit taking**. Changes have already been implemented in a number of jurisdictions, but more **cross-border consistency is needed** to avoid fragmentation and regulatory arbitrage.

o Finally, we have advocated **structural reform of bank managers' remuneration** to discourage the adoption of socially sub-optimal risk strategies. We have come forward with a number of suggestions, arguing that bonuses could be paid in part in assets whose value is tied to that of the parent bank, and a proportion of large bonuses earned in good years could be made repayable in the case of bank failure.

• However, at the OECD we recognise that changing the structure of financial incentives is only half the battle. We also need policies in place which focus on individuals and financial consumers.

o Fostering financial education and consumer protection is essential to equipping the most vulnerable groups with basic skills and competencies needed to efficiently use financial services. G20 Principles on Financial Consumer Protection and on National Strategies for Financial Education developed by the OECD address this.

○ The OECD is benchmarking standards of financial literacy. The PISA Report on Financial Education is the first large-scale international study to assess the financial literacy of young people (age 15). The report showed an almost 2-year gap in financial literacy between the best performing students in Shanghai and the worst in Colombia.

TAXATION – *International Action Can Promote Fiscal Transparency to Discourage Tax Avoidance and Evasion*

- Taxation is an essential element of the trust between governments and citizens. Fair and efficient tax systems underpin the social contract within our societies, acting as a potent instrument for creating equal opportunities for all citizens.

- In an increasingly interconnected world we need global solutions to address tax issues. Too often today, tax avoidance and evasion strategies are taking advantage of the interaction between the tax rules of different countries.

- Our first priority must be to improve global transparency. Our work on tax evasion is beginning to bear fruit, and has now led to the creation of a single common global standard for the *Automatic Exchange of Information* (AEoI).

  ○ Presently, the AEoI has over 60 adherents (all OECD and G20 countries) and the first exchanges will take place in September 2017.

  ○ Crucially, the AEoI will facilitate the transfer of financial account information between countries, to help tax administrations identify funds held in, and transfers between countries, including low or no-tax jurisdictions, on which tax may have been evaded.

- But evasion is not the only problem we face. We also need to take action to tackle *Base Erosion and Profit Shifting* (BEPS), which although legal, means that businesses can shift profits away from the location of economic activity, into jurisdictions where low, or no, tax is paid.

- If we are concerned about inequality, we cannot allow individual households to bear the brunt of the tax burden while MNEs are not paying their fair share.

- We need to employ a coherent strategy to ensure that all businesses contribute fairly to our societies, whose human capital and infrastructure they make use of. At the OECD we started looking at this challenge back in 2013 OECD, which led to the presentation of a 15-point BEPS Action Plan drawing on the experience of a broad range of stakeholders including business, civil society and trade unions.

- The first seven concrete actions of the BEPS Action Plan will be delivered by September 2014, and include recommendations on: strengthening Controlled Foreign Companies rules; limiting base erosion via interest deductions and other financial payments; and making dispute resolution mechanisms more effective.

- One year in, the BEPS project is on track to reform the international tax rules for the 21st century economy, but the need for continued, high-level political support is clear.

- The BEPS project is also essential for developing countries where around 20% of tax revenues are derived from corporate income tax – compared to 8-10% in OECD countries. In these countries, BEPS often result in capital flight, giving MNEs a competitive advantage over domestic businesses that are not able to take advantages of cross-border tax planning.

- We need to recognise that the contribution of tax revenue to more Inclusive Economies is especially important in Developing Countries. That is why the OECD is also pioneering a project on Tax Inspectors Without Borders (8 pilot projects planned or underway). The project transfers tax audit knowledge and skills to tax administrations in developing countries, by deploying experts to work directly with local tax officials on current audits and audit-related issues.

TRADE & LABOUR – Trade Liberalisation Along with Effective International Regulation Can Enhance Labour Rights and Support Environmental Sustainability

- Protecting the rights of workers not only improves their well-being, but ultimately contributes to improvements in productivity and economic growth.

- A number of International Guidelines and instruments are already in place to ensure the protection of workers' rights on a global scale. (i.e. ILO conventions on freedom of association, the right to organise, the abolition of forced labour, etc).

- Today, setting up a new international instrument or institution is probably less important than ensuring effective implementation, and compliance with existing national and international instruments and guidelines.

- We should also not forget to encourage business to respect the rights of workers, so that MNEs do not seek to take advantage of weaker protection of workers' rights in certain countries.

- To address this, we at the OECD have established Guidelines for MNEs covering all major areas of business ethics including human rights, disclosure, employment and industrial relations, environment, combatting bribery, consumer interests and taxation. There are currently 46 adhering countries.

- One of the most important aspects of our role is that we can convince governments, business, trade unions and civil society to develop practical and broadly-supported approaches, as with due diligence and the supply chain, with a focus on human rights and labour risks.

- We have also developed risk-based due diligence systems in the extractive sector through the *OECD Due Diligence Guidance for Responsible Supply Chains of Minerals from Conflict-Af-*

fected and High-Risk Areas. This initiative has helped catalyse a range of private sector actions in the form of auditing mechanisms, tools and assurance programmes for supply chain management which ultimately help to prevent abuse of workers' rights.

TRADE & ENVIRONMENT – Trade Liberalisation Can Bolster Sustainability

- We need to recognise that trade liberalisation can support environmental protection through gains in efficiency and a better use of resources. However, it is also important to understand that it can expose natural resources (forests, fish stocks, water, and minerals) to over-exploitation.

- Reforms to the multinational trading systems should place a greater emphasis on environmental sustainability: eliminating environmentally harmful subsidies and liberalising trade in environmental goods and services.

- Reforming environmentally harmful subsidies would directly benefit the environment, but would also reduce burdens on governments, freeing up funds for increased social welfare. The OECD has led efforts to promote reform of environmentally harmful subsidies and to highlight the environmental and economic benefits of such reform, notably through the publication of the inventory of estimated budgetary support and tax expenditures for fossil fuel.

- Reducing tariffs and non-tariff barriers to trade in environmental goods, such as equipment used to generate electricity from renewable energy sources or to treat wastewater effluent, would lower the cost of environmental protection and correct a playing field that is currently tilted in favour of polluting fossil fuels.

TRADE IN DEVELOPING COUNTRIES - *International Trade Can Be Made to Work for the Benefit of All Citizens in Developing Countries and Emerging Market Economies*

- Global Value Chains (GVCs), which are increasingly coming to dominate international trade, can help to bestow benefits on all citizens. This is a particularly important phenomenon for developing countries. The disaggregation of production into separate stages allows firms to find their place and climb the ladder as their capabilities improve.

- At the OECD, we have charted how GVCs encourage upward movement by rewarding skills, learning, and innovation. Overcoming obstacles to GVC participation pays dividends; developing economies with the fastest growing GVC participation have GDP per capita growth rates 2% above average.

- Developing countries are increasingly involved in GVCs, which offer an opportunity to integrate into the world economy at lower costs, bringing with it enhanced opportunities for sustainable and equitable growth.

- Strong social, environmental, and governance frameworks and policies are important to maximising the positive impact of GVC activities and minimising risks in all countries, especially in developing economies.

- Not all countries, firms and workers are equally prepared for the adjustments associated with more integrated markets. It is crucial to have active labour market policies and investments in education, skills and training – to better match labour supply with demand – as well as adequate social safety nets and competition policies in place.

- Investments in improving supply side capabilities will be needed in many developing countries, in addition to creating an overall policy environment conducive to innovation.

- We need to make sure that GVC participants observe international core labour standards, including establishment and enforcement of occupational health, safety, and environmental standards and related capacity-building for compliance.
- Policies that artificially increase the participation of firms in GVCs through direct government incentives for specific activities and disincentives for other activities will most probably not generate sustainable benefits. Linking with lead firms can be a more solid foundation to build on for many small and innovative firms.

THE GLOBAL FAMILY WITH NEW RULES AND INSTITUTIONAL DESIGN

New Financial Rules and Institutional Design Must Have an Ethical Core

- We need to keep in mind that unethical behaviour in finance and the private sector was one of the roots of the global financial crisis.
- But we can take action to promote a more ethical financial sector. The OECD is currently revising and strengthening its Principles of Corporate Governance that state that "the board has a key role in setting the ethical tone of a company."
- Together we can make use of Guidelines and Principles to create a more ethical business culture. OECD Guidelines on Multinational Enterprises (GoME) call upon enterprises to integrate and disclose social and environmental risk assessment across their operations, which can help to limit negative externalities and internalise positive outcomes.
  - An ethical clause was inserted into Section 1502 of the Dodd Frank Act, which includes reporting requirements for issuers listed on the US stock exchange whose products contain conflict minerals.

- The GoME also advocates that financial institutions undertake due diligence in business relations. Market makers, i.e. stock exchanges and index fund managers, can be key players in undertaking complementary due diligence and pre-screening of companies.

- The National Contact Points of the 46 governments adhering to the OECD GoME have committed to establish a grievance mechanism for interested parties alleging companies' non-observance of the Guidelines.

  - Just last month, thanks to the mediation of the UK National Contact Point, business and civil society came to an agreement to stop oil exploration in Africa's oldest national park, Virunga National Park, in the Democratic Republic of Congo.

- In Finance, the OECD/G20 Principles on Financial Consumer Protection call on jurisdictions to ensure that consumers have access to adequate complaints handling and redress mechanisms. We need to deal with the elephant in the room. By working together we can get tough on international rules to cut tax evasion and avoidance.

- Taking strong action on tax would help us to boost trust in governments, institutions, and markets. After all fair and efficient tax systems underpin the social contract within our societies, supporting equal opportunities for all citizens.

- It is essential to ensure that everyone, especially corporations and multinational enterprises, pay their fair share of tax, to ensure that profits and gains are equally redistributed among members of society.

- Lack of co-ordination between national tax policies often leads to complex tax codes and double taxation which can result in tax avoidance and evasion.

- In an effort to reinforce the role of taxation the OECD, collaborating with the G20, has embarked on two key initiatives to reduce tax evasion and avoidance at the trans-national level: the Automatic Exchange of Information (AEoI) and the Base Erosion and Profit Shifting (BEPS) Action Plan.

- AEoI will establish an international standard on tax information exchange with 60 countries (all OECD and G20 Countries), set to share information by September 2017. It will facilitate the transfer of financial account information between countries, helping tax administrations identify funds held in, and transfers between countries, including low or no-tax jurisdictions, on which tax may have been evaded.

- The BEPS project, drawing on the experience of a broad range of stakeholders including business, civil society and trade unions, will take action to prevent businesses from shifting profits away from the location of economic activity to low or no tax jurisdictions. It will deliver 7 concrete items at the Brisbane G20 Summit (i.e. preventing the artificial avoidance of Permanent Establishment status) with the remaining to follow by the end of 2015.

- At the OECD, we call upon all stakeholders — governments, business and civil society — to join forces in support of the international agenda for global ethics.

Restoring Trust in Government is Essential for Creating a More Inclusive Global Economic System

- Over the last few years we have witnessed a remarkable loss of confidence in government. Levels of confidence are now at a record low (now at 40% in OECD).[2] Electoral turnout is falling across the OECD, with the most educated group hav-

[2] OECD Government at Glance (2013)

ing a 12% higher turnout than the lowest. There is a danger that higher social groups and vested interests might capture the process of policy design and implementation.

- This spectacular loss of confidence is problematic because our governments have an implicit social contractual obligation to minimise uncertainty in the economic, social and political environment of their citizens, particularly with respect to external events over which the latter have limited or no control.

- Lack of trust inhibits decisive action by government to promote recovery because in many cases policies depend on the support and mobilisation of citizens in order to be effective. Governments need to address trust in order to achieve economic and social objectives.

- At the OECD, our work on the issue of trust has highlighted four dimensions where efforts should be focussed:

1. **Firstly, we need to promote reliability:** The ability of governments to minimise uncertainty in the economic, social and political environment of their citizens, and to act in a consistent and predictable manner. This means being good at foresight, risk management and strategic thinking.

2. **Secondly, we need to consider how to increase responsiveness:** Local government can ensure high levels of trust by providing accessible, efficient and citizen-oriented public services that effectively address the daily needs and expectations of tax payers.

3. **Thirdly, we need to ensure that our governments are models of openness and inclusiveness:** the Open Government Partnership (OGP) is a systemic, two-way communication with stakeholders which can help improve transparency, accountability and engagement.

4. **Finally, we need to restore integrity to our institutions:** The OECD aims to generalise good practices through its

instruments on lobbying, revolving doors, conflict of interest, public procurement and new topics such as financing democracy and the role of Justice Institutions.

- Integrity, in particular, is key to restoring trust. Many citizens believe that corruption in government is widespread: it's three-quarters of the population in the US, and almost 90% in Italy, Greece, and Portugal.[3]

- At the OECD, we help countries to strengthen trust in the policy making process by turning knowledge into guidelines and principles in high-risk areas. These include for instance, public procurement, which accounts for 13% of the GDP on average in OECD countries.[4] It also includes lobbying: spending on this more than doubled over the past 15 years, increasing from USD 1.44 billion to USD 3.30 billion.[5]

- We are also combatting the problem of political financing. Many OECD countries have national regulations in place to promote fair competition between political parties and/ or candidates by balancing sources of funding, introducing bans and limits on certain types of donations, and introducing reporting and transparency requirements.

- But we are far from solving the problem of "financing democracy". Over several years we have seen major political careers end in disgrace due to bad practices in this domain. There is also the corollary problem of the increasing dominance of electoral cycles in setting the political agenda — confusing the means with the end.

---

[3] Source: Gallup World Poll2011; & of survey respondents that stated that corruption is widespread throughout the government.
[4] Source: Government at a Glance, 2011
[5] Source: Government at a Glance 2011

For Inclusive Growth to Work Well, the Appropriate Institutions Have to Exist, and Citizens Must Feel that They Can Trust Them

- Our recent report on Inclusive Growth dedicates a whole chapter on the role of institutions and governance in an Inclusive Growth agenda. We found evidence that political and economic disparities tend to reinforce each other.

- The risk is that the views of some socio-economic groups are better reflected in the design and implementation of policies and that policy making itself is captured by the interests of the most privileged groups, who may also contribute to the financing of increasingly expensive political campaigns.

- Well-designed institutions can help improve transparency and contestability, notably by establishing freedom of information legislation and the right to petition governments, opening lobbying to scrutiny, and setting up commissions of enquiry.

- The accessibility of the justice system is an important issue. A legitimate and equally accessible judicial system helps create a level playing field where predictable and independent decisions can be taken.

- Regulators are increasingly responsible for the delivery of a variety of policy objectives, but can be subjected to political pressures or captured by private interests. Governments need to ensure that the appropriate institutional systems and mechanisms of accountability, transparency, engagement and leadership are in place to protect regulatory decisions. (OECD Best Practice Principles for the Governance of Regulators).

- The way policies are designed and implemented matters for Inclusive Growth. An inclusive policy process must be well informed and reflect public interest. It should be inclusive across the policy cycle, which requires effective and representative citizen participation as well as mechanisms to curb the undue influence of money and power.

- Increasingly, governments are partnering with the civil society in the design, implementation and evaluation of public policies. I.e. participatory budgeting, like that undertaken by Seville authority in Spain or the Toronto Community Housing Corporation in Canada, providing taxpayers with a say in how public funds are spent on the services.

- A number of countries are introducing co-production of public services, such as the São Francisco water supply project in Brazil that engages key stakeholders in service planning and delivery. Community involvement is seen as a way to increase inclusiveness, and as part of the solution to addressing service failures and improving policy outcomes.

- Inclusive policy making and service delivery requires an effective decentralisation of policies for better targeted place-based policies. Subnational governments are often much better positioned to plan and manage investment and service delivery "at street level".

- Effective decentralisation for Inclusive Growth requires co-ordination across the whole of government and a clear division of responsibilities for the actions taken at the different levels of government. At the OECD, we are advocating the comprehensive engagement of local governments in the decision making process and delivery.

DISCUSSION OF THE POST-2015 DEVELOPMENT AGENDA AND SUSTAINABLE DEVELOPMENT GOALS

The Post-2015 Development Agenda Should Not Simply Extend MDGs

- We need to look at the Post-2015 Agenda as an opportunity to learn from development experience in the past few decades and to fill in important gaps in the MDGs, which focus largely on poverty and aid in the context of low-income countries, but imperfectly address inequality and vulnerability issues (particularly in middle-income countries).

- By considering those living in poverty as a static group known as 'the poor', the MDGs ignore the reality of poverty and vulnerability.

- In our view, the Post-2015 Agenda should leave space for countries to define their own priorities within broad international development objectives. Rather than focus on selective targets for economic and social development or environmental protection, the aim should be to create an enabling international environment for countries to pursue realistic national plans with their own priorities and policies.

- We also need to ensure that the Post-2015 Agenda captures the "production" elements that were largely ignored in the MDGs. The production structure of a country is related to its capacity to generate sustainable growth and jobs and, therefore, to the human development outcomes and their distribution across the population.

We Need a Global Consensus on an Ambitious Agenda that Bridges Human Development and Environmental Sustainability

- The MDGs showed us the power of a limited number of goals and targets to concentrate global efforts and rally funding and political leadership behind important issues. I believe that the Post-2015 Agenda should be similarly defined to emphasise concise achievable targets.

- But the Post-2015 Agenda is not just a process; it's a call to action. Governments worldwide can and must commit, and they must stand together to produce an action plan that meets the challenges countries face today and tomorrow.

- Our efforts should continue to push for an integrated and coherent agenda, which combines developmental goals with sustainability (SDGs) and inclusiveness targets; stressing the links between poverty, jobs, education, health and environmental degradation, etc.

191

- The OECD fully supports this agenda and has contributed since the very beginning to the design and implementation of global goals and their implementation. We continue to support the UN process as a best supporting actor.

New Goals Need to Focus More on Inequalities In and Between Countries and Be Supported by Better Data

- In the last few years we have seen the limits of what economic growth alone can do for development. Growth has lifted large numbers out of poverty, but many have not progressed to the middle classes, instead getting caught in an intermediate state of "vulnerability".

- Vulnerability occurs for many reasons, but it is often the result of low educational attainment, labour market informalities, and poor social protection, and it leaves many liable to fall back into extreme poverty in the event of adverse shocks [e.g. the 2011 food price spike led to around 44 million falling into poverty].[1]

- In Latin America, many middle class people fall into the vulnerability bracket. In Bolivia, Brazil, Chile and Mexico there are up to 44 million informal middle-class workers, more than 60% of the total middle-class working population of 72 million.[2] Social protection systems fail to reach even half of this population.

- There has been a shift in the geography of poverty with almost 80% of the global income poor (less than $2/day) now living in middle-income Countries. To adjust to this, development should move beyond raising GDP per capita, to focus on income distribution.

---

[1] http://web.worldbank.org/WBSITE/EXTERNAL/NEWS/0,,content-MDK:22833439~pagePK:64257043~piPK:437376~theSitePK:4607,00.html

[2] OECD (2011), *Latin American Economic Outlook 2011: How Middle Class is Latin America?*, OECD Publishing; OECD (2011), *Perspectives on Global Development: Social Cohesion in a Shifting World,* OECD Publishing.

- One of the main innovations of the OECD's Inclusive Growth Initiative has been that inequalities are multidimensional, affecting a number of dimensions essential for well-being: i.e. health outcomes, gender discrimination, education and employment opportunities. We need to be able to better measure inequalities – both monetary and non-monetary.

- The OECD Better Life Index can help to mainstream well-being and multidimensional inequality in developing countries. The index currently covers all 34 OECD countries plus Russia and Brazil, focussing on 11 indicators (including: Education, Jobs and Environment). The OECD well-being for development work further provides a new avenue to start identifying the effect of development policies on several dimensions of well-being both in terms of average achievements and distribution of outcomes.

- More generally, there is a need to support the Post-2015 Agenda with strengthened statistical capacities - e.g. PARIS 21 which aims to promote the better use and production of statistics throughout the developing world by facilitating statistical capacity development, advocating the integration of reliable data into decision making, and co-ordinating donor support to statistics.

- As a key priority, our efforts should focus on completing the MDG on universal access to primary education, whilst moving beyond that to promote access to secondary education. Additionally, there should be a renewed emphasis on quality, and on relating skills learned in the classroom to the local job-market. Increasing educational achievement is a win-win policy goal, which would serve to boost growth, promote job prospects, and improve the income distribution.

- We need tools to measure, monitor and implement. The OECD PISA for Development is well placed to support global efforts. Pilot projects are planned or underway in 6 developing countries: Cambodia; Ecuador; Guatemala; Senegal; Sri Lanka; and Zambia.

The Root Causes of Gender Equality Deserve Particular Attention

- We call for policy makers and decision makers to take into account the underlying drivers of gender inequality in the Post-2015 development framework, which should (1) express its commitment to gender equality through a stand-alone goal – as recommended by the UN High Level Panel on the Post-2015 Agenda – and (2) set gender-specific targets and indicators in the other goals.

- The OECD Development Centre's research on discriminatory social norms through the *Social Institutions and Gender Index* (SIGI) highlights the importance of tackling discriminatory social norms to promote gender equality.

- Our SIGI data highlights the relationship between discriminatory social norms and key development outcomes, such as maternal mortality, educational attainment, poverty reduction and food security.

- SIGI results also demonstrate the extent to which failure to address discriminatory social norms has undermined progress on MDGS. As the only cross-country measure of discriminatory social institutions, the SIGI is a valuable tool for designing effective interventions and evaluating progress towards any Post-2015 goal and target.

- A strong Post-2015 framework will take a holistic view of gender inequalities: 1) addressing girls' completion of a quality education, 2) women's economic empowerment, 3) universal access to sexual and reproductive health and rights, 4) ending violence against women and girls, 5) women's voice, leadership and influence, 6) women's participation in peace and security, 7) women's contributions to environmental sustainability.

- The new framework will need to confront the discriminatory social norms and practices that underlie gender inequality, such as early marriage or tolerance of violence against women.

Keep Aid Commitments and Step up Other Forms of Co-operation

- We should not forget about International aid. It still has a key role to play in supporting the development agenda. In 2013, $135bn in Official Development Assistance was provided – an historic high.

- While aid flows have increased considerably, their allocation patterns continue to overlook the increasing needs of Least Developed Countries. Bilateral aid to sub-Saharan Africa further decreased by 4% in real terms from 2012 (to 26.2 billion, or an 8% decrease from the 28.4 billion recorded in 2011).

- We need to change the spelling of 'Aid' to T-A-X: There should be a greater focus on the ability of developing countries to finance their own development. Projects to support tax collection can help to replenish government coffers. A transfer pricing project in Kenya cost $10 000 and raised additional revenue of $12.9 million – a rate of return of $1 200 for every dollar spent.

- At the OECD, we are undertaking a number of tax-related projects: i.e. Tax Inspectors Without Borders (8 pilot projects planned or underway); Task for Tax and Development (accommodating developing countries' views into BEPS).

- Other resources need to be tapped for development as the global economic stage transforms, opening up opportunities for non-traditional sources of aid, e.g. South-South Cooperation, philanthropic organisations, etc.

EVEN IT UP: TIME TO TACKLE EXTREME INEQUALITY HAS COME

Reflections

OXFAM International

"Some people continue to defend trickle-down theories which assume that economic growth, encouraged by a free market, will inevitably succeed in bringing about greater justice and inclusiveness in the world. This opinion, which has never been confirmed by the facts, expresses a crude and naive trust in the goodness of those wielding economic power and in the sacralized workings of the prevailing economic system. Meanwhile the excluded are still waiting."
"Inequality is the cause of social evil."

Pope Francis, 2013

We are living in a world of paradox: there is a growing recognition among the public, leaders and experts that our economy should truly serve the global common good, and yet the divide between those at the top and the rest continues to widen; our technology and resources provide a real opportunity to end extreme poverty and yet, instead, progress is jeopardized by growing inequality.

In January 2014, *Oxfam* highlighted that the richest 85 people in the world have as much as the poorest 3.5 billion. In July, *Forbes* magazine estimated that that figure had moved down to just 66 people.

A more inclusive economy is within our grasp, if our leaders seize it. But to generate the political will required will need a movement of people across the world, pressing for a more equal society that values everyone and promotes the common good. The good news is that the movement is building. *Oxfam* is part of that movement.

Once again, as with the movement to drop third world debt, people around the world are being inspired by the call of the Holy

See and the Catholic Church to reinstate human beings at the centre of economics. Like Pope Francis, they are demanding that world leaders act to address rising inequality which is holding back poverty reduction and dividing societies.

Through its teaching, through mobilising millions of people for social justice, through its convening of diverse leaders, through its international diplomacy, and through the personal example of Pope Francis, the Holy See is playing a unique and transformational role in advancing the cause of tackling rising economic inequality.

Oxfam stands resolutely with this call. Through our work on the ground across the world with people in poverty we see the damage that rising inequality is causing. Economic inequality is putting lives on the line - more than 1.5 million lives are lost each year due to high income inequality in rich countries alone. A recent study of 93 countries estimated that reducing the income share of the richest 20 per cent by just one percentage point could save the lives of 90,000 infants each year.

Estimates also show that failing to tackle inequality will add hundreds of billions of dollars to the price tag of ending poverty, putting the achievement of any new post-2015 poverty goals in jeopardy.

This is why we believe that tackling economic inequality, as a factor that is also bringing forward other kind of inequalities, is crucial to overcome what His Holiness has called the globalisation of indifference.

Oxfam has set out how, if world leaders choose to do so, they can act to tackle rising economic inequality.

In today's world, it is necessary to overcome tax evasion and tax avoidance practices put in place by wealthy individuals and large companies in the North and in the South, as such practices steal precious financial resources that can be invested in health and education services and in welfare for citizens.

Deliberate policy interventions and political commitments to deliver fair and effective public services - provided according to people's needs and not their ability to pay - can drive down inequality. For *Oxfam*, health and education should be driven by the values of universality, social solidarity, and equity. All people – rich and poor alike – should be allowed to access to the same range of high quality services. When health and education are not free at the point of use, the most vulnerable and disadvantaged people are excluded. Worldwide every year 100 million people are pushed into poverty because they have to pay out-of-pocket for health care.[1] Removing user fees across 20 African countries could prevent the deaths of 233,000 children under the age of five every year.

To finance public services like health and education, fiscal revenues are crucial. Tax is not a dirty word, as it reinforces the social contract between states and their citizens. *Oxfam* supports the concept of 'fiscal justice', whereby we all (individuals and companies alike) pay our fair share – and according to our actual means - in taxes and contribute to building a redistributive and more equal society, in which access to good quality, universal public services are provided irrespective of the extent to which we benefit from them. Combined with greater transparency and accountability mechanisms and the delivery of quality universal public services, a fiscal justice approach strengthens solidarity within and between countries and is a key factor in reducing inequality.

However, tax dodging knows no border and, as much as governments can put in place relevant progressive fiscal policies, regional and international coordination will be necessary to avoid competition over the tax base between states.

Therefore, the need to strengthen existing systems of world governance and to create an effective global policy framework is now of paramount importance. This is particularly evident when we note that, despite the G20 firm commitment to support equita-

---

[1] E.g. *Oxfam International* (2009) 'Blind Optimism: Challenging the myths about private health care in poor countries' and Basu, S., Andrews, J., Kishore, S., Panjabi, R. and D. Stuckler (2012) 'Comparative Performance of Private and Public Healthcare Systems' in *Low- and Middle-Income Countries: A Systematic Review,* PLOS Medicine.

ble and sustainable growth, income inequality has increased since 1990 in all but four G20 countries.

In the last two years the G8 and the G20 have taken some steps on agreeing on an internal multilateral tax information exchange system and delegating to international organizations like the OECD to challenge the policies of tax dodging (base erosion and profit shifting) that were put in place by transnational corporations – but this is only the first step.

The OECD's Action Plan needs to require multinational companies to make public country-by-country reports that will include a breakdown of key financial information (for each country where they operate): number of employees, physical assets, sales, profits, and taxes (due and paid), so that there can be an accurate assessment of whether they are paying their fair share of taxes. The G20 should support these measures.

A second important point for the G20 is to embrace the fight against tax havens, that deliberately behave as 'free-riders' and sap other states' tax base. *Oxfam* estimated that 18.5 trillion USD are hidden offshore in tax havens by wealthy individuals only. Two-thirds of this money is hidden in tax havens related to European countries. Abiding and meaningful definition of tax havens as well as clear sanctions against them should be adopted.

The G20 and OECD are working on this international tax reform, but they also need to create the space for non-OECD G20 countries to join these efforts on an equal footing, and assist them in implementing measures to stem their losses from international tax avoidance that deprives governments of badly needed revenues.

The G20 would also have a great potential to discuss – jointly with other organizations, policy makers from developing and developed countries, and independent experts – a rigorous study of the merits, risks and feasibility of more fundamental alternatives to the current international tax system. A World Tax Authority under the auspices of the UN could independently follow global tax developments and gather statistics; be a forum for discussion on international issues related to tax policy; tackle tax competition by setting common minimum tax rates to prevent a 'race to the bottom' on corporate taxation; exert peer pressure on countries/ jurisdictions that enable companies to be free riders; and develop best practices and codes of conduct on tax-related issues.

Policies to ensure fair wages are a necessary measure – in developed, middle income and developing countries – to overcome inequality. National laws have a crucial role in setting up standards – at national and regional levels – to require companies to change their policies on wages. Despite fears in the US that an increase in the minimum wage would result in job losses,[2] a range of studies have found these fears to be unwarranted[3] and this was also the case when the UK introduced a minimum wage in 1999.[4] In China, where the government has followed a deliberate strategy of raising wages since the recession, spending by workers-turned-consumers is forecast to double in the next four years to **£3.5tn, increasing demand for imported and locally-made goods alike**.[5] If a critical mass of countries were to pursue pro-labour distributional policies simultaneously, there would be significant improvements in aggregate demand and growth, as well as a reduction in poverty and inequality, according to the ILO in its recent report 'Wage-led growth'.[6]

---

[2] Congressional Budget Office report.

[3] Michael Cahill and David Mericle, "What to Expect from a Minimum Wage Hike," Goldman Sachs, March 25, 2014; Congressional Budget Office, "The Effects of a Minimum-Wage Increase on Employment and Family Income," Feb. 2014, http://cbo.gov/sites/default/files/cbofiles/attachments/44995-MinimumWage.pdf; Center for American Progress Action Fund, "Raising the Minimum Wage Would Help, Not Hurt, Our Economy," Dec. 3, 2013, http://www.americanprogressaction.org/issues/labor/news/2013/12/03/80222/raising-the-minimum-wage-would-help-not-hurt-our-economy/

[4] Professor Ken Mayhew Oxford University, ETI presentation Jan 2014.

[5] *The Guardian Financial,* page 3 June 2014.

[6] Wage-led growth ILO.

To ensure human rights protection, the increase in the living wage needs to be coupled with state policies that support workers' bargaining power and international agreements and fora that are able to avoid a 'race to the bottom' business model. Sometimes the business case alone may not be strong enough for such voluntary approaches to deliver decent work on a scaleable basis. This is a responsibility for States and International institutions – such as the International Monetary Fund, World Bank and G20 - to integrate the labour standards into their programs.

In the New Sustainable Development Goals, *Oxfam* believes that a stand alone goal on inequality is a crucial means to increase the awareness of the world community on the need to overcome what is now recognised as a major threat to global peace.

All of the proposals set out by *Oxfam* are workable, practical and achievable. What is needed is the political will. *Oxfam* has witnessed many times the cathartic influence of the Catholic Church and of the Holy See to guide world leaders and civil society on global development, in particular at critical times. The Jubilee 2000 debt campaign represents one of the most shining examples of this leadership.

At present, the encyclical *Evangelii Gaudium* and its calls to abandon the 'economy of exclusion' sets a powerful voice that can help shift the terms of the debate and find space for alternatives to the current economic thinking. This is a welcome and needed call to reduce the inequality gap and ask economic and political decision makers to bring policy and economy back again at the service of human beings.

This implies creating rules that tackle tax evasion and elusion, that increase the capacity of people to access free and public health and education services, that eliminate discrimination and that give back dignity to work with fair wages. We have a common challenge: to build a solid new political and economic orthodoxy that extreme inequality is wrong, and stands in the way of people claiming their rights.

The IMF concurs that current levels of economic inequality are economically damaging. *Oxfam's* work on the ground and the analysis of the world's leading poverty experts confirms that rising inequality is holding back poverty reduction. And the Church has led the way in challenging the moral injustice of such an unequal economy which excludes and degrades so many. Around the world, majorities agree that the gap between the richest and the rest has grown too wide. The campaign to tackle rising and extreme inequality, to even it up, is a transformational campaign that can be won.

THE GLOBAL COMMON GOOD: TOWARDS A MORE INCLUSIVE ECONOMY

Personal Reflection

Tamara Vrooman

President and CEO
Vancouver City Saving Credit Union (Vancity)

Two areas in the participants' Final Statement have especially reso-
nated with me and relate directly to my role leading a financial cooperative that works daily to further the financial, social and environmental
well-being of our 500,000 members and their communities.

First, the statement that "… the active participation of citizens
in their economic actions and of corporations along the lines of
social and environmental responsibility is crucial to tilt the balance
towards the good…" speaks to our approach to banking.

I'll begin by addressing the latter part of that statement first.

In our view, and as we state to our members publicly, the role
of banking is to finance positive change for people and society. We
are working, both in the Vancouver metropolitan region through
our business, and internationally through the Global Alliance for
Banking on Values, to ensure the banking sector is inclusive, transparent and sustainable through our values-based approach.

We have a clear view of the role that financial institutions must
play in society. Banking plays a critical role in preserving, growing
and redistributing capital – serving individuals, families, businesses,
governments and civic institutions. It does this by enabling savings
and investment, providing protection from risks and supporting
the creation of new jobs and businesses. These functions are critical to enabling society to operate in a stable, sustainable way. To

be effective, banking cannot operate in isolation of the people it serves but must act in the best interests of all stakeholders and of society as a whole. Banking must be deeply connected to community, to the many systems that are operating in community, and to how they work together to impact the health of the community.

This is Vancity's purpose – to help communities thrive and prosper by using financial tools in innovative ways that make society better for more people (inclusive), for better outcomes (well-being) and for greater sustainability (environmental outcomes). We don't leave this work to others and/or see it outside of our core business. It is our core business.

As a financial cooperative, our work is underpinned by the seven cooperative principles: voluntary and open membership; democratic member control; member economic participation; autonomy and independence; education, training and information; co- operation among co-operatives; and concern for community.

Resilience to Raise Participation in the Economy

As a financial cooperative whose existence depends on member engagement, Vancity Credit Union is quite familiar with the benefit of an active membership engaged in the governance and direction of our credit union. The virtuous circle is:

- financial education augments financial inclusion;
- financial accessibility and balance engender well-being; and
- financial well-being enables economic transactions and reciprocity.

We also find that this simple circle of well-being strengthens the likelihood of a community voice expressed through our social institutions and offers innovative solutions and problem-solving to benefit all stakeholders, not just a single shareholder.

In the time elapsed since we met July 11-12, global society is even more anxious. There is more being written and expressed about the world risking more financial and economic turmoil, with fewer policy levers available to the ruling technicians of central banks or fiscal mandarins. Six years after the onset of the financial crisis in particular, the Geneva Report released in late September warns that the medicine prescribed (policies approved by the G20 elite) of debt deleveraging and slower nominal growth are in many cases interacting in a vicious loop of further bankruptcy and indebtedness that could put the world economy at risk.

So the question is: can we do better with social engagement than with managerial elites and technocratic agencies who seem crisis prone?

The invitation to recreate a more inclusive economy and overcome reductionism so pervasive in our daily life is to enable widespread participation in our social institutions. Otherwise we are simply complicit in the decay of our democracy as we give up our own action and let our elites (mis)guide us. So we examine how financial education and inclusion contribute to our understanding of economic inclusion and we further acknowledge the institutional support of consumer financial protection laws and protocols.

I'll now address item 3, from the final statement, related to the "fostering of financial education, financial inclusion and financial consumer protection."

Financial Education

We deliver our financial literacy programs to build the knowledge and confidence of our members to make informed decisions about their money. Our financial literacy programs are rooted in who we are as a cooperative – principle five, member education – contributing to our work on financial inclusion as well as offering our members the self-help tools to build their self-reliance.

For example, we have a program for our members that accompanies our credit products. We have observed first hand how self-esteem is often rejuvenated when someone has regained financial balance and has been lifted from the stress of excessive indebtedness. We have observed that financial balance needs institutional support with legislated regulations to protect both civil society and private markets. Vancity invests in financial literacy because one of the first steps on the road to self-sufficiency is financial education – providing the information and tools people need to make sound decisions about money (and markets).

In Canada, November is financial literacy month – ahead of the seasonal and sentimental pressures for consumer spending (often beyond one's means) in our secular society. Vancity and the Vancouver Public Library host a partner program at the library to offer free workshops to understand financial clauses in goods purchased or debt products. Financial literacy, digital literacy, and information literacy are foundational for an engaged citizenry and responsive civil society.

Financial Inclusion

A guiding principle behind Vancity's vision to redefine wealth is to enhance social justice and financial inclusion in our members' lives and communities. A specific example: we know that our members are using so-called "payday loans" much more frequently today than they did 10 years ago. To remedy the downward financial spiral inherent in these high-interest loans, we introduced a "Fair & Fast Loan" for our members. This small credit loan is designed to allow members fast, simple and convenient access to funds at an affordable cost, while managing risk and financial inclusion through a social justice lens. Our goals are to provide fast and convenient access to funds, enable our members to build a credit history, and help members break away from the payday loan debt cycle.

A local community leader said that people using payday loan services are living in what she described as "virtually a parallel world compared to people with a regular paycheque. For someone with unstable income, a crisis can lead to the person having no choice but to take out a payday loan which can, in some cases, lead to a spiral of debt and eventual homelessness."

Financial Consumer Protection

Beyond our individual actions is consumer protection legislation at both federal and provincial levels in Canada. For banks, there is an Office of the Ombudsman for Banking Services and Investments (OBSI). OBSI is not a regulator, nor does it give advice; the office seeks to resolve disputes between participating banking service providers and their customers if they cannot be resolved on their own. The services of the office are free to consumers.

Institutional integrity, like the Office of the Ombudsman, is an essential dimension if civil society is to be engaged in social democracy. Institutional integrity provides a protective pathway to address realities of redistribution of wealth (government) and reciprocity (civil society).

"This alchemy of interests in the common good, however, works only when there are many other diverse institutions" *(PCJP Research Working Paper, p. XII)* – not just the dominant ones led by the ruling elites. It was observed in July at the Vatican that institutions are likely to become extractive (creating negative externalities) the larger and more dominant they become. It is a challenge to be inclusive (creating positive pecuniary externalities) if there is no pluralism of institutions.

The beauty of biodiversity is that there are many paths for participation in an authentic and impactful way as individuals, enabled by financial education. This engagement is often seen in civil society as volunteer leadership which can roll up into a civic voice in electoral matters. An active civil society enhances social democracy and social inclusion. Often the individual initiative connects to convening power of a community or cooperative institution, which in turn is enabled (or held accountable) by a transparent regulatory regime with right and representations – to serve the common good in an effective way.

We at Vancity continue to observe that there is a growing need to increase access to those in our community who are underserved by traditional banking and other types of financial institutions. To further our principle of financial inclusion, we are exploring ways of supporting those who have unmet banking needs.

SOME BASIC ISSUES FOR VATICAN TO CONSIDER

Personal Reflection

Muhammad Yunus

2006 Nobel Peace Prize
Founder of the Grameen Bank

The Catholic Church would like to work to establish an appropriate level of spiritual, social, and material 'capital' in the world. I believe that under the present global economic system, this cannot be done. The present system is an impersonal sucking machine which thrives on continuous sucking of juice from the bottom to transport it to the top. The higher you are in the system, the more juice you are able to suck. It is not because bad people are running the machine, it is because the machine is built that way. The system was not designed to have any moral responsibility. At least that is not in practice. Discussion on moral responsibilities is an after-thought. This machine turns people into money-centric robots.

Business schools pick up the practice and compete to produce market-warriors, to go out and capture market and money. The stock market, which is the ultimate judge of business success, does not grade businesses on the basis of their moral commitment nor on their spiritual orientations. Moral issues were never included in their reporting template.

Social Business

I have been proposing and practicing a new kind of business which is based on the selflessness, replacing selfishness, of human beings. This type of business runs parallel to the selfishness-driven business that rules the world. Conventional business is personal-profit seeking business. The new business, which I am adding, is personal profit-forsaking business. It is a for-profit business, but personal-profit forsaking business. I call it social business – a non-dividend company to solve social problems. The owner can take back his investment money, but nothing beyond that. After getting the investment money back all future profit is ploughed back into the business to make it better and bigger. It stands between charity and profit maximizing businesses. It is designed with the objectives of charity and carried out with the methodology of business, but delinked from personal profit-taking.

Charity is a great concept to help people, and has been used since time immemorial. But it is not sustainable. Charity: money goes out, does a wonderful job, but does not come back. Social business: money gets the job done and then comes back. As a result, this money can be re-used endlessly. It creates independent self-sustaining enterprises, which have their own lives. These enterprises become self-fueled entities.

Business schools today train young people to become business-warriors to capture market and money. They are not given any social mission. If we accept the concept of social business, business schools will also produce social-problem-fighters to bring an end to social problems through social businesses. We would need to create social stock market to attract investors who would like to invest in problem-solving enterprises, without having any intention of making personal profit.

Technology

If the present variety of capitalism continues, the more we advance in technology, improve our infrastructure, spread globalization, and bring 'efficiency' in the system, the more the system will become ruthless in sucking the juice from the enormously wide bottom to transport it to the progressively thinner top.

Income disparity

The present version of capitalism will never deliver equitable distribution of income. A system that is built as a sucking machine cannot bring equitable distribution. It was never put in its DNA.

While 1% of people in the world own half of the world's wealth, 85 individuals own more wealth than all those in the bottom half, and the top half population of the world own almost all the wealth of the world, the bottom half stands no chance. It may get worse, and there is no possibility of getting better.

Indifference or worse

Indifference to other human beings, which has been denounced by Pope Francis, is deeply embedded in the conceptual framework of economics. The theory of economics is based on the belief that a human being is basically a personal profit seeking being. Economic rationality is defined as maximizing personal profit. This encourages a behavior which may be described by a harsher word than mere indifference.

The Capitalist Man does not have any other virtue than selfishness. Real Man is a composite of many virtues. He enjoys relationship with other human beings. He is a caring man. He is a selfless man. He is a trusting man. We have many good examples to demonstrate these virtues. To show that he is a trusting man, take the case of Grameen Bank in Bangladesh. The entire bank is built on trust. There is no effort in this bank to establish relationship with legal glue. It is a lawyer-free bank. It lends out over one and half billion dollars a year to 8.5 million poor women on the basis of trust only. Now it works in many other countries, including the USA, exactly the same way. Its repayment rate is near 100%.

GDP Does Not Tell The Story

As we create a world based on selfishness, people move away from each other. In that selfish world the very way we create measurements of business success fuels more selfishness.

Human society is an integrated whole. It's success or failure should be measured in a consolidated way, not purely on the basis of some purposefully chosen aggregate economic information.

GDP does not tell the whole story. We need something else to do that. It may be GDP minus all human problems (poverty, unemployment, illiteracy, income inequality, status of women, lack of human rights, absence of law and order, lack of technology and opportunities for all people, etc.). Globalisation brings people closer to each other, though not in a friendly way, but in a confrontational posture. Ideally, globalisation should be the process towards building the global human family.

ICT, other technologies, higher levels of creativity, speed of accessing information – these combined forces are changing the world at a faster and faster pace. There is indeed great progress in sight. But there is no global vision driving these changes. Changes are used for commercial purposes. Innovations rush in the direction that businesses see market potential. Nobody is putting up any highway signs to lead the world to its destination. There are lots of amazing breakthroughs, but they don't add up to becoming an unstoppable force to get the world to its destination. Given the power of technology and creativity of human beings today any destination is reachable. But it does not look like anybody is seriously concerned about a destination. We float without direction. In the worse case, in the wrong direction.

The education system is at fault. Young people are never asked to engage themselves in finding out what kind of world they would like to create. They are never told that they are the creators of that world. There is no curriculum in the school to let the students imagine their dream world, what considerations they should put together to construct that dream world. While they are not happy with the world they see around them, they don't know that they can transform this world into their dream world. As a result, even if they want to change the world, they don't know what they will change it into.

Finance

We have created a world for the rich by creating the financial institutions for the rich. If we want to get the poor out of poverty we have to create exclusive financial institutions for the poor.

Finance is power. For the bottom half of the world population, banks do not exist. So they remain powerless.

Today there is a concentration of economic power in a few hands because financial institutions are at their disposal. We talk about land reform for overcoming poverty, because land represents power and independence in rural societies. But we don't talk about credit reform. We don't ask the question of who gets how much of bank credit? Or what percentage of the population gets what percentage of bank credit? This one piece of information will give us the real story on power and powerlessness. Credit disparity is the major cause of income disparity.

We'll have to create new financial institutions if we are worried about income disparity and poverty. Grameen Bank has shown how even the poorest women, and even beggars, can do business with a financial institution provided it is designed for them. Don't ask them to do business with an institution which is designed for the rich.

Not Job Seekers

While the idea of a labour union is an excellent one, the basic assumption of 'once a labour, always a labour' has to be removed. There should be plenty of opportunity for each and every person to quit his job and be an entrepreneur. Social business can make it happen. Every person should have two options, either to work for somebody, or to be an entrepreneur. He should be told about these options in school, when he is growing up. He should be given options for how he should prepare himself, as a job-giver, or as a job-seeker. Even if someone takes up a job, it does not have to be a life-long engagement. He should have the opportunity to move about in both worlds.

No Unemployment

Unemployment means keeping a fully capable person under mothballs. Why should human beings be punished and remain paralysed? A human being is born to be active, creative, energetic, always exploring ways to unleash his own unlimited potential. Why should we allow anybody to unplug him, and deny him the opportunity to use his amazing capacity? Who unplugs him? Why do billions of creative people remain unplugged? Why is our world condemned to miss out on the creativity of almost half the population? This problem is not created by the unplugged people themselves. It is created by our grossly flawed conceptual framework which has drilled into our heads that people are born to work for some privileged people called entrepreneurs. All policies and institutions are built for them. If they don't hire you, you are finished. What a mis-reading of human capacity. What an insult to a human being.

Our education system is built on the basis of the same assumption. It assumes that students should work hard, get good grades so that they can get good jobs.

Young people are never told that all people in the world are entrepreneurs. They are born with two choices, and retain both choices throughout their lives. A job-giver, or a job-seeker, these are his options.

In Grameen Bank we are inspiring the second generation of borrowers' families to believe that they are not job seekers, they are job givers. All children in the world should grow up that way. Institutions and policies should be created to make it happen. Job seeking should become a second choice for any young person. In Bangladesh we have created social business to provide full equity to any young person who wants to create his own business. We provide him support to make him successful.

Why are half the young people in some European countries unemployed? Why are we talking about a lost generation? Why are we accepting it as if it is a fate ordained by God? Are we not insulting God by accepting it as a fate? Is putting them on state charity the only solution? Is this how we uphold human dignity, by putting young creative people on state charity? What about giving them opportunity to explore their own creative power? How can we take something away which God has given them?

Have we ever asked them if they can start an enterprise of their own? If they can, what would they need? Have we ever thought of coming up with supports which they need? We have created social business funds in Bangladesh to provide exactly that type of support. Young people are loving it. Why not try it in Europe? The Catholic Church can easily create social business funds to solve the problem of youth unemployment in Europe? If it works for Europe, it will change the world forever. Someone has to take the initiative. We cannot just sit and watch a whole generation of young people fall through the cracks of theory because we are too timid to question the wisdom of our theoreticians.

We have to redesign our theory by recognizing the limitless capacity of a human being, not just relying on 'invisible hands' which remain invisible because they do not exist. We have to design new concepts, new institutions. This is where the Catholic Church can play the most important role.

State charity

If we can demonstrate that nobody needs to remain unemployed, it would easily lead to a society without poverty and without charity. Unemployment is an artificial creation of our faulty conceptual framework. It is not natural to human beings. Human beings are doers, and go getters. Theory has the audacity to put them in chains. Theory should not be allowed to punish human beings – the greatest creation on earth. We should be the one to punish theory by scrapping it.

We should make sure that the word 'unemployment' soon gets unemployed. When we build a new world we know for sure in that world the word 'unemployment' will not make sense to anybody. Nobody would be able to figure out how a person could remain idle. They would suspect something related to his health, but not his lack of opportunities.

In our conceptual framework we should not allow anything which is derogatory to the human spirit. Theory should reflect us, human beings should not be squeezed in to fit into narrow theory. Theory must keep enough room to accommodate the fact that human beings thrive in this world by constantly making the impossible possible. People should have the final word on their fate, not the theory.

Helping people in distress is the prime responsibility of the state. State charity must be applauded for doing an excellent job of taking care of its citizens in distress. But still higher responsibility of the state will be to make sure that people can come out of their distressful situation as soon as possible so that they can end their dependence on the state.

Human beings are all about independence and freedom, and the constant search for their own worth, not about dependence on anyone. Dependence diminishes human beings. One's mission on this planet is to make it a better place for everybody. One should not be put in a situation where he remains dependent on the state all his life, then passes it on to the next generation, who in turn, passes it on to the third generation, creating an unending series. State charity has created this situation for many people in Europe. We have the technology and methodology to bring an end to this. All that is needed is a determined initiative.

Taxation

Taxation is needed to overcome the deficiencies of the market mechanism in creating common goods. With the introduction of social business we'll have to revisit this proposition. State is no longer the only creator of social goods. Citizens can create social businesses to do that. Through social businesses, citizens can create better and efficient healthcare, education, and many other social services more efficiently, creatively, and sustainably than the state. Every society then will have three options for providing common goods, a) through public sector intervention, b) through social businesses, or c) through for-profit private sector intervention. They should compete and collaborate to bring the best common goods to the people.

In most countries the tax administration is extremely corrupt; big money in the government exchequer makes politicians corrupt, and too powerful to listen to citizens' voices. Also works done by public money in most cases are low quality, and inefficient. I would feel more comfortable seeing citizens organising social businesses to create common goods. Citizens can bring more creative power, and technology to solve people's problems, than the governments can. Once government creates a programme for offering social good, it cannot be stopped, even if it is un-needed, or totally inefficient and corrupt, for political reasons. Governments are not good at closing down any service. But if a social business does not work, it will have its natural death. It does not become a burden on citizens.

International Financial Institutions

All international financial institutions (IFI) should be redesigned to work both with governments and non-government sectors. Each IFI should create a social business fund at the headquarter level which, in its turn, will create country level funds. Country level funds should take initiative in organising social business design competitions regularly within the country and invest in the top business plans. They should build communities of social businesses within the country, and among countries.

These funds can offer management services to manage and supervise social businesses on behalf of the government, private sector, and foundations. They can also work as match-makers to set up joint venture social businesses with local and international companies.

IFIs must focus on projects which are sustainable, and make sure recipient countries or the private sector do not get burdened with debt. They may include a sustainable sub-project within a larger unsustainable project even if the sub-project is a very small part of the larger project. This will keep the issue of sustainability alive within the project. This sub-project may be created as an independent social business run by citizens, not by government.

Bilateral aid

Bilateral aid agencies may follow the same procedure as suggested in the case of IFIs, create country level social business funds, and generate social business projects to invest, and act as a match-maker for social business joint ventures between donor country companies and local partners. These local funds will grow in size because each year the country will receive more aid in the fund. Donors will have reason to feel happy that unlike the present system, a part of their money will continue to recycle, and continue to solve problems long after the money was given.

Conclusion

Each human being is an enormously creative and entrepreneurial being. The conceptual framework of present capitalist theory is too narrow and very undignified for him. It reduces him to a selfish robot. We need to design a theory keeping in mind the true human being, not a distorted and miniaturized version of him. A true human being is a selfless, caring, sharing, trusting, community-building, friendly human being. He is, at the same time, also the reverse of all these virtues. Which one of these virtues he'll promote, which ones he'll suppress will depend on the world around him. We need to give him opportunities to bring out the right virtues. Today we don't give him that opportunity. We are stuck with the opposite. That's where the trouble begins.

FINAL STATEMENT

SEMINAR ON THE GLOBAL COMMON GOOD

The Pontifical Council for Justice and Peace is grateful to the undersigned experts and academics who gathered at the Pontifical Academy of Sciences on July 11-12 to discuss the urgent questions of a more inclusive economy and governance for the common good.

Pope Paul VI challenged his fellow Church-leaders to enter into "dialogue with other Christian brethren and all people of goodwill, to discern the options and commitments which are called for in order to bring about the social, political and economic changes seen in many cases to be urgently needed" (*Octogesima Adveniens* § 4). This is exactly what we undertook to do throughout the weekend's sessions.

More specifically, according to Pope Francis, we cannot understand the Good News of Jesus Christ – the gospel of dignity and fraternity, of justice and peace – without being aware of real poverty, i.e., by turning our backs on the scandal of exclusion or blindly hoping that it will take care of itself (cf. *Evangelii Gaudium*, § 54). Quite on the contrary, it will be by putting the human being back into the heart of economics and politics, by welcoming the participation of the poor, that poverty can be overcome and the planet safeguarded.

Final Statement

As a fruit of the discussions, we participants, joined by others who wish to add their names, are pleased to put forward the following final statement of concern and engagement:

Beyond the Globalisation of Indifference: Towards a More Inclusive Economy

In the face of the many unresolved issues brought to the fore by the financial crisis and our ongoing inability to bring an end to endemic poverty and exclusion, there is substantial agreement between us that, as a human community, we must recover our moral compass and re-examine the assumptions of our economic theory to be more realistic and based on a more complete view of the human being and of the world.

People welcome the job creation, healthcare improvements and the many other benefits that today's economy has provided. Globalisation in a positive sense has the potential to bring people together. Nevertheless, many people experience a severe loss of value and morals in political and economic life, and furthermore, the means and instruments of our economy, such as money, are accorded more importance than the proper end or goal of that same economy, that is, sustaining a good life for the human community. Similarly, human beings are frequently treated as means to an economic end, and not as the reason why economic activity take place at all. The experience of social businesses demonstrates that people can be active in creating their own work and enterprises and so make a secure future for themselves. We must put people and their wellbeing at the centre of our economic and political life.

An economic system is like a natural environment. It requires diversity to strengthen its resilience. We therefore acknowledge the contribution of various actors to the economy, and in particular women and rural workers, and support the ongoing development of the many different organizational forms (for profit corporations, cooperatives, productive not for profit entities, ethical or sustainable banks and businesses, social business, and so on). They contribute to the production of social capital, as well as economic value, as an expression of economic democracy and for the fulfilment of the human being. Inadequate regulation must not be allowed to harm this biodiversity.

On the basis of this shared vision of the human person and the central elements on which our economic thought must be founded, we share a consensus that welcomes existing reforms of the global economy, and the financial system in particular, but also that this must go much further. It is equally important to empha-size that no structural reform leading to greater inclusion can be ultimately successful unless there is a conversion of the human heart. Without a recovery of the virtue of gratuitousness and the willingness to make moral judgments, allowing our action to be guided by them, no structural reform can be sure to bring about positive outcomes.

With these premises in view, we strongly endorse and we com-mit ourselves to supporting the following reforms aimed at achiev-ing a more inclusive economy:

1. The adoption of ambitious and inclusive Sustainable Devel-opment Goals centred on human dignity and a new global climate agreement in 2015 which, apart from their impor-tance in themselves, are also critical opportunities for mak-ing a breakthrough to more effective global institutions. By doing so, we have a chance to eradicate poverty, support worker protection, environmental standards, tax revenues, and financial regulation, and confront inequality.

2. The multilateral work led by the OECD/G20 on the Auto-matic Exchange of Tax Information and Base Erosion and Profit Shifting (BEPS), and in confronting the "too big to fail" problem in the international banking system. At the same time, we call on the G20 to be more ambitious and explicit about the ethical framework that informs its deliber-ations, helping to enhance its legitimacy.

3. The fostering of financial education, financial inclusion and financial consumer protection, equipping the most vulnera-ble groups so that they may access finance more easily, effi-ciently use financial services, make informed financial choic-es and be protected against the effects of unfair practices. We support the creation of banks for the poor.

4. The fight against persistent structural unemployment, grow-ing youth unemployment and the lack of security and pro-

tection for informal and rural workers are worldwide scourges. We urge policy-makers to take strong actions in order to promote access to decent and quality jobs to all segments of the societies, to promote access to education for skills, both of which are essential to human life and dignity.

5. The various initiatives of the UN and civil society to combat, in particular, child labour, discrimination against women, human trafficking, international crime, corruption and money laundering.

Finally, we believe, based on the transformations which are already taking place under our very eyes, that the active participation of citizens in their economic actions and of corporations along the lines of social and environmental responsibility is crucial to tilt the balance towards the good, and that rules should be created to stimulate the development of civic and corporate virtues.

In conclusion, the Holy Father exhorted us to resist a throwaway or discarding culture: "If the human person is not at the centre, then something else gets put there, which the human being then has to serve."

Vatican City, 12 July 2014

1. Card. Peter K.A. Turkson, President
2. Bp. Mario Toso, Secretary
3. Dr. Flaminia Giovanelli, Under-Secretary
4. Rev. Prof. Helen ALFORD
5. Mr. Bertrand BADRÉ
6. Rev. Fr. Paulo C. BARAJAS GARCIA
7. Prof. Leonardo BECCHETTI
8. Prof. Simona BERETTA
9. Ms. Laura BERRY
10. Mr. Peter BRABECK-LETMATHE
11. Prof. Luigino BRUNI

12. Ms. Winnie BYANYIMA

13. Prof. Michel CAMDESSUS

14. Dr. Mark J. CARNEY

15. Ms. Celine CHARVERIAT

16. Mr. Paolo CONVERSI

17. Mr. Renato CURSI

18. Mr. Enzo CURSIO

19. Rev. Dr. Michael CZERNY

20. Prof. Partha DASGUPTA SARATHI

21. Ms. Marike DE PEÑA

22. Prof. Séverine DENEULIN

23. Ms. Amira ELMISSIRY

24. Hon. Amb. Francesco Paolo FULCI

25. Mr. Juan GRABOIS

26. Dame Pauline GREEN

27. Lord Brian GRIFFITHS

28. Mr. José Ángel GURRÍA

29. Prof. André HABISCH

30. Dr. Heinz HÖDL

31. Mr. Steve HOWARD

32. Hon. Amb. Monica JIMENEZ DE LA JARA

33. Dr. Donald KABERUKA

34. Ms. Lamia KAMAL-CHAOUI

35. Dr. Steve KAYIZZI-MUGERWA

36. Dr. Mukhisa KITUYI

37. Dr. Kalpana KOCHHAR

38. Prof. Huguette LABELLE

39. Mr. Pascal LAMY

40. Mr. José Ignacio MARISCAL TORROELLA

41. Rev. Fr. Pierre MARTINOT-LAGARDE

42. Hon. Amb. John McCARTHY
43. Mr. Curtis McKENZIE
44. Prof. Branko MILANOVIĆ
45. Ms. Amina MOHAMMED
46. Mr. Moussa Djibril MOUSSA
47. Rev. Msgr. Bernard MUNONO
48. Rev. Msgr. Osvaldo NEVES DE ALMEIDA
49. Ms. Chisom OKECHUKWU
50. Ms. Ngozi OKONJO-IWEALA
51. Rev. Msgr. Paul PHAN VAN HIEN
52. Dr. Philipp ROESLER
53. Mr. Michel ROY
54. Dr. Onno RUDING
55. Prof. Jeffrey SACHS
56. Bp. Marcelo SÁNCHEZ SORONDO
57. Mr. Kartikey SHIVA
58. Dr. Vandana SHIVA
59. Mr. José Maria SIMONE
60. Mrs. Livia STOPPA
61. Dr. Jomo SUNDARAM
62. Mr. Raymond TORRES
63. Mr. Tebaldo VINCIGUERRA
64. Ms. Tamara VROOMAN
65. Prof. Mohammad YUNUS
66. Prof. Stefano ZAMAGNI
67. Rev. Dr. Augusto ZAMPINI

The Catholic Justice & Peace Commission of the Archdiocese of Brisbane-Australia has expressed the wish to join in this *Final Statement*.

APPENDIX

THE GLOBAL COMMON GOOD: TOWARDS A MORE INCLUSIVE ECONOMY

DISCUSSION PAPER
Vatican City, 30 June 2014

Preface

In his Apostolic Exhortation *Evangelii Gaudium*, Pope Francis seeks to awaken consciences to the scandal of a humanity which, despite ever greater potential at its disposal, has yet to succeed in overcoming some of the social plagues that humiliate the dignity of the person. In line with the *Magisterium* of his Predecessors, the Holy Father declares his emphatic opposition both to "ideologies" that defend the absolute autonomy of markets and financial speculation, and to an attitude of indifference that characterises today's political, economic and social situation.

To such elements of irresponsibility and of social disintegration, one must respond with a determined search for an economy based on respect for the dignity of the human person – an inclusive economy, supported by justice, temperance and the culture of gift and gratuity, capable of marking a substantial change in the conditions, styles and models of life of all humanity, preserving and improving the environment for current and future generations.

1. Introduction

The first observation of the Social Doctrine of the Church, as well as of social ethics founded on integral human development, is that every political and social action should have a clear anthropological perspective;[1] in fact, economic and social systems do not

[1] Cfr. Pope Francis, Apostolic Exhortation *Evangelii Gaudium*; Benedict XVI, Encyclical Letter *Caritas in Veritate*.

automatically serve human dignity; rather, they should always be guided by our responsible action inspired by human dignity and, accordingly, carried out with a right intention, oriented by wise national and international policies, and supported by appropriate levels of spiritual, social and material "capital".

Economic globalisation has above all been produced by markets opening up and therefore by the flow of capital and by great migratory movements which often involve unacceptable suffering. This globalisation is bringing about a slow but gradual "economic" convergence among States in terms of GDP, even if its realization still seems very far away. This is, however, not always accompanied by a similar "structural" convergence in terms of infrastructure, physical capital, access to new technologies and quality of institutions, and still less a "social" convergence of citizens of the various States, in terms of education, social capital, equitable distribution of benefits and quality of life.

On the other hand, while globalisation has undeniably helped greatly to increase aggregate wealth in total and of many individual States, it seems just as true that globalization has worsened the gaps between the different social groups. Both political and economic analyses confirm what is clearly observable from the point of view of ethics and moral theology,[2] namely, that worldwide or global inequality is increasing because of globalisation: the averages of national income hide enormous income disparities between those who have the skills and means needed to take advantage of ongoing progress, and those who instead remain marginalised and excluded from the dynamics of the market. The most recent scientific studies show a world divided into three major social sectors, regardless of national borders. In 1% of the world population is concentrated half of global wealth; another 47%, considered the global middle class, controls a little less than the other half; and the remaining 52% of humanity shares the "crumbs" with less than $2

[2] Cfr. Pope Francis, Apostolic Exhortation *Evangelii Gaudium*.

per person per day.[3] International efforts to promote development have successfully favoured economic convergence between States, but have neglected convergence among people within individual States. In the last quarter century, in fact, the rate of growth of the poorer countries has been higher than that of the richer ones, even though inequalities between individuals have dramatically increased.

This rapid synthesis of today's distribution of wealth at the world level still does not encompass all global problematics, for ecological consequences should also be taken into account, as these risks becoming unsustainable and disastrous.

2. Anthropological and Social Reductionisms of Today's Economic Thought and Activities

The *globalisation of indifference* denounced by Pope Francis is not only a psychological distortion produced by individualistic and utilitarian attitudes but corresponds, more profoundly, to an anthropological vision based upon reductionist views of *man*, of *economic activities* and their related *values*.

The first reductionism is one that sees the human person as an economic agent driven primarily by self-interest or egoism. The social sciences are now confirming what the Social Doctrine of the Church, together with other social-ethical approaches, has always affirmed: self-interest is a less rational form of existence in comparison with co-operation, because being in relationship is an essential part of the human person. Likewise, both traditional ethical doctrines and the new sciences of human behaviour recognize that, in interpersonal relationships, cooperation is not a foregone conclusion but requires the practice of social virtues, which are fruit of each person's authentic development. Authentic relationship requires trust, which always entails a "social risk" because it means put-

[3] Cfr. Branco Milanovic, "Global Income Inequality by the Numbers: in History and Now – An Overview," The World Bank, November 2012.

ting oneself in another's hands, entrusting oneself to his or her responsibility, and running the risk of being let down. Therefore, trust must always be cultivated and sustained. *It is the prime responsibility of institutions and civil society to encourage all those initiatives capable of establishing and nourishing these personal and social virtues and putting them into practice.*

The second reductionism is to see the subjects of economic activity – enterprises whether private or public – as entities oriented towards simply producing goods and services or maximising profit for the owners of the capital. This vision can lead to countless injustices, for example, the recent tendency towards relocating production only for the sake of profit, wherever the protection of labour and ecology is weaker, resulting in the widespread erosion of workers' rights and of the natural environment. In reality, companies (both public and private) are also a particular social and productive unit which deeply affects the lives of all those they touch: investors, employees and workers, suppliers, local communities, consumers, at both national and international levels.

Businesses cannot be driven only by the pursuit of the maximisation of production or of profit for the owners of capital. Nevertheless, the many existing norms and institutions have still not succeeded in finding a synthesis between the interests of owners of capital and the national and international common good. *It seems necessary to favour collaboration among governments, civil society organisations, citizens' groups and businesses, so that each of these recognise, assume and promote social and environmental sustainability as one of their essential goals.*

The third type of reductionism refers to the concept of "value" in economics. The "wealth of nations" is not merely the flow of goods and services produced somewhere during a given measure of time (e.g., GNP or GDP). Rather, it is the pool of cultural, natural, economic, social and spiritual goods that a particular community and its individual members may enjoy. Among these are certain fundamental rights that stand out, including religious freedom, the freedom and possibility to form and maintain a family, and access to education. Accordingly it would be fundamental to develop new composite indicators to serve at both national and international levels as criteria for evaluating the impact of economic policies. Similarly, both economic thought and governmental activity should *help the process of globalisation to realize its truer and fuller vocation: the integration of humanity as one family*, rich in its multiplicity of difference and cultures but freed from dreadful inequalities.

3. To Recover the Human Roots of the Economy and, Overcoming the Reductionisms, to Civilize Globalisation

The market economy has historically represented an important means or instrument for expressing free human creativity, for social inclusion and for support of democratic political culture. However, when the three above-mentioned reductionisms have prevailed, the economic system has lost this potential. History moreover teaches us that the most significant and long-lasting economic experiences are those in which the market has succeeded in respecting and integrating itself with social realities which express all the human dimensions, including the transcendent one, without reducing man to a mere producer and consumer. It is about developing a constructive synthesis – and also integration – of the market (the vocation to entrepreneurship and generation of wealth), civil society (reciprocity), and national and international institutions (redistribution of wealth). Such a harmonious coexistence among economic, political, civil, cultural and religious institutions, aimed also at transforming the interests of the individual into the interests of the common good, is the polyarchy which the Social Doctrine of the Church proposes.[4]

Such a positive integration, moreover, demands a renewed consideration of the dimension of time, a dimension which the

---

[4] Cfr. Benedict XVI, Encyclical Letter *Caritas in Veritate*, 47 and 57.

logic of today's economy and of its cultural manifestations tends, rather, to ignore. The ICT revolution is constantly reducing the time needed to make economic choices, consequently limiting the possibility of honouring motivations other than profit alone. The depth of time from which we come (history) and to which we are destined (the future) can be missing from today's economic culture and also from civic culture, with a consequent erosion of those institutions that give meaning, significance and substance to social life.[5] We need to restore a "polyarchic governing" of society with a broad long-term horizon, guided and harmonised by public institutions and inspired by those fundamental values in order to overcome the above-mentioned social and anthropological reductionisms.

Such polyarchic governance is also called to analyse carefully the various facets of finance, trade, labour, work and taxation, and their complex interrelationships.

4. Relationships Amongst Finance, Trade, Labour, Work and Taxation in the Era of Globalisation

4.1 Finance

Finance is an essential component of national and global economic functioning. It allows using time and trust as fundamental factors of economic development. Finance in fact collects savings in order to use them efficiently and allocate them to the most profitable uses; it anticipates the value of activities and spreads

---

[5] "A constant tension exists between fullness and limitation. Fullness evokes the desire for complete possession, while limitation is a wall set before us. Broadly speaking, 'time' has to do with fullness as an expression of the horizon which constantly opens before us, while each individual moment has to do with limitation as an expression of enclosure. People live poised between each individual moment and the greater, brighter horizon of the utopian future as the final cause which draws us to itself. Here we see a first principle for progress in building a people: time is greater than space" (Pope Francis, *Evangelii Gaudium*, 222).

them over space and in time; it creates mechanisms of insurance and risk-sharing in economic activities; and it facilitates the coming together of economic resources or capital, ideas, productive capacity, etc. Without financial activity in the broadest sense, the progress of humanity would not have been possible.

There have however always been distortions, sometimes even severe ones, in the finance area: financial agents have often tended to lend only to those who could provide economic guarantees equal to or greater than the sum of the loan requested and for considerations independent of the results of financial activities, giving rise even to usurious conduct. Modern instruments of finance, meant to facilitate credit or insure eventual risks, have moreover become, in practice, instruments of reckless speculation, encouraged by asymmetric incentives of earnings for finance operators. It is also noteworthy that, in the absence of norms and rules, fiancial activities do not necessarily tend towards competitivity but rather towards the formation of oligopolies, with a great capacity to lobby politically,[6] and this may make their maximisation of short-term profits in favour of shareholders their sole and primary objective, thus distorting the very meaning of the financial activity and the democratic essence of certain decisions by States at national levels and inter-governmentally, to the grave detriment of the world economy.

In response to these issues, a consensus is emerging on the elements that can guide national and international financial activity so that it always serves human dignity and integral human development. In this spirit, it is necessary to return to the true

---

[6] The 2014 Report of *Corporate Europe* highlights the imbalance of power between the financial lobbies and those of civil society and NGOs. Finance spends 30 times as much on lobbying than any other industrial pressure group (according to conservative estimates, Euro 123 million per year with about 1,700 lobbyists at the EU). The relationships between the representation of the financial lobbies and representation of NGOs or trade unions in consultation groups are 95 to 0 in the stakeholder group of the ECB and 62 to 0 in the *De Larosière Group on financial supervision in the European Union*.

and legitimate social functions of financial activity, favouring the encounter between saving and productive investments. What would serve this end is not only a true ethical assumption of primary responsibility towards the stakeholders of such activities, but also prudent and responsible reflection on the relationships of the national and international banking system with the central banks and intergovernmental bodies. This may help prevent the financial bubbles and crises with their serious repercussions, not only for the economy generally but even for the more essential availability of basic resources.

The efficiency and velocity of financial transactions are not ultimate goals but intermediate values, that is, features which must necessarily be harmonized with higher overarching values of precaution, stability and the common good in the sense of service to integral human development. Accordingly, the objective of fiancial regulation cannot be to maximise the velocity of trading and the infinite growth of liquidity. *Finance can and must do better by returning to its own mission of serving the common good.*

4.2 Trade

As with finance, so trade has always been a part of human social behaviour and a means towards cordial relations among peoples. It has allowed societies to overcome the limitations of autarchy, allowing each region to specialise in those activities that enhance its *genius loci*. Coming together, specialising in unique products and exchanging goods have in turn led to gains in effiiency and a better use of resources. Yet many times in history, trade has been used as a means of ensuring national and cultural supremacy and generally, like all economic activities, becomes an oppressive idol when absolutised and when subordinated to partisan needs and values.

The current world trade system has been an important means of economic convergence between many developing countries and so-called developed ones.[7] However, it seems that the rules of trade agreements in force have not always benefitted every individual citizen, nor have they really served to prevent international trade from eroding labour rights and environmental sustainability. Moreover, this increased participation of poor countries in trade has sometimes had negative impacts on their local social fabric, through the erosion of economic protection of various kinds of economic-social capital such as crafts, small and local businesses, family farms, special services, etc.

In general, the poorest segments of the population have gained substantial benefits from globalization when the positive results of international trade have been accompanied, at the national level, by social policies aimed at guaranteeing all residents a minimum dignity of life and by economic policies aimed at creating decent and sustainable work for all.

4.3 Trade, Social Responsibility and Labour

One of the aspects of today's global economic system is the exploitation of the international imbalance in labour costs, due to the presence of billions of people living on less than two dollars a day. Not only does this imbalance disrespect the dignity of those who feed this reservoir of cheap labour, but it also destroys sources of employment where labour is more protected without, however, creating new permanent sources of employment elsewhere. Therefore the question is whether the private mechanisms of competition and of the market, together with current national and international regulations, are capable of facilitating the positive convergence of labour rights and environmental protection.

---

[7] One of the causes of the acceleration of economic growth in developing countries during the last 20 years, more specifically since the end of the Uruguay Round and the creation of the WTO, has been their substantially greater participation in world trade.

First, the norms of labour law and trade-union freedom, which are by now a legal patrimony of all humanity, must be respected and implemented everywhere. In recent years, the international community has also been developing an important environmental legal corpus that still needs to be strengthened, respected and applied everywhere. In addition, at various national and international levels, there is ongoing reflection on the social and environmental responsibility of companies and other economic operators, which should be promoted and whose conclusions should be applied.[8]

Environmental protection and labour law must always promote the growth of all citizens' dignity and wellbeing in all States, adapting to the structural conditions of the poorest countries and to the heterogeneity of social situations without, however, justifying any attempts at protectionism.

4.4 Work: An Essential Element of Human Dignity, Beyond Any Sort of Exploitation

Today's social surveys confirm what the Social Doctrine of the Church has always affirmed: access to work which is useful, meaningful and adequately remunerated is natural to man and essential for a dignified life. Unemployment, or lack of decent work, is accordingly one of the most serious consequences of an economic system disconnected from human dignity. Beyond the high economic costs of such situations, the most dramatic social and personal damage, on the part of those who lack access to decent work, is the loss of their sense of dignity and self-esteem.

---

[8] One may think, for example, of a tax on the demand side that favours products from businesses with high social and environmental stewardship (initiatives such as the Social Business Initiative in the EU), or rules for access to contracts that set minimum thresholds of social environmental and fiscal responsibility. One could also stimulate the growth of a market of information on the social, environmental and fiscal quality of businesses that would allow citizens to favour those enterprises which best create socially, environmentally and fiscally sustainable value.

The growth in value and productivity generated by technological progress, which often eliminates many jobs, must be accompanied by prudent political orientations in order to create new job opportunities not only in the for-profit sector but also in non-profit areas (science, art, religion, local and international services and development, protection and repair of the environment, etc.). An essential component of such guidelines should be a marked improvement both quantitative and qualitative in access to education at all levels.

The defence and protection of decent work cannot be left to market forces alone. One can look again to the previously mentioned polyarchic governance which, in this case, would seek the right balance between capital and labour, thanks also to the indispensable help of responsible business and union organisations.[9]

4.5 Taxation

Taxes, duties, tariffs, and other indirect levies are used to finance public institutions and activities for the common good and can also serve as a means for correcting or adjusting the processes of financial, commercial and labour-market globalisation. Taxation not oriented towards the common good, however, can create artificial and unfair advantages in international trade, and promote international financial speculation and the exploitation of labour.

It is urgent to carry out initiatives that ensure appropriate fiscal transparency nationally and internationally, so as to discourage tax avoidance and evasion, which result in unfair competition between small/medium-sized businesses and large ones. In addition to traditional legal systems of oversight and enforcement of tax laws, it would be helpful to create mechanisms that transform fiscal responsibility into a competitive

[9] Cfr. Benedict XVI, Encyclical Letter *Caritas in Veritate*, 25 and 64.

advantage rather than its opposite,[10] while at the same time promoting responsible public and private consumption.

5. Towards Renewed International Financial Institutions

One of the major paradoxes of the globalised economy and finance is the political inability to foresee and govern the fluctuations in domestic and international markets that have significant world consequences, even for those countries not involved in the concrete finance activities and for the poorest populations. The global financial architecture has to be rethought. International financial organisations, in harmony with governments, must play a prominent role in the governance of international finance in order to mitigate negative externalities and allow the "internalisation" of positive outcomes, adopting a vision of the economy and of development founded on the primacy of the human person.

6. The Perspective of the Social Doctrine of the Church

A new ethical perspective on the world economy, constructed from an integral vision of man, involves a constant effort to overcome the reductionisms of man, of socio-economic organisations, and of values. This requires going beyond the thinking that relies on mere technological development ("laissez-faire") and on the self-regulation of systems to resolve world economic problems, or on neo-statist approaches which require strong and exclusive regulation at the national government level, converting people into simply passive subjects of the State.

---

[10] For example, once the required transparency in accounting were assured, it would be helpful to draw up a system for rating fiscal responsibility. Thus, market mechanisms (civic pressure from below) and institutional mechanisms (minimum levels of fiscal responsibility necessary for submitting tenders) could stimulate fiscal responsibility and turn it into a competitive advantage. Similar results can be obtained by establishing internal systems of fiscal compliance which, when oversight were not exercised, would render the companies or the internal comptrollers responsible for omissions and violations.

Integral and non-reductionist visions of man, such as proposed by the Social Doctrine of the Church, offer, instead, a fundamental guide for personal behaviour, for collective action, and for policy, in order to build up a national and world economic governance centred on the dignity and responsibility of the human person, on solidarity and on the universal destination of goods.

6.1 Development, and the Protection of Human Dignity, as well as Institutional and Cultural Diversity, are Prior and Superior to the Market

Economic estimates and national and international government planning must start from the recognition of the diversity of practices and various types of institutions, result of human dignity and freedom. Global economic thinking based only on free trade or, contrariwise, on a statist view with totalitarian tendencies, will be in irreconcilable conflict with cultural and institutional diversity and will tend to cancel such diversity out, because the only value is to maximise the flow of goods and services and their profits, or otherwise nationalism and class struggle. Therefore, it is necessary to defend all those social forms – the fruit of solidarity and subsidiarity, including social entrepreneurial or community entrepreneurship – which represent a value in themselves, over and above their monetary value on the market or their utility for a social goal defined *a priori*. The market, including the global market, should become that space where local varieties can express themselves, interact and be improved, rejecting a deterministic and reductionist vision of man and of society.

6.2 Application of the Principle of Subsidiarity at the Transnational Level

Organisations of civil society including trade unions – characterised by their associative nature, not founded on profit and representing the rich variety of expressions of the human person – should be able to play a rightful role in monitoring the activities of international institutions and of multinational enterprises, in order to better promote a human and ecologically sustainable globalisation oriented towards real integral human development.

In this regard, we urge that amendments be agreed to the statutes of international financial organisations, founded to meet the post-World War II challenges, so that they become effective manifestations of the international community understood as the Family of Nations. These renewed international institutions should contribute to rewriting economic rules which convey the idea that efficiency is generated not only by private property and by free trade, but also by policies that ensure competition, transparency, the transfer of technology, and *trust*, founded on a shared notion of the nature and dignity of man which should ground and orient all political and economic actions.

Everyone should agree that development must be equitable, democratic, sustainable, and at the service of the integral dignity of the human person and of families. For the orientation of their actions and for scientific analysis, the agencies of development assistance, international financial institutions and the academic sector, should therefore be encouraged to include and use, among their benchmarks, indicators of the distribution of human wealth, of integral human development, of respect for the environment and of local characteristics.

No single global and comprehensive legal system exists, nor does any global government; given the vast richness and diversity of human beings, it seems difficult that such could ever exist. Nevertheless, this unlikelihood should not make it impossible to conceive of global regulatory regimes involving a multiplicity of actors such as intergovernmental organisations, non- governmental organisations and other international bodies or agencies: a true *polyarchy,* in other words, to deal effectively with issues and problems that cannot be addressed or resolved only by national governments.

Finally, patterns of life and personal consumption, social life, and international relations should be based on respect for a complete notion of human dignity and on the resulting promotion of integral human development and on the establishment of a culture of reciprocity, manifested also in economic organisations marked by reciprocity.

7. Conclusion

By way of overall conclusion, seeking to to humanise the economy must also entail an intrinsic requirement to **grasp transcendent dignity of every person, distinct yet inseparable in his/her relationality**. The reduction, by contrast, of human experience to what is "calculable" in utilitarian terms constitutes an *a priori* ideological view which that very experience contradicts.

Social life is much more than simple contractual relationships or hollow political constraints. It is the realisation of a range of values and culture expressed in a complex of social relationships (many of which also have economic value) hosted or at least protected by a complex of institutions. Such institutions preserve, increase and transmit those values, allowing for the building up of truly free people.

The reductionism of the person, of action and of economic values to egoism or selfishness, fails to appreciate social virtues such as trust, good will, reciprocity and cooperation, and depreciates them as mere inclinations of nature irrelevant to the building-up of civilisation. The technical narrowing of economic thought and the reduction of human sociability to the market allow a hegemonic expansion of purely economic relations, ignoring and destroying those relations which express the spiritual richness of the human person and of our sociability, history and culture. Likewise, political and economic action which, to be effective, needs to strip man of everything that cannot be marketed, opens the way to new forms of statism and tyranny. The great problems arising from globalisation can be solved, not in the theoretical radicalisation of neo-statism versus neo-liberalism, but in a healthy flowering of those forms of organisation which express the richness of human relationality and which can characterize a modern civil economy.

If economic and social research and their consequent political action would effectively address the old and new problems in our society, they can no longer confine themselves to a technical-mathematical approach of economic behaviour radically detached from every anthropological consideration. If the economy only continues to fortify its analytical and technical apparatus without overcoming its self-obsession (its reference only to itself), it will be less and less able to grasp reality effectively, and so to suggestive effective lines of action.

In summary, the message that the Social Doctrine of the Church wants to convey in the current debate about global economic governability is the following: market systems are, in essence, organised systems of values. Therefore, a culture of possessive individualism will produce different results from a culture of reciprocity in which individuals, even if motivated by personal interests, get involved in fraternal relationships; or a culture of cooperative competition will lead to different results from a culture of positional rivalry.

Consequently, the criticisms of Pope Francis of the current economic situation, in line with all of his Predecessors, consist of two major elements. On the one hand, today's situation of inequality and of exclusion is in no way acceptable and must be addressed with urgency and sincerity. On the other, social construction, of which the economy is just one component, is possible only on the basis of a culture and human action based on an anthropological perspective that recognizes the full dignity of the human person and all the values and virtues that from it flow.

THE GLOBAL COMMON GOOD: TOWARDS A MORE INCLUSIVE ECONOMY

Vatican, 11-12 July 2014

RESEARCH WORKING PAPER

DISCLAIMER: This Research Working Paper is an academic essay produced independently by Professors: Leonardo Becchetti from the University of Rome "Tor Vergata", Luigino Bruni from the University "Lumsa di Roma", André Habisch from the Catholic University of Eichstätt-Ingolstadt, and Stefano Zamagni from the University of Bologna and John Hopkins University, SAIS Europe. The essay does not necessarily represent the position of the Holy See. The Paper carries the names of the Authors and should be cited accordingly.

Edited by
Leonardo Becchetti
Luigino Bruni
André Habisch
Stefano Zamagni

0. Premise

History does not proceed "linearly". What we are experiencing now is truly an "exceptional" period in history. 23% of world output since the time of Christ's birth to the present was produced after the year 2000, and 28% of the "history of humanity" (if history is defined as the total number of years lived by all human beings who have ever appeared on earth) since the birth of Christ to the present was experienced in the last century. In almost all OECD countries, the period from 1970 to 2011 saw a spectacular increase in life expectancy of around ten years. Humanity seems to be on a launch pad. There is a high risk that this will become a tower of Babel destined to collapse unless we can accompany the irreversible nature of technological progress with an ability to manage these advances in a context of social and environmental sustainability and integral human development.

The phenomenon of globalisation and that of the third industrial revolution make it urgent and necessary to update our principles and values in the light of the *res novae* of a rapidly changing world. It is because of today's desperate quest for novelty and change that we feel the need for reflection in order to develop and follow up on the insights that Pope Francis has drawn together in the exhortation *Evangelii Gaudium*. The Pope sought to shake the conscience of humanity regarding the scandalous situation in which, although the potential of humanity continues to grow, yet we have not succeeded in breaking down certain disgraceful structures that humiliate the dignity of human beings. Our attention is called to avoid the tendency to find comfort in the erroneous belief that the splendid destiny of progress in markets and finance is almost certain to lead us towards a better future. The economy does not run on autopilot, and Adam Smith's "invisible hand" that would reconcile the sum of individual self-interests with the common good is valid under conditions that are so hard to satisfy that they have practically never been met. Even competition, although it brings benefits to consumers, is not the natural outcome of the interaction of market forces but is achievable only through action by the appropriate authorities to combat the slide towards oligopolistic concentration.

That is why Pope Francis warns us that "we can no longer trust in the unseen forces and the invisible hand of the market". He declares his opposition to "ideologies which defend the absolute autonomy of the marketplace and financial speculation". On this point we read in *EG*: "*In this context, some people continue to defend trick-*

le-down theories which assume that economic growth, encouraged by a free market, will inevitably succeed in bringing about greater justice and inclusiveness in the world. This opinion, which has never been confirmed by the facts, expresses a crude and naive trust in the goodness of those wielding economic power and in the sacralised workings of the prevailing economic system. Meanwhile, the excluded are still waiting". The moral consequence of this insidious determinism is the plague of moral indifference. *"To sustain a lifestyle which excludes others, or to sustain enthusiasm for that selfish ideal, a globalisation of indifference has developed. Almost without being aware of it, we end up being incapable of feeling compassion at the outcry of the poor, weeping for other people's pain, and feeling a need to help them, as though all this were someone else's responsibility and not our own".* The Pope also reminds us that *"as long as the problems of the poor are not radically resolved by rejecting the absolute autonomy of markets and financial speculation and by attacking the structural causes of inequality, no solution will be found for the world's problems or, for that matter, to any problems".*

In this context, the Church's social teaching provides a perspective that strives for an inclusive economy, supported by justice, and the culture of fraternity and reciprocity. With the enormous opportunities provided by technological progress and knowledge, if our societies are faithful to the ideal of the full development of the human person, then they can do better, much better. It is this that we wish to explore and consider on the eve of an important occasion like the target date for the Millennium Development Goals in 2015, and the launch of reflection to define the new Millennium Sustainable Goals that will indicate the direction and targets for the years to come.

1. Introduction

The economic system works with immense potentiality and redress mechanisms that are, however, not automatic. They work if activated with the right intention and appropriate levels of spiritual, physical, human and social "capital". The great global contradiction in history has been the rapid growth of affluence in some areas of the world but not in others that have remained cut off and at the margins. Globalisation has sparked this contradiction by transforming the misery of the latter into a threat to the affluence of the former. The transformation of markets from local to global and the possibility of near-instantaneous transfer of "weightless goods" (audio, data, images and money) from one place to another on the planet, means that one billion people living below the threshold of extreme poverty, with their low cost of labour, compete with workers in countries accustomed to living with much better wages and better safeguards. This gradually erodes those wages and safeguards. High-income countries, therefore, can no longer bail themselves out alone but need the poorest countries so that they can maintain their welfare and youth employment that are threatened by relocation and by the erosion of national production. That is why working for the deprived and efforts to promote their dignity is no longer the heroic choice of missionaries. It is necessary and urgent for all to defend the rights and protections that have been achieved. The good thing about globalisation is that it makes us more and more interdependent by uniting in a common destiny the rich, the emerging and the poor of the planet.

The opening of markets in itself and the related movement of capital and the often distressing movement of migrants have set in motion very slow mechanisms of convergence and adjustment. According to the principle of the "conditional convergence" theory (verified for the most part by econometric studies in recent decades), poor countries on average recover ground compared to rich countries if they can catch up in terms of conditional convergence factors such as education, social capital, infrastructure and physical capital, access to new technologies and quality of institutions. Average rates of global growth, for years higher in poor countries than in rich countries, confirm this trend. Even if things continue like this for many years, convergence would still take a very long time (many decades, and for larger gaps more than a century if we extrapolate the current growth rates, assuming that they will continue to be the same in the future). In addition, as noted, behind the average national income huge gaps lie concealed. In some cases they are increasing within a country between those who have high levels of education - and therefore have the absorptive capacity to allow them to master information, knowledge and technology - and those who are marginalised and excluded from the market. In the world today, the 85 richest people own assets that approximately equal those of the poorest half (3.5 billion) of the world population. Over the last ten years, five percent of the major income earners in the world (the booming global elite) have increased their income by 60%. Behind them we are witnessing the decline of the global middle class who are being pressed by the low labour costs of the relocating emerging global middle class. Last of all there are still one billion impoverished people living below the absolute poverty line ($1.35 a day) and altogether 2.7 billion who live on less than two dollars a day. *We cannot accept these figures if we are to avoid the globalisation of indifference.*

The crucial question of our time is, therefore, how long those at the bottom of the pile will have to wait in hope for adjustment mechanisms to be activated more vigorously through the commitment of virtuous citizens, businesses and institutions. The question in reality is much more complex. Emphasis on only one dimension of economic well-being can lead to unsustainable growth that brings about environmental disasters as we try to satiate our craving for more. No doctor can try to solve the problem of a limb by administering a medicine that damages other parts of the body and leads to death. Similarly, we can only think in a multi-dimensional perspective of creation with an economic value that is environmentally and socially sustainable. In this regard, we must rid ourselves of three reductionist views **of human beings, of business and of value**.

As to the first form of reductionism, we know that the economic and social sciences are unanimous in recognising that selfishness is a lower form of rationality with respect to cooperation. It is lower from the point of view of both economic fertility and human flourishing because a person's value lies in that person's belonging to networks of relationships. However, cooperation is not a foregone conclusion in interpersonal relationships because it requires the practice of social virtues that are not innate. Trust is a "social risk" because it means putting oneself in the hands of another and running the risk of being betrayed. To trust and to be trustworthy expose us to the risk of lack of reciprocation, and therefore they must be cultivated and supported. It is the primary responsibility of institutions and civil society to promote all initiatives that can encourage these virtues.

As for the second type of reductionism, we must not think of businesses as being production black-boxes. Productive organisations, as well as producing goods and services, also have a profound effect on the character of all those who have dealings with them: investors, employees, suppliers, local communities and consumers. The companies that move at the international level are driven by the pursuit of profit maximisation to locate in countries where the cost of labour and of environmental protection are lower. Meanwhile, international regulations and institutions that are able to find a new synthesis between individual interests and the common good, are still struggling to emerge. That is why civil society organisations and citizens' groups that carry out vicarious work by respecting a system of global rules that is not yet in place, are asking businesses to join in setting targets for social and environmental sustainability. This is to ensure that globalisation does not change from being a mechanism that produces upward convergence to a mechanism that generates a race to the bottom regarding rights and protection of labour and the environment. If companies play their role properly in the context of a transparent and competitive market, they create value for their stakeholders. We think of the businesses that operate in markets at the "base of the pyramid" (C.K. Prahalad) of the global distribution of income.

They meet the needs of poorer consumers that would otherwise remain unmet. In this respect new technologies can play a large role in the dissemination of information and the acquisition of new knowledge, as is the case with the spread of mobile phones among people in the most marginalised rural areas of the globe.

To address the third type of reductionism, it is necessary to redefine the concept of value in economics. The "Wealth of Nations", a modern Adam Smith would say today, is not merely the flow of goods and services produced in its territory in a given unit of time (GDP). It is rather the stock of spiritual, cultural, natural, economic and social goods which a given community can enjoy. The problem of the economic depression is serious as it greatly aggravates the issue of unemployment and debt, and so too are the risks of growing impoverishment that deplete the real wealth of the community by destroying those stocks. It is for this reason that it seems essential to continue to encourage all those efforts developed at transnational level as well as national to build new composite indicators to be used as reference for impact assessments, environmental and social, of economic policies.

In order to tackle the great problems of our time, it is therefore necessary to resolve the three reductionisms that prevent the release of the full potential and positive energy that people, communities and businesses can unleash in social and economic life. It is a case of helping the process of globalisation to fulfil its authentic vocation to the full: the joining of humanity as one family, rich in its diversity of cultures and differences but freed from appalling inequalities and from a lack of global institutional references. There would be a solid economic and social fabric capable of releasing individual potential according to the logic of the common good, a logic by which the fulfilment of each person is oriented to the development of the community.

In the chapters that follow, we shall detail aspects of this enormous project that involves all of us and in which we are all active participants. In the second chapter the present economic phase will be analysed from a historical perspective focused on the relationship between the market and institutions, a relationship that highlights the risk that the evolution of economic systems today may lose contact with their roots. In the third chapter we shall address the specific nodes of finance, commerce and work. In the fourth chapter we shall address the question of the functioning of international institutions and their reform. In the fifth there will be some concluding remarks.

2. To recover the historical roots of the market economy in order to civilise globalisation

"The channels of communication are not only physical, but moral, too. Straight, easy and safe roads: rivers, and ferry routes; utility work machines, these come first. But we need moral channels too" (Antonio Genovesi, Naples, 1765).

Our time is characterised by extraordinary growth in wealth and technology, unknown to past generations. The human family has achieved huge successes in combating deprivation, in the dissemination of information worldwide, and in life expectancy, wealth and education. At the same time, if we compare our potential with our achievements, we cannot be satisfied at a time when almost one billion people, mostly located in sub-Saharan Africa, are still living in extreme poverty. Extreme poverty, misery, deprivation and exclusion have been the human condition for thousands of years, while welfare and prosperity have remained limited to a very small portion of the population to this day. What is no longer ethically acceptable nowadays, however, is the contrast between our impressive capacity to create wealth and resources and the still too high number of people excluded from the possibility of a decent life in terms of welfare and rights. In other words, the problem of inequality is at the heart of the social question today. This is the social justice that has been at the centre of the Social Doctrine of the Catholic Church from its earliest beginnings – *Rerum novarum*,

1891 – right up to recent documents like John Paul II's *Centesimus Annus* (1991), Benedict XVI's *Caritas in Veritate* (2009) and, finally, Pope Francis' *Evangelii Gaudium* (2013).

The market economy has been one of the main tools of social inclusion and democracy in past centuries, but in recent decades, due to the phenomenon of 'financialization', our economic system has been reducing its capacity to increase wealth and opportunities. Much of speculative finance is a network of zero-sum games, if not actual gambling, that deny the very nature of market interactions, namely that of a cooperative network of relationships of mutual benefit. This was pointed out by the great economists of the 17th to the 19th centuries such as Smith, Ricardo, J.S. Mill, Marshall, the Neapolitan Antonio Genovesi and many others.

2.1. Market and society. In the under-soil of our civil and economic culture there are two opposing growing trends. The first is a gradual rapprochement between the culture and languages of the many variants of the capitalist economy. The second trend, in contrast, is a growing opposition based on an ethical evaluation of the market. This leads some to see the capitalist market as the solution to all our economic and civil ills, while others consider it to be the cause of all moral, social and political evil.

The first would like a society that is led and managed only, or mainly, by market values and instruments (from the privatisation of common goods to the buying and selling of organs). Others would banish these values and instruments from all morally relevant areas of human life, and keep them controlled and restricted in size. With globalisation and the financial and economic crisis, this ideological confrontation that has lasted at least two hundred years has entered a new phase. We believe that the new synthesis and new constructive dialogue that we need are something different and are not ideological.

We should first recognise that the history of the real world has taught us that the real markets are much more vital, promiscuous, non-ideological and surprising than imagined and described in both views mentioned. The most significant and lasting economic experiences, those that have increased the true welfare of the people, democracy and the common good all over the world, were all experiences that arose from the market and from civil society. The real market worked well when it pervaded social spaces and when it learned to live in and include the peripheries. The great and long history of the relationship between markets and civil life, between contract and gift, is primarily a story of friendship and alliance.

2.2. Institutions matter. This working paper, then, is a call for a critical reflection on the relationship between market economy, wealth creation (and hence the vocation of entrepreneurship), poverty and inequality. The methodological starting point of our analysis is however, a positive attitude towards the market as an expression of creativity, freedom and, at least potentially, inclusion. At the same time, we believe that the market alone is not sufficient to ensure wealth creation and social justice, because this requires other equally essential principles and institutions, such as reciprocity (civil society) and the redistribution of wealth (government).

The market economy was the fruit and result of the encounter between Christianity, Judaism and Greek and Roman cultures. A key role was played by spiritual movements like the Franciscans and Dominicans. There was first the Catholic and later the Protestant "spirit". The market economy became a civil entity thanks to the interplay between the pursuit of individual interests and the action of institutions.

Nowadays the global market economy is suffering from a lack of proper economic and political institutions. The market itself is an institution, and it produces civil benefits if it is accompanied by other institutions. People's lives become poor and nations fall into decline when societies create, select and nurture "extractive" institutions, developing them and making them grow when there are already "inclusive" institutions present (Daron Acemoglu and James Robinson, *Why Nations Fail*, 2012).

On closer inspection, the boundary between extractive and inclusive institutions is not so sharp, because the two forms co-exist within the same community or nation, and, more importantly, they can be transformed from one form to another. In all societies there are institutions created for the sole purpose of looking after the interests of a few groups of people. However, it is still true that many institutions that start out inclusive become extractive with time, and institutions that are created extractive become inclusive. European history gives us clear examples of this, and the present situation of the financial market is equally eloquent.

2.3. Polyarchy and biodiversity. The market economy would never have emerged at the end of the Middle Ages without specific institutions: guilds, corporations, courts, banks, big fairs, abbeys and monasteries. Some of these were intentionally oriented towards the common good (brotherhoods, hospices for the poor, pawnshops...), but many others (like corporations) were created to protect and promote the interests of their members (bakers, shoemakers, apothecaries ...), and thus ensure monopoly revenues for certain classes of merchants.

The civil strength of urban communities succeeded, however, in turning the interests of individuals into the interests of many, and not infrequently of everyone. Many achievements of modernity, both political and civil, are the result of both extractive and inclusive institutions.

Many of the economic institutions are extractive and were originally closed, but it is their coexistence with other political, civil, cultural and religious institutions that often opens them up and elevates their original interests. The common good requires more than altruism, benevolence and philanthropy. The *"Wisdom of the Republics"*, as the philosopher Giambattista Vico pointed out, lies primarily in being able to create institutional mechanisms capable of transforming even private interests into the Common Good.

This alchemy of interests in the common good, however, works only when there are many other diverse institutions, in a social and political context characterised by what Pope Benedict XVI's *Caritas in Veritate* called an "institutional polyarchy" (CV 57). The "plurality of institutional forms of business" and financial institutions, furthermore, are also essential for the accomplishment and for the freedom of the market (CV 47).

Economic and financial *biodiversity* is essential for fertility and wealth just as diversity is essential in biology. In fact, institutions are likely to become extractive and not become inclusive if there is no pluralism of institutions, if no new institutions come into being or if they are not placed next to all the others.

The "lodge of the merchants", the palace of the "captains of the people" and the convent of Saint Francis often took up the different sides of the same square in the European Middle-Age cities. Each developed in contact with the others, without mergers, confusion or incorporation. Democracy, welfare and rights emerged from this constant mutual exchange, clashes and control, and from the co-existence of peers in the same square. Today, the global economic institutions are experiencing a strong extractive drift because other global institutions, whether political, cultural or spiritual, are having less contact with them on a reciprocal basis.

2.4. Time. Finally, institutions were, in all civilisations, the main guardians or "keepers" of time. In the relay race of generations, when the race is over, institutions allow for yet another goal to be reached, ensuring that the rules of the game are respected and maintained, that there is reason to continue to run and that the passage of time continues to make sense (that is, to have direction and meaning).

These institutions, including the economic ones, had and still have an important role. Banks, for example, were the transmission belt of wealth and employment between the generations.

They knew how to preserve and increase the value of time. When banks go astray, the value of time is forgotten. It is no longer served, but rather used for speculative purposes. Banks thus tend to act "against nature" and damage the Common Good, both yesterday and today.

Today, however, we are experiencing *an eclipse of time*. The logic of the capitalist economy and its culture that is undisputedly dominating much of social and political life, do not know the dimension of time. Their cost-benefit analyses cover just a few days, months or a few years - under the most generous assumptions. A radical tendency of our financial capitalism is in fact the progressive shortening of the time period available to make economic choices, and therefore to choose policies that are increasingly driven by the same economistic culture.

The industrial revolution first, and then the computer and finally the financial revolution, subtracted time from economic choices, until they had reduced the time needed for some highly speculative operations to fractions of a second.

The depth of time from where we come (history) and where we are bound (the future) is absent from our economic culture. As a result it is also missing from our civic culture, from the training of economists and from the education system: "*People live poised between each individual moment and the greater, brighter horizon of the utopian future as the final cause which draws us to itself. Here we see a first principle for progress in building a people: time is greater than space*". (Pope Francis, *Evangelii Gaudium*, 222).

In the global financial economy the new "lodges of the merchants" have grown too much. They have bought the neighbouring buildings. If economic institutions are left to themselves in the global village, they will eventually be the only inhabitants of squares that in turn will become increasingly more deserted. We must fill our global village squares with new institutions again if we want to see new welfare, new social inclusion and new democracy.

2.5. Globalisation and humanising markets. It is certainly true that globalisation is a positive-sum game that increases aggregate wealth. However, it is also true that it exacerbates the contrast between winners and losers. This fact is linked to the emergence of a new form of competition, unknown until recently: positional competition, according to which the "winner takes all and the loser loses everything" – the so-called "superstar effect" as understood by Shermin Rose. Why is literature on the subject so hotly divided? A credible answer comes from a recent work by Branko Milanovic (2011) who distinguishes between *world* and *international* inequality.

International inequality considers the differences in the average incomes of various countries, unweighted ("1st concept of inequality" according to Milanovic) and duly weighted to account for the size of the population ("2nd concept of inequality"). World inequality, on the contrary, also takes into account the inequalities in income distribution within the individual countries ("3rd concept of inequality"). Well, it is world or global inequality that is increasing as a consequence of globalisation. Indeed, in order to decrease the 3rd concept of inequality, two conditions must be met: I) poor and densely populated countries must grow at a faster rate than rich countries; II) this must occur without causing an increase in inequality within these countries.

Now, while the first condition is more or less satisfied, the second condition is virtually absent. In fact, over the last quarter of a century, the growth rate of the poorest countries has been higher than that of the richest countries (4% versus 1.7%). So why should we be concerned about the growth of global inequality? It is because it is a principal cause of conflict and ultimately of civil war. Conflict can be visualized as "trade gone awry". If a country's gains from trade are not as high as that country thinks it should receive, this becomes a major determinant of conflict, which might in the end jeopardise peace itself. That is why the search for a system that integrates socially responsible trade, one that is also capable of taking into consideration the "pains from trade" (Verdier, 2005), is a duty from which responsible people must not escape.

A related aspect concerns the relationship between globalisation and poverty. Over the past two decades, poor countries have increased their participation in world trade, so much so that to-day they can be said to be more globalised than rich countries. Yet, there is very little evidence to prove this relationship and even the scanty evidence available only indirectly deals with the link between globalisation and poverty.

Three general propositions deserve special attention: a) contrary to the Heckscher-Ohlin theory of international trade, the poor in countries with a lot of unskilled labour do not typically gain from trade expansion; b) globalisation generates both winners and losers among the poor and this creates social instability to the extent that it destroys social cohesion: c) the poor segments of the population obtain the largest benefits from globalisation when national governments endeavour to enhance welfare policies aimed at improving the capabilities of life of their citizens, rather than improving merely their living conditions.

Humanise the market, don't demonise it: this is the slogan that describes the challenge confronting us to-day. That is why we cannot consider any solution to the many and grave problems now afflicting our societies that would delegitimize the market as a social institution. If people continue to demonise the market, it really will become hell. So, the real challenge is the humanisation of the market. The Social Doctrine of the Church will never be able to accept any step backwards in this regard. Those who cultivate the concept of time as *kairos*, and not merely as *chronos*, know that difficulties are surmounted by transforming visions of the future into reality – and not with operations that would wind back the clock of history. Although the temptation to return to times gone by is understandable, it certainly cannot be justified by those who fully embrace an anthropology based on the human person. While they reject individualism, they can never pass over to the opposite side of communitarianism. In both cases the final outcome would be nihilism.

3. Finance. Trade. Work.

3.1 Finance

Finance is a tool that has tremendous potential for the proper functioning of economic systems. Good finance allows savings to be pooled in order to use them efficiently and allocate them to the most profitable uses; it transfers the value of assets in space and in time; it implements insurance mechanisms that reduce exposure to risk; it allows those who have disposable income but not productive ideas to meet with those who, conversely, have productive ideas but no funding. Without this coming together, the creation of economic value of a community would remain in a state of potentiality.

Unfortunately, the finance with which we are dealing today has largely escaped from our control. Financial intermediaries often fund only those who already have money (as they can put up collateral equal to or greater than the amount of the loan requested). The vast majority of derivative instruments were constructed potentially to achieve insurance benefits, but instead they are bought and sold for very short-term speculative motives with the opposite result. Paradoxically, they put at risk the survival of the institutions that have them in their portfolio. Systems that use asymmetric incentives for managers and traders (with profit sharing, bonuses and stock options and no penalty in case of losses) are constructed in such a way that they encourage people to take excessive risks. This makes the organisations for which they work structurally fragile and at risk of failure. A further element of dangerous instability is given by the tendency of these organisations to aim for profit maximisation (which is not the same as seeking to attain lawful and reasonable profit) because they place the well-being of shareholders over that of all other stakeholders. Banks that maximise profit through distorted incentives will find it increasingly profitable to channel resources to the business of speculative trading or to activities whose rates of returns are greater than those in lending activities.

The evolution of finance in recent decades has made it clearer than ever before that markets, especially where the returns to scale are increasing, do not at all tend spontaneously towards competitiveness but towards oligopoly. Indeed, the gradual easing of rules and forms of control (such as that on the separation between investment banking and commercial banking), have gradually led to the creation of an oligopoly of intermediary banks too big to fail and too complex to be regulated. The illusion of regulators has therefore produced a serious problem of balance of power for democracy itself. The *Corporate Europe Observatory*[1] issued a report in 2014 that highlights the imbalance of power relations between the financial lobbies and those of civil society and NGOs: the finance lobby spends 30 times more than any other industrial pressure groups (according to conservative estimates, they spend 123,000,000 euro per year with about 1,700 lobbyists in the EU). The relationship between the representation of financial lobbies and the representation of NGOs or trade unions in consultation groups are 95 to 0 in the stakeholder group of the ECB and 62 to 0 in the *de Larosière Group on financial supervision in the European Union*.

This dominance of finance not only in terms of lobbying power but also in ease of access to information, knowledge and technologies has enabled the managers of large financial oligopolies to appropriate huge revenues at the expense of all other stakeholders. In confirmation of how this all distorts the use of resources, there is the recent abandonment of infrastructure projects that would have enabled better mobility of vehicles and people. And, compared to this, the recent construction of a tunnel between New York and Chicago that cost hundreds of millions of dollars in order to reduce by three milliseconds the trading time of some operators that benefit from the laying of the cable to achieve an information advantage that is to the detriment of others.

[1] http://corporateeurope.org/sites/default/files/attachments/financial_lobby_report.pdf.

The disasters produced by this kind of finance are obvious to all. In a recent working paper of the International Monetary Fund,[2] Laeven and Valencia calculate this effect, following the crisis of 2007, to be an increase in the debt / GDP ratio of 70 percentage points in Iceland and Ireland and more than 20 percentage points in Greece, Germany, UK, Belgium and the Netherlands. In Italy, the impact has been more limited (8%), but the risks are very high given the levels of the Italian public debt. It is also estimated that the financial crisis has caused a gap of 65 billion dollars in the budgets of low-income countries.[3] No one can have any doubt that this model of finance is largely ineffective as well as harmful (as evidenced by the authoritative reports by Vickers in the UK and Liikanen in the European Union). Reforms have been introduced out of necessity.

First, there has been a return to the separation between commercial banking and investment banking. This is to ensure a sacrosanct greater transparency and effectiveness of monetary policy to stimulate the economy. It is not acceptable for banks to use the resources of depositors in high-risk proprietary trading operations when depositors believe that they have been made available for lending. It is not effective stimulation of monetary policies when central banks provide ample liquidity in the banking system for the provision of credit to businesses when this cash is used for speculative transactions. Countries like the USA, UK, France and Germany have moved in this direction with laws ranging from the prohibition on proprietary trading to rules on ring-fencing between commercial divisions and trading divisions, but such laws remains at the moment largely irrelevant because of the deadlock on im-

---

[2] Fabian Valencia & Luc Laeven, 2012. "Systemic Banking Crises Database: An Update". IMF Working Papers 12/163, International Monetary Fund.
[3] http://www.oxfam.org/en/policy/impact-global-financial-crisis-budgets-low-income-countries.

plementation regulations.[4] Forms of bank bailouts based on the socialisation of losses borne by taxpayers are not fair. That is why we talk about the primary responsibility of the bank stakeholders (shareholders, bondholders and depositors). On the other hand, it is equally unfair to make depositors responsible, as they are often unaware of the fact that the banks are dedicated to speculative trading instead of traditional banking activities.

Second, reform is needed in the systems of remuneration of managers and traders, not only for reasons of equity, but also in order to defuse the incentive for excessive risk-taking that jeopardises the stability of the system.

Third, it is essential to complete initiatives already started that ensure appropriate fiscal transparency through country by country reporting mechanisms so as to discourage tax evasion and avoidance. The OECD has calculated that tax avoidance leads to unfair competition between small and medium-sized businesses and large enterprises, resulting in a higher tax burden for the former as they do not manage to exploit the mechanisms of circumvention. Once the necessary accounting transparency is secured, it would be useful to establish the rating charts of fiscal responsibility in order to stimulate it through market mechanisms (pressure from citizens at the grassroots) and institutional mechanisms (minimum levels of fiscal responsibility required to participate in invitations to tender), and to turn it into a competitive factor. Similar results can be achieved through the mandatory integration of internal offices for tax compliance that, in case of lack of vigilance, would make companies or internal auditors more directly responsible for violations and omissions.

Fourth, it is essential to define rules that restore the balance of power and the representation of interests of different pressure groups in order to avoid the excesses referred to above. The rules

[4] http://www.astrid-online.it/Regolazion/Atti-dell-/STRUCTURAL/ Comm-UE_SWD_resilience_transparency-impact- assessment_en.pdf.

define equal representation in the organs of consultation and establish maximum limits on the number of lobbyists who may have access to the institutions.

Fifth, it is necessary to discourage, with fiscal mechanisms such as a small tax on financial transactions at global level, the impatient and high-frequency trading of financial capital that produces continuous disturbances on the markets by linking the dynamics of price sensitive sectors, such as those of raw materials, to speculative factors that are completely disconnected from the real dynamics. This produces financial bubbles and crises. On this point it should be emphasised that efficiency and speed of transactions are values but not ultimate ends, insofar as they must be in tune with the superior and higher-level values of precaution, stability and the common good. Nobody would suppose that the purpose of traffic laws is to maximise the velocity of circulation, and likewise the objective of financial regulation cannot be the maximisation of the speed of trade and the infinite increase in (in most cases apparent) liquidity.

It is not a case of setting good finance against bad finance, or of granting certificates for ethical behaviour to deserving operators. It is to understand that finance can and should do better, much better, to serve people and the common good, by returning to its original purpose.

3.2 Trade

Trade has always been considered to be an instrument of rapprochement between peoples. Economic theory teaches us that through trade you can overcome the limitations of autocracies by allowing each region to specialise in those activities that enhance its *genius loci*. Meeting, exchange and specialisation in turn determine the efficiency gains that enable better use of resources. As it unfortunately has happened with other sectors of the economy, in this one too the instruments of trade per se that are providentially placed at the service of human beings, are becoming oppressive idols when they are made absolute and when they are subordinated to partisan values and needs. From this point of view it seems appropriate to seriously revise the rules of free trade agreements.

This is to ensure that free trade does not become a goal to which labour rights and environmental sustainability are sacrificed rather than a means that should promote the rights and empowerment of each person.

As previously noted, the fundamental problem of the global economic system is the imbalance in living standards that automatically translate into imbalance in labour costs between different areas of the globe. The presence of hundreds of millions of people living on less than a dollar a day and billions of people living on less than two dollars a day is a formidable reservoir of cheap labour that businesses often have the urge to use and so reduce costs by outsourcing parts of their supply chain. The bottom line today is therefore to check whether the spontaneous mechanisms of competition and the market (relocation, price competition) and the policy rules of national and international institutions are capable of producing mechanisms of upward convergence of labour rights and care of the environment by ensuring social and environmental sustainability.

In order to trigger virtuous mechanisms, the spontaneous force of the relationship between demand and supply of labour is not enough, even though in some areas important processes of wage growth have been initiated due to the process of productive delocalisation. Because there is, and always will be, a worker who is poorer and able to compete with a richer one, it is necessary and appropriate to accompany these automatic mechanisms with regulations that can accelerate upward convergence. Take, for example, a tax system on the demand side that awards the products offered for sale which come from sectors with high social and environmental responsibility while penalising those that have been obtained through below minimum acceptable standards (as urged by initiatives such as that of the Social Business Initiative in the EU).[5] There could also be regulations for access to public procurement which set minimum thresholds for social, environmental and fiscal responsibility in order to be allowed to compete. It is also necessary to stimulate the growth in marketing information on social, environmental and corporate tax quality of companies that would allow citizens to "vote with their wallet". This would reward those companies at the forefront of efficiency in multiple dimensions, or businesses that are leaders in the creation of economic value that is socially, environmentally and fiscally sustainable.

We know that there are responsible business people operating in various parts of the world who are struggling to define quality standards in the way in which the production process is organised and in the way in which people compete in the market arena. There are also business people (such as the new generation of impact investors) who go further and try to be agents of change for a more inclusive economy and creators of true social innovation for the benefit of the entire community. It is time to recognise their leading role, and awareness of their efforts should reach broad sectors of public opinion. Above all, there should be support, in various forms, for business associations that, despite many difficulties and often misunderstandings, aim to put into practice *The Vocation of Business Leaders* (2012). It is certainly true that virtue is more contagious than vice, but this happens – as Aristotle would say – when virtue is made known.

3.3 Work

The availability of more extensive information on subjective data, such as life satisfaction, makes it possible today to substantiate with empirical evidence aspects unexplored until recently by socio-economic surveys. Research on the determinants of life sat-

---

[5] http://ec.europa.eu/internal_market/social_business/index_en.htm

isfaction gives ample confirmation of the existence of a sort of natural law with regard to the key factors for the flourishing of human life. Of these, the most important appears to be the condition of unemployment. An equally important fact is that these studies show that the cost of unemployment in terms of unhappiness is certainly higher than the wages earned. This is demonstrated by all those cases in which redundant workers reject as unsatisfactory the offer of financial compensation equal to their wages made by employers who are called by the courts to reinstate the workers to their original occupation. What the unemployed lose, in addition to salary, is their self-esteem and social reputation. For this reason, one of the priorities that the organisation of economic life in a global society must set is the creation of conditions for full employment.

The obstacles are many. The first pitfall is paradoxically technological progress as it increases the productivity of capital goods that save work. This unstoppable process is progressively reducing the demand for routine jobs for which increasingly intelligent machines can replace human work at a lower cost. At the same time, growth in value generated by productivity increases and by technological progress should allow for the creation of job opportunities in other sectors and in more creative and leisure activities. Until some time ago, there was optimism that the net balance between the creation of jobs in some sectors and the elimination of jobs in others would be positive. At this stage in which robotics has and will have a growing role and many capital goods will be able to function under the guidance of computer programs without (or with very limited) human intervention, that optimism is disappearing.

At the individual level the challenge posed by these changes is an increasing need for training. This is essential in order to escape from the trap of routine jobs that are in declining demand and subject to competition by reduced labour costs. It is needed in order to access "creative" jobs and to develop an absorptive capacity which is critical in order to take advantage of advances in technology. All efforts to remove barriers to access education, from primary to higher education, are therefore urgent and absolutely meritorious. At the aggregate level the challenge of creating jobs is achieved not only and not so much through the alchemy of contractual forms that promote higher or lower rigidity in the creation and destruction of jobs. It is done by supporting investment in infrastructure and removing all the obstacles that make it especially difficult to create social businesses. From this point of view, the most important factors are efficiency in civil justice, a reduction in the costs of bureaucracy and access to network technologies.

A commitment to increasing the number of jobs is not enough if it is achieved through the creation of temporary jobs. These offer little dignity and only increase the worrying phenomenon of the working poor. Another crucial factor to consider is that of the quality of the job. This includes, in addition to salary, a number of important factors such as the physical quality of the work environment, human relationships with colleagues, creativity of the work, and the possibility of harmonising time at work and time for family life.

We must not leave the defence and protection of the dignity of work to market forces alone. The one market mechanism that could promote growth in salaries and quality (labour demand exceeding supply) only works in some limited circumstances, and certainly cannot function when there is a giant "reserve army" of the needy who live below the absolute poverty line. Similarly, globalisation often makes national laws for the protection of the dignity of labour ineffective. Paradoxically, it risks causing greater difficulties in countries that raise the bar for rights and protections thus increasing the likelihood of businesses relocating that hitherto had been producing on the territory. We stress once again the need to integrate both incentives for responsible consumers and public rules (access to contracts, tax rewards for socially responsible supply chains) that can foster processes from the bottom up (and not from top to bottom) in terms of the dignity of labour.

The aim of economic activity is not free trade per se to which labour rights and people's rights are sacrificed. Furthermore, rewarding supply chains that are socially and environmentally sustainable should not overlook the protectionist intent of rich countries towards poor countries. It should rather promote growth in dignity and well-being at work of everyone in all countries. Human beings are the same everywhere in the world! In building a system of regulations and rewards, it is advisable to define standards of quality of work that are modulated to take account of the starting positions of the various countries and the diversity of living conditions and purchasing power in different parts of the world.

4. On the "res novae" of present times: consequences for institutional design

4.1. The old international economic order

For some decades now, society has been undergoing continuous change at an increasing pace, both in developed and in emerging and developing countries. We have seen interrelations between people and nations multiply at a growing rate, changes in power balances between countries and blocs, new armed conflicts and terrorist threats, the intensification of migration, a deep financial and economic recession, proposals to reappraise the state's role and suggestions for a new range of corporate social responsibilities, demands for new human rights, a growing awareness of the effects of poverty and economic inequality, and new ways of thinking about leadership in our world.

All of this is changing our view of the sciences that we usually describe as social or human: economics, sociology, social psychology, history, law, political science, human geography, demographics and philosophy.

This change is taking place at an increasing rate due to the multiplication of events that overlap and interfere with each other, calling for a rapid response from experts, politicians and social leaders. Against this background, it is a fact that social scientists – with certain exceptions – continue to be influenced by great ideas developed in the past as well as by the grand narratives of times gone by. Confusion and often despondency result when they realise that the "old" categories of thought and traditional research approaches no longer apply today. Too often, because of mental laziness, and perhaps also for the defense of vested interests, they rely on representations of a reality that has become obsolete. It is a case, then, of resuming the journey with a spirit of humility – there are no definitive and objectively true answers in the social sciences – and above all with willingness to be open to interdisciplinary and intercultural debate, without preconceived exclusions for reasons of "political correctness".

The emergence of a global economic order is the most characteristic feature of our age. As already mentioned, globalisation entails many dimensions, and the most relevant is the creation of a global financial market. The increasing importance of the financial structure compared to the real situation of the economy is posing a new paradox. At a time when we would need more regulation, precisely because financial markets are intrinsically unstable, we have less. This is because international financial institutions are weaker, in relative terms, than the domestic ones, or even non-existent.

An important implication of the paradox noted above is revealed by the recent financial crisis. It has shown its peculiar nature that reflects a new characteristic in international capital transactions. Although capital and goods markets are increasingly integrated, policy has largely remained a national matter. Most scholars see the importance of institutions in the new global financial environment. The need to introduce a new global financial architecture can be seen as a first step towards the regulation of the international monetary system.

Indeed, the conditions under which institutions such as the World Bank and the IMF were founded no longer exist. There are structural flaws in the current system which was originally designed in 1944 at Bretton Woods for the Western world (and not for developing countries) to regulate the current account imbalances. Yet there are too many different ideas on what institutions should be, what they should do and how they should do it. The frequency and magnitude of international financial crises testify to the huge asymmetry existing between an increasingly sophisticated, yet unstable, international financial system, and the institutions that regulate it. The world lacks the kind of institutions that financial globalisation requires. The case for the provision of emergency lending by the international financial community, such as the International Monetary Fund (IMF), can be addressed on a theoretical basis.

More generally, a world in which large nations direct their macroeconomic policies to domestic goals (and can afford to do so), and where markets are integrated, generates *externalities* for third countries, especially for the smaller developing economies. It is crucial that international economic organisations, international financial institutions in particular, play a leading role in *internalising* the positive *externalities* and in mitigating the negative ones.

4.2. In search of new institutions

A pragmatic contradiction should be noted at this stage. The proposals so far submitted for a new international financial system, while they assign to the G8 a major role in the steering of the monetary system, they do not contemplate any form of policy coordination, not to mention cooperative behaviour, among the G8 members themselves. Yet, it cannot be denied that the international repercussions of the domestic policies of the largest countries are a major determinant of financial stability.

The rise in economic interdependence, associated with globalisation, means that even large segments of a population may be adversely affected by events that have occurred in 'distant' places. For example, side by side with the well known 'depression famines', contemporary reality has also experienced 'boom famines'. The expansion of the scope of the market – in itself a positive phenomenon – means that the capacity of a social group to gain access to food depends, often in an essential way, on what other social groups do. For example, the price of a primary commodity can also depend on what happens to the price of other products. The nation state, by adopting wrong economic policies, can undermine the capacity of certain sections of the population to gain access to food (the Soviet famine of the 1930s and that of Cambodia at the end of the 1970s are clear examples of this).

In short, it should be recognised that today's major social and economic problems are more a question connected to institutional structures than to the lack of resources and know-how. The institutions that are involved are not only economic institutions but also political and juridical institutions. To recognise this means to increase our responsibilities, since institutions are made by human beings. History has shown that a new international order has always been established at the end of a war for supremacy.

We can see the example of the Thirty Years War, the Napoleonic Wars and the Second World War. All of these are events that, after destroying the old order, left behind *tabulae rasae*, on which the victorious powers were able to inscribe the rules of the new order. No such situation exists today.

Firstly, there is no agreement on who actually won the Cold War (assuming that there was a winner). Secondly, there is no agreement on whether we are living in a unipolar or multipolar world, or on which countries should be counted among the great powers today. There is no agreement because we are still far from defining the yardsticks for qualification as a great power.

Another important feature of this age is the number of *agents* that are seeking to play a major part in the process of building the foundations of a new international order. One might say that international affairs have become a 'participatory democracy' issue, which helps to explain why it is becoming increasingly difficult to reach an agreement quickly. Bretton Woods and the Uruguay Round are a case in point. Bretton Woods was completed in a few months with the decisive impulse of two men (J.M. Keynes and H.D. White), while the Uruguay Round took ten years of bitter negotiations among a dozen major parties plus about 100 international governments in the background.

A third feature that is unambiguously typical of the present phase in our history is the radical change that has occurred in the international distribution of economic and military power. For over three centuries the international system was dominated by the Western powers, with the centre of gravity in the North Atlantic. Even the Cold War was a struggle between two 'visions' belonging to the same European civilisation. Today, economic power has shifted towards the Pacific and East Asia areas that are now becoming the centre of gravity of world history, for better or for worse. This means that the emerging Asian powers will increasingly demand a part in designing international institutions.

But these (such as the United Nations Security Council, the World Bank, the IMF, etc.) are dominated by the ideas and the interests of the Western powers that are not doing enough to redress a situation that has now become untenable. As always occurs in international relations, where power and authority coincide, the emerging powers, dissatisfied with the status quo, are doing everything they can to change the situation.

These considerations lead us to address the vast issue of cultural relations in the global village. How are we to distinguish between cultural interaction and cultural imperialism? How can we organise cultural diversity so as to prevent a breakdown in communications and the development of potentially closed communities? The mismatch between centripetal globalisation processes and centrifugal isolation processes, and between interaction and fragmentation, is certainly a danger and threatens to undermine the common destiny of the whole of humanity. It is not enough merely to condemn different forms of 'fundamentalism' without asking how these have come about and without seeking to look at the dark side of our Western universalism.

4.3. The perspective of Catholic Social Teaching

So what is to be done? There is a variety of different ways to respond to the challenges of the twenty-first century.

There is the way that we might call 'laissez-faire fundamentalism' that advocates a plan for technological transformation driven by self-regulating systems, with the abdication of politics and above all with the loss of any possibility of collective action. It is not difficult to see the risks of authoritarianism, resulting from the democratic deficit, that are inherent in such an approach.

A second way is the neo-statist approach which postulates a strong demand for regulation at the level of national government. The idea here is to revive, albeit partially renovated and streamlined, the areas of public intervention in the economy and in social spheres. However, it is clear that this would not only produce undesirable effects but could even lead to disastrous consequences in the case of countries in transition. Indeed, the implementation of new free-market policies would, under current conditions, damage the already low levels of prosperity in developing countries.

Lastly, there is the strategy favoured by Catholic Social Teaching. (It may be of interest to recall that for centuries, the Catholic Church used the expression *doctrina civilis* to refer to teachings about the economic and political order. It was only after the pontificate of Leo XIII that *doctrina civilis* become *doctrina socialis*). What are the distinctive features of this approach? Five pillars sustain it.

  a. Economic calculation is compatible with diversity of behaviour and types of institutions. It is therefore necessary to defend the weaker kinds of enterprises and to learn from them for the future. This means that the selection filter must certainly be present, but it should not be too fine, precisely in order to make it possible for any solution that exceeds a certain efficiency threshold to survive. The global market must therefore become a place in which local varieties can be improved, which means having to reject the determinist view, according to which there is only one way of operating in the global market.

It should not be forgotten that globalisation inevitably levels down all the institutional varieties that exist in every country. There is nothing surprising about this because the rules of free trade clash with cultural variety, and they consider institutional differences (for example: different welfare models, education systems, views of the family, the importance to be given to distributive justice, and so on) to be serious obstacles to their propagation. This is why it is essential to remain vigilant in order to ensure that the global market does not eventually constitute a serious threat to economic democracy.

b. The application of the principle of subsidiarity at the transnational level. This requires that the organisations of civil society be *recognised* and not *authorised* by states. These organisations should have a function that is more important than mere advocacy and denunciation; they should play a full role in monitoring the activities of transnational corporations and international institutions.

What does this mean in practice? Civil society organisations ought to play public roles and perform public functions. In particular, these organisations should bring pressure on the governments of major countries to get them to sign an agreement that is able to drastically curb the benefits resulting from the sudden withdrawal of capital from the developing countries.

c. Nation-states, particularly those belonging to the G8, must reach an agreement to modify the Constitutions and statutes of international financial organisations, thus superseding the *Washington Consensus* which was created during the nineteen-eighties following the Latin American experience. This ultimately entails writing rules that express the idea that efficiency is not only generated by private ownership and free trade, but also by policies such as competition, transparency, technology transfer policies and so on. Over-borrowing and domestic financial repression are the unfortunate consequences of the application of this partial, distorted and one- sided view of things.

It should be remembered that in a financially repressed economy, inflationary pressure drives a wedge between domestic deposits and loan interest rates. The result is that domestic enterprises are artificially induced to seek to borrow abroad, while domestic savers are encouraged to deposit their funds overseas.

d. The Bretton Woods institutions, the UNDP and the other international agencies should be encouraged by civil society organisations to include in their development parameters the indicators of the distribution of human wealth as well as the indicators of multidimensional wellbeing that take into account the concept of wealth of nations as presented in the introduction. (It includes not only economic goods, but also spiritual, cultural, environmental and relational goods). These indicators must be taken into adequate consideration, both in the elaboration of international rankings and when drafting intervention and assistance plans. Pressure should be brought to bear in order to gain acceptance for the idea that development must be *equitable, democratic and sustainable.*

It is the lack of institutions (not bureaucracies!) at the global level that makes so many problems of our age hard to solve, especially the environmental problem. As markets become more globalised, the transnational institutional landscape is still that of the immediate post-war world. One could argue that perhaps there are enough international treaties, and enough contracts at the domestic level to regulate relationships between individuals. The analogy is dangerously misleading, because contracts concluded within a country can be enforced by that country's national state, while there is no transnational authority capable of enforcing treaties between states.

On the whole, it is hard to see how the present state of affairs can continue. While the market, in its great variety of forms, has by now become global, the configuration of governments has remained essentially national or at the most international.

What is required is that *International Governmental Organization* (IGOs) be established by national governments. (An example of an intergovernmental network of national regulators is the Basel Committee on Banking Supervision, which includes representatives of 27 national banking supervisory authorities). The fact that there is no single global and comprehensive legal system, and no global government, does not imply that it would be impossible to conceive of global regulatory regimes made up of bodies such as IGOs and NGOs (*Non-governmental organizations*) that deal with issues and problems that cannot be addressed or resolved by national governments alone.

e. Finally, a rich fabric of non-utilitarian experiences should be created on which to base consumption patterns and, in more general terms, lifestyles that are capable of enabling a *culture of reciprocity* to take root. In order to be credible, values have to be practised and not only voiced. This makes it of paramount importance that those who agree to take the path towards a transnational civil society must undertake to create organisations with a *modus operandi* that hinges around the principle of reciprocity.

5. In conclusion

To conclude. We can say that the search for a way to humanise the economy in itself contains a question of a relational nature that should be carefully looked into and satisfied as well as possible, if we want to avoid far-reaching side effects. Indeed, the proper functioning of an economic system depends also on whether certain concepts and certain ways of life have achieved dominance or not. Individual behaviours are embedded in a pre-existing network of social relations that cannot be thought of as a mere constraint, as mainstream economists continue to argue. Rather, they are one of the driving factors that prompt individual goals and motivations.

It seems to us that the central problem in the current transition towards a post-Fordist society is to understand how to act so that individuals may be at liberty to decide on procedures for the supply of goods and services that they themselves require. What is at stake here is not so much freedom to decide the overall *composition* of goods to be produced (more private goods or more public goods; more commendable goods or more relational goods, etc.), but freedom to decide *how* that composition should be achieved. This is why we cannot depend on the efficiency principle alone in deciding what and how to produce.

Many admirers of the free market, understood as a social institution, seem to overlook the fact that it is the very hegemonic expansion of impersonal relations that slowly, but inexorably, is destroying the whole system of social norms and conventions that constitute a civil economy, thereby paving the way for the success of new forms of statism.

Today it is imperative that we admit that the hypertrophic growth of both the state and a market that excludes explains the many problems that cripple our societies. In a situation like this, the solution will not be found in the radicalisation of the public economy versus a private economy, or neo-statism versus neo-liberalism, but in a healthy flourishing of the forms of organisation that shape a modern civil economy.

The most damaging consequence of a narrow-minded (and obsolete) notion of market, still predominant to this day, is to lead us to believe that behaviour inspired by values other than the pursuit of self-interest relentlessly push the economy to disaster. By en-

L

couraging us to expect the worst of others, such a vision eventually brings out the worst in us. Moreover, in the end it immensely hampers the enhancement of inclinations such as trust, benevolence and reciprocity, since that vision perceives these inclinations to be merely inborn peculiarities of human nature, unrelated to the civilisation process taking place in our societies. That is why it is essential to promote the presence of different types of businesses (capitalist, public, cooperative, social, benefit corporations, etc.) in our market economies.

It is a fact that the reduction of human experience to the "accountancy" dimension of utilitarian calculus is not only an act of intellectual arrogance; it is belied by actual experience. Today, we have come to the point where even the most "detached" observer cannot but admit that if we want to deal with the new problems in our society – such as the endemic aggravation of inequalities, the scandal of hunger, recurrent and serious financial crises, the rise of conflicts of identity in addition to the traditional clash between interests, the paradoxes of happiness, unsustainable development, and so on – research simply can no longer be confined within a sort of anthropological limbo.

To sum up, the main message that Catholic Social Teaching wants to convey is the following. It is by now a well recognised fact that market systems are consistent with many cultures, conceived as viable patterns of behaviour or, more generally, as organised systems of values. In turn, the type and degree of congruence of market systems with cultures is not without effects on the overall efficiency of the systems themselves: in general, the final outcome of market- coordination varies from culture to culture. Thus one should expect that a culture of possessive individualism will produce different results from a culture of reciprocity where individuals, even if motivated by self-interest, entertain a sense of fraternity. In the same way, a culture of cooperative competition will certainly produce different results from a culture of positional competition. However, cultures must not to be taken for granted.

Cultures respond to the investment of resources in specific cultural patterns, and they also depend on the witness given by those who put activities into operation. The proper functioning of an economic system depends also on whether or not certain conceptions and ways of life have achieved a dominant position among the population.

Pope Francis is well aware of the fact that secularism is trying to banish Christianity from public discourse and to make it irrelevant. He is reacting strongly to the attempt of global capitalism, understood as a model of social order, to impose itself as a kind of new immanentistic religion.

Nowadays, efforts to cover up the full extent of the religious nature of global capitalism takes place in two ways. On the one hand, decisions with moral content are presented in technical terms – e.g. fundamental human rights, it is argued, have to be limited for the sake of efficiency. On the other hand, technical arguments about the choice of means, such as the choice between the option of "more market" and that of "more state" are presented as if they were ideological issues. Efforts to de-mask such projects are one way to demonstrate the intellectual relevance as well as the proactive approach of Catholic Social Teaching in today's world.

LIST OF PARTICIPANTS

International institutions

1. **BADRÉ Bertrand** (France), Managing Director and CFO of *World Bank Group*
2. **CARNEY Mark J.** (Canada), Chairman of the *G20's Financial Stability Board*
3. **GURRÍA José Ángel** (Mexico), Secretary-General of the *Organisation for Economic Co-operation and Development* (OECD)
4. **KABERUKA Donald** (Rwanda), President of the *African Development Bank*
5. **KAYIZZI-MUGERWA Steve** (Uganda), Director of the Research Department at the *African Development Bank*
6. **KITUYI Mukhisa** (Kenya), Secretary-General of the *United Nations Conference on Trade and Development* (UNCTAD)
7. **KOCHHAR Kalpana** (India), Deputy Director, Strategy, Policy and Review of the *International Monetary Fund* (IMF)
8. **MOHAMMED Amina** (Kenya), *UN* Assistant Secretary General; *UN* Secretary-General's Special Adviser on the Post-2015 Development Agenda
9. **SUNDARAM Jomo** (Malaysia), Assistant Director-General and Coordinator for Economic and Social Development of *Food and Agriculture Organization* (FAO)
10. **TORRES Raymond** (France), Director of the *International Labour Organization* (ILO) Research Department

Academic institutions

11. **DASGUPTA SARATHI Partha** (India), Professor Emeritus of Economics at the *University of Cambridge*, Fellow of St

John's College, Cambridge – England, member of the Pontifical Academy for Social Sciences

12. **DENEULIN Séverine** (Belgium), Professor of International Development, *University of Bath* – England

13. **MILANOVIĆ Branko** (Serbia), Presidential Professor, *City University of New York Graduate Center* – USA

14. **SACHS Jeffrey** (USA), Professor of Sustainable Development and Director of the Earth Institute, *Columbia University* – USA

Business corporations

15. **BRABECK-LETMATHE Peter** (Austria), Chairman of *Nestlé*

16. **FULCI Francesco Paolo** (Italy), President of *Ferrero SpA*

17. **GREEN Pauline** (Great Britain), President of the *International Co-operative Alliance*

18. **GRIFFITHS Brian** (Great Britain), Vice-Chairman of *Goldman Sachs International*

19. **MARISCAL TORROELLA José Ignacio** (Mexico), Former Chief Executive Officer and Current Director of *Grupo Marhnos*, Director of *Grupo Bimbo*

20. **SIMONE José Maria** (Argentina), President of *UNIAPAC International*

Civil Society

21. **BERRY Laura** (USA), Executive Director of *Interfaith Center for Corporate Responsibility* (ICCR)

22. **BYANYIMA Winnie** (Uganda), Executive Director of *Oxfam International*

23. **DE PEÑA Marike** (Holland), Chair of the Board of *Fairtrade International* (FLO)

24. **GRABOIS Juan** (Argentina), Co-founder of the *Excluded Workers Movement* and Confederation of Popular Economy Workers – Buenos Aires
25. **HÖDL Heinz** (Austria), President of CIDSE
26. **HOWARD Steve** (Australia), Secretary General of the *Global Foundation*
27. **LABELLE Huguette** (Canada), Chair of the Board of Directors of *Transparency International*
28. **LAMY Pascal** (France), Former President of the *World Trade Organisation* (WTO) and Honorary President of *Notre Europe*
29. **OKONJO-IWEALA Ngozi** (Nigeria), Former Vice-President and Corporate Secretary of *World Bank*
30. **ROESLER Philipp** (Germany), Managing Director of the *World Economic Forum*
31. **ROY Michel** (France), Secretary General of *Caritas Internationalis*
32. **SHIVA Vandana** (India), 1993 *Right Livelihood Award*, Board member of the *International Forum on Globalization*
33. **VROOMAN Tamara** (Canada), President and CEO of *Vancity*, member of the Steering Committee of the Global Alliance for Banking on Values
34. **YUNUS Mohammad** (Bangladesh), 2006 *Nobel Peace Prize*, Founder of the *Grameen Bank*

Assistants

35. **CHARVERIAT Celine** (Belgium), Advocacy and Campaign Director of *Oxfam International*
36. **ELMISSIRY Amira** (Zimbabwe), Assistant to the President of the *African Development Bank*
37. **KAMAL-CHAOUI Lamia** (France), Advisor of the Secretary-General of the *Organisation for Economic Co-operation and Development* (OECD)

38. **MARTINOT-LAGARDE Rev. Fr. Pierre** (France), Special Adviser for Socio-religious Affairs *Emerging and Special Partnerships Unit – International Labour Office* (ILO)

39. **MOUSSA Moussa Djibril** (Chad), Protocol Assistant of the *African Development Bank*

40. **OKECHUKWU Chisom** (Nigeria), Assistant of Ms. Ngozi Okonjo-Iweala

41. **SHIVA Kartikey** (India), Assistant of Ms. Vandana Shiva

Scientific Committee

42. **ALFORD Rev. Sr. Helen** (Great Britain), Dean of the Faculty of Social Sciences, Pontifical University St. Thomas Aquinas "Angelicum" – Rome

43. **BECCHETTI Leonardo** (Italy), Full Professor of Economics, University of Rome "Tor Vergata", President of the supervising committee of *Banca Popolare Etica*

44. **BERETTA Simona** (Italy), Full Professor of Economics, Catholic University of the Sacred Heart - Milan

45. **BRUNI Luigino** (Italy), Full Professor of Economics, University LUMSA – Rome

46. **CAMDESSUS Michel** (France), Honorary Governor of the Bank of France

47. **CONVERSI Paolo** (Italy), Desk Officer of International Organisations, Secretariat of State, Holy See

48. **DAL TOSO Msgr. Giampietro** (Italy), Secretary of the Pontifical Council "Cor Unum"

49. **GIOVANELLI Flaminia** (Italy), Under-Secretary of the Pontifical Council for Justice and Peace

50. **HABISCH André** (Germany), Professor for Christian Social Ethics and Society, Catholic University of Eichstätt-Ingolstadt

51. **NEVES DE ALMEIDA Msgr. Osvaldo** (Brazil), Desk Officer for Relations to the United Nations, Secretariat of State, Holy See

52. **RUDING Onno** (Netherlands), Former Member of the Pontifical Council for Justice and Peace

53. **SÁNCHEZ SORONDO Bishop Marcelo** (Argentina), Chancellor of the Pontifical Academy of Sciences

54. **TOSO Bishop Mario** (Italy), Secretary of the Pontifical Council for Justice and Peace

55. **TURKSON Cardinal Peter K. A**. (Ghana), President of the Pontifical Council for Justice and Peace

56. **ZAMAGNI Stefano** (Italy), Full Professor of Economics, University of Bologna, member of the Pontifical Academy of Social Sciences, Adjunct Professor of International Economics - Johns Hopkins University

VATICAN PRESS